ARABIA AND THE BIBLE

THE LIBRARY
OF
BIBLICAL STUDIES

Edited by

Harry M. Orlinsky

Arabia
and the Bible

By

JAMES A. MONTGOMERY

Professor of Hebrew and Aramaic
University of Pennsylvania

Professor of Old Testament
Literature and Language
Divinity School of the
Protestant Episcopal Church
in Philadelphia

PROLEGOMENON BY

GUS W. VAN BEEK

KTAV PUBLISHING HOUSE, INC.
1969

FIRST PUBLISHED 1934

New Matter
© Copyright 1969
KTAV PUBLISHING HOUSE, INC.

Library of Congress Catalog Card Number: 68-25721
Manufactured in the United States of America

CONTENTS

To my friend Fullerton
with happy memories of
Jerusalem and Oberlin

PROLEGOMENON

It was not my privilege to know James A. Montgomery, because there was a very real generation gap between us. His study of Arabia was completed long before my interest in the Peninsula began. If he were alive today, he would be filled with pride that his Haskell Lectures—delivered at Oberlin College in the spring of 1930, and subsequently published in 1934—have stood the test of time, and are now being reprinted. And this is as it should be. For these lectures, published as *Arabia and the Bible,* are the best treatment of all aspects of the relationship between the Arabian Peninsula and ancient Canaan and Israel that has yet been written. Nowhere else are the ethnic, cultural, and economic connections between these regions explored in such depth and with such competence as in this book. Here, Montgomery brought together all information then available that dealt with the impact of Arabian cultural influence on the Bible. Nor was his presentation entirely one-sided. Although it was not central to his theme, he also dealt in summary fashion with the influence of biblical peoples and ideas on the pre-Islamic and early Islamic, cultures of Arabia, and especially with the important role played by Jews in Arabia during the early centuries A.D.

This book is a product of sound scholarship. Montgomery showed considerable breadth in his selection of sources which included studies in the fields of geography, linguistics, literature, and archeology, all of which he scrutinized with the utmost care. In his selection of material, he displayed a remarkable ability to discriminate between the more important and the less significant in an area in which he was not primarily a specialist. He interpreted the assembled data with balance and good judgment. He was not always correct, as we now know with some 35 years of research in Arabia separating the publication of the book and its reissue now. But he was more right than wrong, and this reflects his disciplined intuition which was bred by his intimacy with the ancient Near East. When the evidence on opposing sides was of equal weight, he presented both sides succinctly and refrained from choosing one or the other. Even when he chose what has proven to be the wrong side, he did so with reason. We owe a great debt, then, to this scholar who brought together diverse source material and presented a coherent synthesis of the many currents that moved on different levels between Arabia and Palestine in biblical times. So far as I know, he never set foot on the Arabian Peninsula, and yet he displayed a familiarity with this land, borne of long acquaintance and indeed friendship.

In the following pages, I shall review some of the major theses of Montgomery which have to be modified in varying degrees as a result of the archeological and literary research that has taken place during the past 35 years. This is intended to supplement Montgomery's text, bringing it up to date, to show how the relationship between Arabia and the Bible should be viewed as of 1969.

A major premise of the book that requires clarification at the beginning is that Arabia and the Desert are not synonyms, as Montgomery assumed throughout; they belong to different categories of meaning, although they are related.

Desert is an environmental term meaning an arid region with a limited flora and fauna, and commonly populated by nomadic peoples whose culture represents an adaption to the environment. Arabia, on the other hand, is a geographical designation, the name of a specific region. To be sure, much of that region is desert, but some sections cannot be included under this definition, belonging instead to mountainous and coastal environmental zones with all that those zones imply in terms of sedentary peoples with different forms of culture.

Unhappily, as a result of Montgomery's confusion of Arabia and "desert," the reader is led to believe that the influence of the desert on ancient Israel is the same as the impact of Arabia, and this is simply not true.

That the desert exerted a tremendous hold on Israel throughout biblical times is certain, and we owe a debt of gratitude to Montgomery for pointing this out so forcefully. Israel's origins took place in the Desert of Sinai. There a group of slaves with distant memories of nomadic tribal beginnings in northwestern Mesopotamia and in Canaan were welded into a people. There this generation of slaves was replaced by a new generation of lean and hungry fighters, as is sometimes bred in arid wastes. There the timid ones, who were ready to return to Egypt after seeking to enter the land from the south, were supplanted by wiry men with stamina, whose dream of a land flowing with milk and honey enabled them to conquer the Amorite Kingdoms east of the Jordan, and then successfully attack the city states of the hill country of Canaan. There moral and cultic law was given, and the covenant with its contractual relationships between God and the people was reestablished on a new and firmer footing.

In later times, Israel's desert origins in Sinai were remembered as the Golden Age, when its faith was purified, tempered, and fashioned in the heat of the desert. After the settlement in Canaan and the transformation of the people from nomads to agriculturalists—with all the concomitant problems that threatened national life, the foremost of which was the assimilation of Canaanite agricultural religious practices—the prophets sought to preserve the identity of Israel by recalling God's faithfulness when Israel was utterly dependent upon Him in the desert, and by urging a strict adherence to its obligations under the Covenant. But this is a desert ethos which is separate from Arabia itself. Indeed, many of the peoples of the Arabian Peninsula shared a similar view, conditioned by the waste lands which were their homes.

The cultural influence from Arabia is reflected in other ways. Geographically, Israel was always oriented toward the east and south after its entry into the promised land under Joshua. While its roots in the Patriarchal Age were in northwestern Mesopotamia, its orientation from this time on was toward Arabia. Israel never looked seaward. Having settled in the hill country, several centuries passed before Israel controlled the southern Mediterranean coastal land, which was then held by Philistines and Canaanites. Even in the time of the monarchy and later, the northern portion of the coast which had the good harbors was never held by Israel, but rather by the Phoenicians and their successors. Indeed, nowhere south of Acco was there a decent harbor until the port constructions of the Roman Period. For this reason, Israel concentrated on control of land routes connecting Egypt with Syria and Mesopotamia on the one hand, and with Arabia on the other. As Wright correctly noted, throughout Israel's history its most important emporium was Gaza, a city at the intersection of important land routes, but located some three miles from the sea.[1]

Montgomery correctly noted that there is no formidable geographic barrier between Palestine and the Arabian Peninsula. Once the Jordan River is crossed, the highland plateaus of eastern Palestine give way gradually and naturally to the mountains and plains of the Arabian desert. This open frontier facilitated the passage of people, trade, and the flow of cultural expressions between Arabia and

Palestine.

The relationships between ancient Israel and Arabia are limited to two categories: ethnic and commercial. Nowhere in the Bible is there an expression of fear of Arabia as a seat of aggression. The major spawning grounds of armed invasion of Israel were Egypt, Syria, Mesopotamia, and Persia, as well as such minor sources as Edom and Transjordan. Nor is there any record of significant political influence from any tribe or state in the Arabian Peninsula, with the possible exception of Midian at the time of Moses. Similarly the Bible contains no suggestion of a threat from Arabia to the cultural identity of Israel, or even of cultural borrowing from that region. The greatest cultural danger was the indigenous Canaanite-Phoenician religious ideas and ethical values, as well as sporadic perils from the cultic life of Mesopotamia and, though to a lesser extent, Egypt.

Ethnic relations were another matter. From the point of view of Israelite historiography and genealogy, Israel's closest relatives—aside from their distant ancestors in the Haran region—were the peoples of the Arabian Peninsula. According to the J document (Gen. 10:21-31), Israel and many of the Arabian groups are descended from a common ancestor, Eber (or Heber, as spelled in the Vulgate): Israel from one of Eber's two sons, Peleg, and the Arabian peoples from the other, Joktan (*yqtn*). The latter includes two of the most prominent South Arabian states, Hazarmaveth (Hadhramaut) and Sheba (Saba). Accordingly, they are closer cousins to the Israelites than the latter's more immediate neighbors, the Canaanites, Amorites, Jebusites, and others who are descended from Ham.

According to the short genealogy in Genesis 25:1-4, which seems to be derived from narrative sources, this relationship is even closer. Here, Abraham, by his second wife, Keturah, is the father of Jokshan (*yqshn*), and Jokshan—probably the same name as Joktan in Genesis 10:25 f.[2]—is the father of Sheba, and some of the North Arabian peoples, such as those of Dedan and Midian. This makes

Sheba a direct grandson of Abraham, and the first cousin of Jacob and Esau.

The later P document, on the other hand, has some of the Arabian peoples descended from Ham (Gen. 10:6 ff.). Accordingly, Seba, Sheba, and Dedan among other South Arabians are sons of Cush, and therefore presuppose an African origin. Montgomery explained this derivation as ". . . based on historical and political motives" (p. 42), meaning, as he put it, "Without doubt there was an early exchange of populations between Arabia and Africa, especially across the strait of Bab-el-Mandeb, a close relation, illustrated in later political history, which may well have suggested the African origin of South-Arabian peoples." Of the supposed African element in Arabia in early times, there is not as yet a shred of evidence. In prehistoric times, the Red Sea—even at Bab el-Mandeb—was a formidable barrier, and the successive cultures of southern Arabia have little if any relationship to contemporary cultures in Sudan, Ethiopia, and the Horn of Africa, as shown by the lithic industries.[3] We now know that in the protohistoric and historic periods, i.e., after the 12th or 11th century B.C., the influence went in the other direction, from Arabia to Africa. The fact is that the P document here reflects the Sabaean colonization of Ethiopia, which certainly took place no later than the 7th century B.C. and perhaps as early as the 10th century B.C. In a real sense, there were two Sabas— one Arabian, the other African—with the latter probably owing allegiance to the former for several centuries, perhaps throughout most or all of the first millennium B.C. This is almost certainly the source of the confusion in the two names, Seba and Sheba, that appear in Genesis 10:7. It was not until the beginning of the Christian Era that southern Arabia came under strong influence from Africa, in this instance, Ethiopia.[4]

It is also of interest that, according to P, the descendants of Abraham and his Egyptian concubine Hagar, through their son Ishmael, included many of the tribes of North

Arabia. Furthermore, Moses' wife, Zipporah, was a Midian-
ite according to Exodus 2:16-21 and 18, and one can
reasonably suppose that in this formative period, there were
many other unions between Israelite and Arabian peoples.

Montgomery's treatment of these ethnic relationships in
Chapter III, "The Hebrews and Their Cousins the Arabs,"
is excellent. It is a succinct and clear summary, incorporat-
ing many diverse sources as well as Montgomery's own
balanced ideas. A number of details have been subsequently
corrected by other scholars, especially Speiser and Albright,[5] but his work still stands as the basic study of
Israel's connections with its neighbors in the Arabian
Peninsula. What emerges is a keen awareness among the
early Israelites of their common origin with the North and
South Arabs. In general, the earlier the documentary source,
the closer the relationship.

A further problem concerning the identification of the
peoples of Arabia involves the location of the Sabaeans.
Montgomery and many other scholars of his period took
it for granted that the Sabaeans originally lived in northern
Arabia, and later migrated to the south. This assumption
was based on the fact that two Sabaean kings, Itiamara and
Karibilu, who are mentioned in the Annals of Sargon and
Sennacherib respectively, could not have ruled in the
southern part of the Arabian Peninsula because of the great
distance separating it from Mesopotamia, and must therefore have lived in the northern part of the region.

In the years since Montgomery's book appeared, no evidence supporting this assumption has come to light. It
should be noted that in neither reference does the Assyrian
king claim to have conquered these Sabaean kings; both
are represented as paying tribute only. Indeed, Sargon
states that he conquered some tribes of Arabia, and received tribute from others. The probable explanation is that
there were Sabaeans in northern Arabia who were there to
preside over the administration of caravan facilities and to

guard the trade routes. As such they represented an extension of the influence of the Sabaean State into the north.
As Assyrian interest reached southward from Mesopotamia,
it inevitably came in contact with this northern extension
of the Sabaean trading communities. To maintain continued freedom to engage in trading activities, it seems likely
that the South Arabian State paid tribute to the mightiest
land empire in the Near East at that time.

So far as we know, the Sabaean State was always centered in the south, with its capital at Marib. On the basis
of the pottery at Marib, the site was certainly occupied as
early as the 9th century B.C., and in all probability goes
back to at least the 11th century. Furthermore, based on
the archeological work of the past decade, it is quite clear
that the culture of northern Arabia was totally different
from that of southern Arabia and had its own cultural
sphere. It is not yet possible to describe the exact orientation of this northern culture in pre-Nabataean times, although the points of similarity that it shows with South
Arabian culture are few.

This is to say that, if the Sabaeans were originally centered in northern Arabia, we should expect to find there
precursors of the artifacts and cultural motifs found in
southern Arabia, since migrating people inevitably carry
with them their traditional material culture, and do not give
it up immediately upon entering a new land. Yet the material culture of northern Arabia, i.e., the al-Öla and Teima
regions, is entirely different from that of southern Arabia.
The questions of interest now are: How far north did South
Arabian culture extend? How far south did northern Arabian culture reach? And at what point, or in what area, did
they meet, and what were the cultural effects of that meeting? In this connection, it should be mentioned that a third
cultural zone in the eastern provinces of Saudi Arabia,
along the south side of the Persian Gulf, seems to have
greater affinities to the cultures of Mesopotamia than to
those of either North or South Arabia.

While the interchange of peoples between Palestine and Arabia may have been more significant than even the biblical authors themselves realized, it was trade between the regions that seems to have captured their imagination.

Most biblical allusions to Arabia deal with caravan traffic and trade in luxury goods, chiefly gold, frankincense and myrrh, spices, and the like. This suggests that Arabia played a prominent role in the economy of ancient Israel, a role which we have only begun to define. The key to this role is the distribution of frankincense and myrrh, two commodities whose total world production was controlled as a monopoly by the South Arabian states.[6] Indeed, in economic importance, the domination of the production and distribution of frankincense and myrrh was to the ancient kingdoms of southern Arabia what the oil industry is to the Arabian states today.

The earliest evidence of commercial relations with Arabia is related in I Kings 10:1-13 (and its parallel in II Chronicles 9:1-12) where the visit of the nameless Queen of Sheba to the Court of Solomon is described. The biblical authors state that the Queen of Sheba had heard of Solomon's fame, and came to test him to see if the reports concerning his wisdom and prosperity were true. This suggests that the trip of 1,500 miles across difficult terrain was made for the purpose of intellectual discussions and to satisfy the Queen's curiosity. Incidentally, she brought with her—presumably as royal gifts—spices, gold, and precious stones.

It must be remembered that the major caravan route, by which these commodities were carried to the north, kept to the east, or desert, side of the range of mountains paralleling the Red Sea along the west side of the Arabian Peninsula. At Dedan (modern al-Öla), a track branched off leading to Mesopotamia by way of Teima. The main route continued northward along the King's Highway to Syria and Anatolia. Secondary tracks must have led from this route to the cities in the hill country of Palestine such as

Jerusalem, Bethel, and Samaria. Trade destined for the Mediterranean lands was carried by a major route that branched off, crossed the Arabah and the Negev, and terminated at Gaza. These routes are known to have been used in Roman times, and they must have been in use long before that period.

As the preeminent monarchs in the entire Near East in the 10th century B.C., David and Solomon must have controlled the King's Highway in eastern Palestine as well as the route crossing southern Palestine leading to the Mediterranean by which frankincense and myrrh were distributed to consumer nations. The paramount objective of the Queen of Sheba's visit, then, must have been to conclude an agreement covering the distribution of these substances, which were the life blood of South Arabian economy. Access to markets was the *sine qua non* of this incense-based economy. It may not be accidental that immediately before the account of the Queen of Sheba's visit is the description of Solomon's Red Sea fleet which was perhaps operated on a contract basis by Hiram of Tyre, and which was based at Ezion-geber. Possibly the competition of this fleet, which threatened Sabaean commerce along the established caravan routes, prompted the Queen of Sheba's visit. It is also possible that this discussion between Heads of State resulted in a reciprocal agreement whereby Solomon's fleet was given access to African and Arabian ports controlled by the Queen of Sheba, while the security of the northern section of the caravan routes and points of distribution was guaranteed by Solomon. In any case, it is increasingly clear that the Queen of Sheba's visit to the Court of Solomon would today be called an economic mission.

It is not accidental that the only objects imported from southern Arabia—or objects reflecting an Arabian style— are incense burners found at Tell Jemmeh and Samaria, and a South Arabian clay stamp discovered at Bethel. The latter, found by James L. Kelso in his excavations in 1956, can only be understood as evidence of frankincense trade.[7] Since we know that Jeroboam established a sanctuary at Bethel to prevent the citizens of the northern Kingdom from feeling the need to worship Yahweh in Jerusalem, and since we know from I Kings 13:1 that Jeroboam himself offered incense at Bethel, and since the incense burned on the altar almost certainly contained frankincense, Bethel is one of the places where evidence of South Arabian incense trade could be expected. The clay stamp in question is indisputably South Arabian in origin: it is made of typically South Arabian paste; it is lettered with a South Arabian text; and an identical stamp with an identical text was found and recorded in a squeeze by Theodore Bent in Wadi Du'an, Hadhramaut, in the year 1895.[8]

That more objects from Arabia have not been found in Palestinian sites is probably due in a large part to the fact that, until quite recently, no one could identify Arabian artifacts. Nothing was known about the material culture of Arabia, and items that did not fit into the repertory of Palestinian material culture, and could not be associated with any other culture, were probably discarded as anomalies. As archeologists become increasingly knowledgeable about Arabian culture, it is quite likely that more Arabian products will be identified in sites in Israel and elsewhere in the Near East and Mediterranean Basin.

Thus Israel's relations with Arabia consist, on the one hand, of close ethnic relationships going back to the Patriarchal Age, and on the other, of commercial relations made necessary by Israel's geographical setting along the principal trade routes of antiquity.

Since James Montgomery completed his study of the relationships between Arabia and the Bible, a number of major discoveries relating to these relations have been made through increased archeological exploration and excavation. It must be remembered that at the time of

the Haskell Lectures in 1930, only one structure had
been excavated in all of Arabia. That building was a
Temple located at Huqqa, some distance north of Sanaa,
Yemen, which had been cleared by Carl Rathjens and
Herman von Wissmann in 1928.[9] By 1930, no competent
archeological reconnaissance had as yet been made, although epigraphic expeditions had been moderately frequent in the late 19th century. While some notes were
made on various sites, these were at best haphazard and
inspired little confidence in their accuracy.

Since that time—and especially following World War
II—our knowledge of the Peninsula has been revolution-
ized by a number of archeological surveys and excavations covering most of Arabia. To be sure, some regions
are better known than others, because of a greater concentration of research effort. Preliminary or full archeological surveys have been conducted in most of Arabia: in
Wadi Beihan by Richard LeBaron Bowen, Jr.,[10] in Oman
and Dhofar by Ray L. Cleveland,[11] in the Yemen by
Ahmed Fakhry[12] and the writer, in the Hedjaz by William
L. Reed and Fred V. Winnett,[13] and by Peter Parr and
John Dayton; more thorough-going surveys in the eastern
province—along the Persian Gulf—have been carried
on by Geoffrey Bibby, and in the Hadhramaut and southern
Saudi Arabia by the writer.[14]

Excavations have been carried out at Hureidha by Gertrude Caton Thompson, at Timna' and Hajar Bin Humeid
in Wadi Beihan, at the Marib Temple (Mahram Bilqis)
in Yemen, and in Dhofar by the archeologists of the
American Foundation for the Study of Man. Of these,
Hureidha was published in a splendid monograph in 1944,[15]
and the sites excavated by the American Foundation for
the Study of Man have for the most part been published,
and some are in the process of study and publication at
this time; to date, four volumes have appeared, and at
least two more are projected.[16]

Since the appearance of *Arabia and the Bible*, archeological field work has added several thousand graffiti and texts to the repertory of South Arabian inscriptions. For the most part these consist of personal names, burial inscriptions giving the name of the deceased and his clan, dedicatory texts, and building inscriptions. Few are annalistic or historical documents which would provide a framework for detailed historical reconstruction. The texts, however, have made possible the broad-scale reconstruction of the development and chronology of South Arabian palaeography, especially by W. F. Albright and Albert Jamme, and a tentative historical framework by Albright, Jamme, and Jacques Ryckmans.[17]

One dispute of major significance that raged at the time Montgomery wrote this book was the controversy over the proposed high chronology versus the low chronology for southern Arabia.[18] This question had ramifications for the culture history of the entire Peninsula, because events and trends are interrelated everywhere in this region. The proponents of the high chronology held that the states of Ma'in and Qataban preceded Saba, and they placed the beginning of the Minaean State in the second millennium B.C. Those who argued for a low chronology gave priority to Saba, dating the *Mukarrib* period in the eighth century B.C., and fixing the beginnings of the Minaean and Qatabanian states in the late eighth and seventh centuries B.C. respectively.

The first major breakthrough was made by F. V. Winnett in 1939.[19] He demonstrated that most of the kings of Ma'in belonged to the period between 400 and 100 B.C., by showing Minaean influence in some of the Late Lihyanite inscriptions from North Arabia, and by examining all other relevant evidence. The *coup de grace* to the high chronology was delivered by the excavations conducted by the American Foundation for the Study of Man at Timna' in 1950. There, a pair of bronze lions with infant riders were found which were made in the Hellenistic style of the first century B.C.[20] On the bases of these lions were inscribed the names of the two workmen who refurbished the building on which these magnificent pieces of sculpture had been mounted. The names of these craftsmen also appeared in an inscription on the wall of the building, in which it was stated that they undertook this work during the reign of a well-known Qatabanian king, Shahr Yagil Yuhargib. Thus this king must have reigned during Hellenistic times, rather than in the eighth century B.C. as dated in the high chronology. The solution of the problem of chronology was a giant step forward in the study of Arabian archeology.

It is now clear that there were several major cultural regions or centers in Arabia during biblical times. These include: South Arabia, North Arabia, the coastal region along the Persian Gulf, and Eastern Arabia (Muscat and Oman). The most distinctive and best known of these to date is that of southern Arabia. This culture was centered on the desert side of the triangle formed by the mountains of Yemen on the west, by both the mountains and desert plateau of South Yemen on the south, and the sands of the Rub'al-Khali on the north. It did not emerge from a long, evolving, indigenous tradition, but burst upon the South Arabian scene fully developed. It was brought by a group, or more probably several groups, of emigrants from somewhere in the North, perhaps along the agricultural fringe of the Fertile Crescent—to judge from the relationships manifest in their language and material culture—at various times between the 15th and 12th centuries B.C.

South Arabian culture was characterized from the beginning by a unique and complex system of irrigation agriculture, the remains of which are found in every cultivable valley east and north of the watershed, and on many of the plateaus. This system utilized both flash flood run-off and wells as sources of water, rather than perennial rivers and springs as were used in the Fertile Crescent. The flash flood installations included the use of earthen diversion dams—sometimes faced with stone— which deflected the torrents of water into large earthen canals. The canals carried the water to stone-built sluices, which diverted it into smaller channels for distribution over the fields. The most completely investigated system is found near Hajar Bin Humeid in Wadi Beihan,[21] and the best preserved and largest system—which has not yet been studied in detail—is located in Wadi Dhana, near Marib, Yemen.

This culture was also marked by a tradition of urban living not unlike that found in Mesopotamia, Syro-Palestine, and Egypt during the same period. Settlements ranged in size from small towns of four or five acres, to large cities—such as Marib—which covered an area of about 150 acres. All exhibit about the same level of town planning, or lack of it, that characterized contemporary towns and cities of the North. Construction was of both mud brick and stone, with the later achieving some of the most intriguing forms and designs in the history of ancient Near Eastern architecture. Especially noteworthy is elaborate recessed wall paneling in combination with dentil-like projections, false louvers, and lattice windows, which is found in both full size buildings, such as the Marib Temple (Mahram Bilqis),[22] and in reduced scale on furniture[23] and incense burners. Two beautiful styles of masonry occur: marginally drafted pecked masonry which has a long history of development in the region,[24] and fine ashlar masonry—trapezoidal in section when viewed from the top—dressed with flat or slightly convex faces.

All of the arts of contemporary civilization were included in this culture. Writing was exceptionally common, as attested by the great number of inscriptions. The South Semitic language was written in a beautiful alphabetic script—perhaps the most beautiful of all of the alphabets of the ancient Near East—consisting of 29 consonants. Inscriptions of varying subject matter and length were carefully carved on stones such as gneiss, limestone, and alabaster, cast in bronze, and incised on pottery. The many graffiti indicate that many of the common people, including caravaneers and shepherds, knew how to write; this suggests that education was widespread in the population.

The cult featured a highly developed pantheism in which astral, planetary, and moon gods and goddesses predominated. Temples were probably located in every town as well as in the cities, and many achieved considerable size and elegance. The best examples feature an open court, surrounded by a peristyle, with the sanctuary at one end. All included some form of water installation, which must have functioned for ritual cleansing. All had many dedicatory statues and plaques in alabaster or bronze seeking or expressing gratitude for divine favor.

Some forms of technology reached an advanced stage of development. Great quantities of objects, including sculpture, furniture, and vessels, were carved from alabaster (calcite), marble, limestone, steatite, and brucite, with a technical skill and competence in cutting, shaping, drilling, and polishing that rivaled that shown in the stone carvings of Egypt and Mesopotamia. No ancient sculptors —even those of Greece—rendered the head of a bull with greater sensitivity and realism than the South Arabian sculptor,[25] and the intricate carving of stone chests with facades resembling recessed panelled buildings had no equal until Roman stone furniture carvers reached the pinnacle of their craftsmanship. Metallurgy also achieved an advanced stage of development. Iron, bronze, brass, silver, and gold were all worked. Study and analyses of bronze artifacts have disclosed that bronze was cast using the lost wax technique, and the first evidence of the drawing of bronze wire in the ancient Near East has recently come to light.[26] Ceramics, on the other hand, do not show the advanced manufacturing techniques known in the Fertile Crescent. But some decorative styles betray a northern tradition, which indicates not only contact between the regions, but more importantly the existence of some common ceramic ideas which extended from the Caucasus to southern Arabia.[27]

While most of the South Arabian cities stand on tells, and the resulting height provided an obvious military advantage, few of the towns and cities had defensive enclosure walls. This suggests that their history was comparatively peaceful and less marred by regional conflicts and international wars than the contemporary lands of the Fertile Crescent. This is supported by the relatively small number of annalistic inscriptions recounting battles and victories in the region. Such peacefulness was in part due to their geographic isolation from the political wars of the great nations in the North. It may also be explained as a lack of fighting prowess, which is no better portrayed than by Strabo, who states that in the campaign for Marib, Aelius Gallus inflicted 10,000 casualities on the South Arabians while losing only seven of his legionaires.[28] Even allowing for considerable exaggeration, the picture that emerges shows a lack of military expertise among the South Arabians. It seems probable that their emphasis was always on commercial relations rather than on military conquest, and in this political stance they closely resembled the Phoenicians.

The mainspring of South Arabian economy was the production and distribution of frankincense and myrrh. As noted above, traffic in these substances brought immense wealth to the South Arabian states throughout the first millennium B.C., reaching its peak during the Roman period when, in the first century A.D., Pliny the Elder described the South Arabs as "the wealthiest race in the world."[29] From the list of imports to the South Arabian

ports along the Red Sea and Gulf of Aden prepared by
the anonymous Greek-speaking ship captain who wrote
the *Periplus of the Erythraean Sea,*[30] it is clear that the
South Arabs purchased only luxury goods, which points
to both a surplus of wealth and a self-sufficiency with
regard to the production of the necessities of life. These
luxury goods included the finest imports from abroad:
bronze lions with baby riders and other sculpture such as
figures of Heracles and Sabazios styled in the Hellenistic
manner; brass goblets patterned after Megarian bowls;
a table top made of Egyptian blue and set with a border
of triangular inlays, perhaps from Persia; Arretine pottery
from Italy; glazed ware from Anatolia and southern Russia;
and a small bronze figure of a Salabhanjika from India.

With the present state of our knowledge of South Arabian economy, it is virtually certain that James Montgomery
erred when he attributed the ". . . degradation of economics
of Arabia. . . ." to the supplanting of the traditional caravan routes by the Greek and Roman shipping fleets oper-
ating out of Egyptian Red Sea ports. He suggested that
once these ships had captured the Indian Ocean trade, the
stability of the South Arabian kingdoms was in jeopardy,
since the political well-being of a state depends on the
soundness of its economy. While such competition played
a role in the decline of southern Arabia's international trade,
it is an oversimplification to consider it the sole or even the
major cause of the decline of the South Arabian states. Indeed, the author of the *Periplus of the Erythraean Sea* (for
example, paragraph 16) indicates that in the middle of the
first century A.D., at a time when Greek and Roman shipping was already quite active in the Red Sea and Indian
Ocean, the Arabs were very much involved in sea trade,
and there is no reason to think that this traditional involve-
ment in maritime commerce ceased with the entry of the
Greeks and Romans into the region.

More significant for the decline of the South Arabian
economy was the rise of Christianity. While churches made

use of frankincense in their religious rites, the amount consumed in this manner was in no way comparable to the vast quantities used in pagan religious practices such as the burning of bodies on funeral pyres covered with frankincense. It must be remembered that Pliny the Elder tells us that on Poppea's funeral pyre, her husband—the Emperor Nero—lavished a full year's production of all Arabian frankincense.[31] This suggests that among wealthy Romans and others under the influence of Roman culture, it must have become a contest for status to see how much incense could be consumed with the body. It seems clear, therefore, that when the cremation of frankincense-covered bodies ceased with the coming of Christianity, the demand for frankincense must have fallen considerably. The loss of demand, then, rather than the competition for distribution of the product by sea is surely the major reason for the deterioration of South Arabian economy. Its effect on these kingdoms was probably as great as the collapse of the demand for petroleum products would be to Saudi Arabia, Kuwait, Iraq, and Iran today if oil were suddenly replaced by another source of energy by the great petroleum users of the western world.

It also seems likely that this sudden weakening of the economy was accompanied by a gradual culture fatigue. There was no longer sufficient imagination and determination to respond in new and different ways to the challenges of the changing world in which the South Arabs found themselves. A major thrust to regain supremacy in East African and South Asian trade, or the concentration of efforts on producing other revenue creating products—such as increasing the export of alabaster and gold—might have saved South Arabian economy. But the culture no longer inspired such efforts among people. Furthermore, the commitment to South Arabian religious beliefs and practices was no longer of sufficient strength to enable the South Arabs to resist the alien religious systems of Christianity, Judaism, and Zoroasterianism which successively pressed in on the traditional paganism. The elasticity in the culture was gone, with the result that they met the demands of their time not with resiliency and new ideas, but with resignation and retreat. It is probable that some of the migrations from southern Arabia to the North took place at this time.

Elsewhere in Arabia, the cultures are much less well defined. In North Arabia, there has still been no excavation, and our information is limited solely to that gleaned from surface surveys. The pottery collected in the course of these survey trips at major sites within the region, such as al-Öla (ancient Dedan) and Teima, differs considerably from site to site. Whether these differences reflect contemporary variation within the culture, or illustrate time change, cannot be determined as yet, because of a lack of deep excavation at one or more sites. Little of the pottery bears any resemblance to that from pre-Islamic South Arabia, except for a few shreds from Medina, suggesting that pre-Nabataean North Arabia belongs to a different cultural sphere from southern Arabia. While great strides have been made in the recovery of Nabataean civilization in Israel and Jordan through both excavation and survey by Nelson Glueck, Peter Parr, and others, important information on the southward distribution of the culture has been obtained from surface surveys in the Peninsula.

The Eastern Province of Saudi Arabia, the region fronting on the Persian Gulf, is also beginning to yield data on the culture of this area. Pottery collected on the surface of one of the major sites, Thaj, and a description of the ruins have been published by P. W. Lapp, Peter Parr, and J. P. Mandaville,[32] and surface reconnaissances have been carried on by Geoffrey Bibby for the National Museum of Denmark. The material cannot be associated with that from any other known culture in the Peninsula, and probably indicates that this region is a separate center of culture. It must be remembered that according to Strabo, this region was inhabited by Chaldaeans,[33] who had strong ties with southern Mesopotamia in particular. Indeed, a cylinder seal in a private collection, which is said to have been found in the Eastern Province, can be confidently assigned to the Jemdet Nasr style of the Late Prehistoric Period in Mesopotamia, at the beginning of the third millennium B.C. The orientation of this culture, therefore, was probably always toward Mesopotamia.

Eastern Arabia, including Muscat and Oman, has not been sufficiently explored as yet to shed light on its cultural history. Ray Cleveland, the only archaeologist to work in the region, was unable to locate any evidence of pre-Islamic occupation in a short season of field work.[34] Everyone agrees, however, that the region must have been inhabited during this period, and it is hoped that future surveys will disclose pre-Islamic sites that will enable us to define the culture.

This Prolegomenon, then, corrects the more fundamental mistakes that Montgomery made, and presents a brief summary of the status of our knowledge of pre-Islamic Arabian cultural history today. There are other errors in this book, but most are of so little consequence that they are not worth correcting. In general, the errors that Montgomery made reflect not poor judgment but a deficiency in information. This introductory chapter, therefore, more properly supplements Montgomery's discussion, bringing it up to date in the places where it is needed. Some interpretations presented here were anticipated by Montgomery; others were not. Perhaps after working through Montgomery's text, the reader should return to the Prolegomenon and go through it again, if he wishes to place this book in perspective.

From my vantage point, I am filled with admiration and respect for James Montgomery and *Arabia and the Bible*. He was a great man; and this is a great book.

Gus W. Van Beek
Curator, Smithsonian Institution
June 20, 1969   Washington, D.C.

FOOTNOTES

[1] G. E. Wright, *Westminster Historical Atlas to the Bible* (Philadelphia, 1945), p. 18.

[2] It seems likely that the names *yqtn* and *yqshn* go back to an original semitic *yqthn*; in one dialect the *th* (shin 1) became *sh* (as *thalath* became *shalosh*), while in another dialect, the *th* (shin 1) became an emphatic *teth* partially assimilating under the influence of the emphatic *qoph* (as *hithsadeq* became *histadeq*).

[3] G. Caton Thompson, "The Evidence of South Arabian Palaeoliths in the Question of Pleistocene Land Connections with Africa," *Pan-African Congress on Prehistory, Proceedings of the Third Congress, Livingstone* (London, 1957), pp. 383 f.

[4] G. W. Van Beek, "Monuments of Axum in the Light of South Arabian Archaeology," *Journal of the American Oriental Society*, 37 (1967), pp. 113-122.

[5] See especially, E. A. Speiser, "Man, Ethnic Divisions of," *The Interpreter's Dictionary of the Bible*, Vol. III, pp. 235-242, which is the best recent study of both the ancient and modern ethnic relationships. For detailed studies of Dedan and Massa' and related tribes, see W. F. Albright, "Dedan," *Geschichte und Altes Testament* [the A. Alt Festschrift] (Tübingen, 1953); and "The Biblical Tribe of Massa' and Some Congeners," *Studi Orientalistici in onore di Giorgio Levi Della Vida*, Vol. I (Rome, 1956).

[6] For a full discussion of these commodities and their economic importance, see G. W. Van Beek, "Frankincense and Myrrh," *The Biblical Archaeologist Reader*, Vol. 2 (New York, 1964), Anchor Book A250b, pp. 99-126 (*The Biblical Archaeologist*, 23, 2 [Sept. 1960], 69-95).

[7] G. W. Van Beek and A. Jamme, "An Inscribed South Arabian Clay Stamp from Bethel," *Bulletin of the American Schools of Oriental Research*, 151 (1958), pp. 9-16.

[8] A. Jamme and G. W. Van Beek, "The South-Arabian Clay Stamp from Bethel Again," *Bulletin of the American Schools of Oriental Research*, 163 (1961), pp. 15-18.

[9] C. Rathjens and H. von Wissmann, *Vorislamische Altertümer* (Hamburg, 1932).

[10] R. LeB. Bowen, Jr., "Archaeological Survey of Beihan," *Archaeological Discoveries in South Arabia* (Baltimore, 1958), pp. 3-34.

[11] R. L. Cleveland, "The 1960 American Archaeological Expedition to Dhofar," *Bulletin of the American Schools of Oriental Research*, 159 (1960), pp. 14-26; "Preliminary Report on Archaeological Soundings at Sohar (Oman)," *ibid.*, 153 (1959), pp. 11-18.

[12] A. Fakhry, *An Archaeological Journey to Yemen* (Cairo, 1952).

[13] W. L. Reed and F. V. Winnett, "Report on the Arabian Expedition of 1962," *Bulletin of the American Schools of Oriental Research*, 168 (1962), pp. 9-10; "Report on the Archaeological Expedition to Ha'il in Northern Saudi Arabia (1967)," *ibid.*, 188 (1967), pp. 2-3.

[14] G. W. Van Beek, G. H. Cole, and A. Jamme, "An Archaeological

Reconnaissance in Hadhramaut, South Arabia—A Preliminary Report," *Smithsonian Report for 1963* (Washington), pp. 521-545.
[15] G. Caton Thompson, *The Tombs and Moon Temple of Hureidha (Hadhramaut)*, in *Reports of the Research Committee of the Society of Antiquaries of London*, XIII (Oxford, 1944).
[16] R. LeB. Bowen, Jr. and F. P. Albright, *Archaeological Discoveries in South Arabia* (Baltimore, 1958); A. Jamme, *Sabaean Inscriptions from Mahram Bilqis (Marib)* (Baltimore, 1962); R. L. Cleveland, *An Ancient South Arabian Necropolis* (Baltimore, 1965); G. W. Van Beek, *Hajar Bin Humeid* (Baltimore, 1969). In addition to these monographic studies (in the series, *Publications of the American Foundation for the Study of Man*), there have been a host of articles on both general and detailed subjects.
[17] W. F. Albright, "The Chronology of Ancient South Arabia in the Light of the First Campaign of Excavation in Qataban," *Bulletin of the American Schools of Oriental Research*, 119 (1950), pp. 5-15; "The Chronology of the Minaean Kings of Arabia," *ibid.*, 129 (1953), pp. 20-24; "A Note on Early Sabaean Chronology," *ibid.* 143 (1956), pp. 9 f. A. Jamme, *op. cit.* and the bibliography cited there. J. Ryckmans, *L'institution monarchique en Arabie méridionale avant L'Islam (Ma'in et Saba)*, in *Bibliothèque du Muséon*, 28 (Louvain, 1951).
[18] For a detailed discussion, see J. Tkatsch, "Saba'," *Encyclopedia of Islam* (London, 1934), pp. 12-15.
[19] F. V. Winnett, "The Place of the Minaeans in the History of Pre-Islamic Arabia," *Bulletin of the American Schools of Oriental Research*, 73 (1939), pp. 3-9.
[20] Berta Segall, "The Lion-Riders from Timna'," in *Archaeological Discoveries in South Arabia (1958)*, pp. 155-178.
[21] R. LeB. Bowen, Jr., "Irrigation in Ancient Qataban (Beihan)," *ibid.*, pp. 43-131.
[22] F. P. Albright, "Excavations at Marib in Yemen," *ibid.*, pp. 223-225.
[23] G. W. Van Beek, "A New Interpretation of the So-Called South Arabian House Model," *American Journal of Archaeology*, 63 (1959), pp. 269-273.
[24] G. W. Van Beek, "Marginally Drafted, Pecked Masonry," in *Archaeological Discoveries in South Arabia*, pp. 287-299.
[25] See the group from Timna', for example, in R. L. Cleveland, "Representations of Bulls," *An Ancient South Arabian Necropolis*, pp. 36-43.
[26] M. E. Salmon, "A Survey of the Composition and Fabrication of Bronze Artifacts from Hajar Bin Humeid," *Hajar Bin Humeid*, pp. 373-386.
[27] G. W. Van Beek, *ibid.*, pp. 356 ff.
[28] *The Geography of Strabo* (Loeb Classical Library), 16.4.24.
[29] *Natural History* (Loeb Classical Library), VI. xxxii. 162.
[30] W. H. Schoff, translated and annotated edition of *The Periplus of the Erythraean Sea* (London, 1912), paragraphs 24-28.
[31] *Natural History*, XII.xli.83.
[32] P. W. Lapp, "Observations on the Pottery of Thaj," *Bulletin of the American Schools of Oriental Research*, 172 (1963), pp. 20-22; P. J. Parr, "Objects from Thaj in the British Museum," *ibid.*, 176 (1964), pp. 20-28; J. P. Mandaville, "Thaj: a Pre-Islamic Site in Northeastern Arabia," *ibid.*, 172 (1963), pp. 9-20.
[33] *The Geography of Strabo*, 16.3.3.
[34] See n. 11 above.

PREFACE

THIS volume contains the substance of the Haskell Lectures for 1930, which I delivered at Oberlin College in the Spring. Those Lectures, as conditioned by their presentation before an audience, were intended to be informative, and with the same object of information they may be of interest to the larger reading public. Despite the vast interest in the archæology of the Bible their subject has been scantily treated in English, although it has had far more extensive vogue in German. There are at hand the invaluable volume of Hogarth's *Penetration of Arabia*, his accompanying brief *History of Arabia*, Margoliouth's stimulating Lectures on the *Relations between Arabs and Israelites*, and for the scientific exploration of Arabia the noble series of Musil's volumes published by the American Geographical Society; for the literary illustration of the Bible such books as George Adam Smith's *Early Poetry of Israel* and Duncan B. Macdonald's *Hebrew Literary Genius*. But this volume may still have a place as presenting a reasoned survey of the particular relations between biblical history and Arabia, and it is hoped that its brief massing of evidence may turn the eyes of thoughtful readers towards that inscrutable land for more light on the Bible.

I have thought it well to document the book with references. These may be ignored by the more casual reader, who will however remark that there is authentication for all important statements. But for the more serious student—and even for professional scholars Arabia is often a sealed book—the references may lead him to pursue further investigation, and so achieve for this volume the chief purpose of any publication, the stimulus to further inquiry.

Arabia and the Bible

I have to thank the President and Faculty of Oberlin College for the honor they conferred on me in tendering me the Haskell Lectureship, and for their delightful courtesy on my visit. And my sincere obligations are due to my friend and colleague Professor Speiser for reading through a manuscript in perverse condition and for giving me his corrections and suggestions.

J. A. M.

ABBREVIATIONS

THE following abbreviations are used: AV, Authorized, or King James, Version; RV, British Revised Version; SV, American Standard Version; JV, The Holy Scriptures, published by the Jewish Publication Society; RVV, the latter three in agreement; EVV, all these Versions in agreement.

I

THE BIBLE AND ARABIA

IT is a commonplace to discuss the dependence of Palestine, the land of the Bible, upon the two great neighboring civilizations of the valleys of the Nile and the Euphrates. Assyriologists and Egyptologists have for long disputed over the merits of the respective fields in regard to their bearing upon the civilization and religion of the people of the Bible. In the eighteenth century it was vogue among the philosophic Illuminati to hold that the Hebrew religion was derived from the wisdom of Egypt, that Moses was an apostle of its culture to his rude people, that Israel's monotheism was based upon the alleged lofty tenets of the Egyptian religion. Within the past generation arose in Germany the so-called Pan-Babylonian School, which has found in Babylonia the mother and mistress of art and science and philosophy, and discovered the original of Israel's religion in the speculations of Babylonian thinkers.[1] And so Abraham was an evangelist of the esoteric monotheism cultivated in the Sin or Moon god cult at Ur and Harran to the West-Semite barbarians, and thus Israel's religion derived through him as spiritual father ultimately from Babylonia—a radical enough hypothesis, but with conservative results in its alleged confirmation of the biblical data as to the antiquity and lofty character of the religion of Abraham. The pendulum of theory of origins has since swung westwards to Egypt; the high antiquity of its culture has been demonstrated and the evolution of man out of primitive stages

---

1. Cf. Jeremias, *The Old Testament in the Light of the Ancient East* (Eng. tr., 1911); also his *Handbuch der altorientalischen Kultur* (ed. 2, 1929).

can be mapped out most clearly in the valley of the Nile; the monotheism of Akhenaten in the fourteenth century would then give the *milieu* if not even the actual source of the biblical religion of the One God; and literary *rapprochements* between the Bible and Egypt have been increasingly discovered.[2] How much these hypotheses of explanation depend upon sensational archæological discoveries appears just now in the return of interest to the Babylonian field in view of the extraordinary discoveries at Ur.[3] Quite naturally in the unfolding panorama of ancient civilization the eye not only of the layman but also of the scholar tends to focus upon those two poles of brilliant culture between which lay the modest land of Palestine.

Meanwhile archæologists have been pursuing their researches in the less colorful Palestinian soil and attempting to measure from the scattered finds the proportions of Egyptian and Mesopotamian influence in that land. But the same science has equally opened up other vistas. In the Great Sea to the West has been rediscovered the ancient Ægean or Minoan civilization, a third focus of the culture of the Near East. How great its influence was upon the arts of Palestine is demonstrated in the excavations;[4] the Proto-Greek Philistines were

2. See Breasted, *A History of Egypt,* and his Presidential Address before the American Historical Association in the *Am. Hist. Review,* Jan. 1929; G. A. F. Knight, *Nile and Jordan* (1921); T. E. Peet, *Egypt and the Old Testament* (1922); A. S. Yahuda, *Die Sprache des Pentateuchs,* vol. I (1929), with stress upon the Egyptian affinities of the Pentateuch. For the problem of the relation of the Egyptian Wisdom of Amenemapt and the book of Proverbs see the *Commentary* by Oesterley (1929), Excursus I.

3. See C. L. Woolley's recent volumes, *The Sumerians,* and *Discoveries at Ur,* and C. J. Gadd, *History and Monuments of Ur* (1929). Compare the discussion by G. A. Barton, 'Origins of Civilization in Africa and Mesopotamia,' in *Proc. Am. Phil. Soc.,* 1929, pp. 303 ff., and at length, V. G. Child, *The Most Ancient East* (1929), e.g., pp. 218 ff.

4. See *The Cambridge Ancient History,* vol. II, chap. 16; Glotz, *Ægean Civilization* (Eng. tr.).

Israel's neighbors and rivals in the land of Palestine to which those outsiders have given their name.[5]

The uncovering of the history of the Hittites in Asia Minor, or Anatolia, offers another fresh and fascinating vista.[6] Here we stand on surer historical footing, because actual documents, Egyptian, Akkadian,[7] Hittite, enable us in good part to precise Hittite history, to know its dynasties and fix its chronology for several centuries in the second millennium B.C. The Hittite 'empire' appears to have comprised a conglomerate of races, in which, however, the Indo-European element dominated, and now the earliest-known documents of that group are being deciphered. Scholarship has had perforce to approve the biblical data concerning the movement of these northern, non-Semitic stocks into Palestine from early days. We recall the Hittites at Hebron in Abraham's day, while we know that a Hittite dynasty sat on the throne in Jerusalem in the early fourteenth century. The tradition of this ancient relation is preserved by Ezekiel: "The Amorite was thy father and thy mother a Hittite," 16:3. In consonance with Akkadian usage the Bible knows Syria as the land of the Hittites, e.g., Jos. 1:4. The ancient oracle that "God enlarge Japheth and he shall dwell in the tents of Shem," Gen. 9:27, enshrines the record of this ancient immigration into Semitic lands. Other non-Semitic stocks from the north are coming to be recognized as settled in Palestine, e.g., the Horites (for-

5. The original meaning of 'Palestine' occurs quaintly in AV at Ex. 15:14, Is. 14:29, 31, following the ancient Versions.

6. D. C. Hogarth, *Kings of the Hittites* (1926); J. Garstang, *The Hittite Empire* (1929); *The Cambridge Ancient History*, vol. II, chap. 11.

7. I follow the new usage of this word, denoting the language of Babylonia-Assyria, and replacing the older clumsy term Assyrian, which was used philologically to include Babylonian.

merly understood to be the Troglodytes of the land), related now by scholars with the Hurri of northern Mesopotamia.[8]

These imposing fields of archæological research and results have tended to obscure another land, nearer indeed to Palestine, but one the study of which has not yet shown itself very articulate, except among a small group of investigators. I refer to the Hinterland of Palestine, on east and south, to which we may give with full historic propriety the name Arabia. For its merit to be included among the great groups of civilization which mightily affected Israel, its land, its history, and its religion, may be cited some words of the distinguished German Orientalist, the late Hugo Winckler. After enumerating the three civilizations which had their bearing upon our Bible, the Babylonian, Egyptian, and that of Anatolia, he rightly proceeds to maintain:[9] "The Arabic field can be included with those other three as the fourth center of culture. If we shall see in Arabia the home of the Semitic peoples, to which Israel also belongs, so we must expect that all that can be established concerning the life and character of Arabian peoples is fitted to disclose to us Israel's life and thought in its primitive conditions." And a trenchant statement by the contemporary Scandinavian scholar, Ditlef Nielsen, may be quoted as presenting the vast scope of this relation between Israel and Arabia in enforcing the value of the biblical tradition for our understanding of Semitic origins; he says,[10] "The Hebrews alone among

8. See Prof. E. A. Speiser's fresh and original volume on the subject, *Mesopotamian Origins: The Basic Population of the Near East* (1930), to which add now his monograph, 'Ethnic Movements in the Near East in the Second Millennium B.C.,' *Annual Am. Schools Or. Research*, 1933, pp. 13–54.

9. In Schrader, *Die Keilinschriften und das Alte Testament*, ed. 3, p. 7.

10. *Handbuch der altarabischen Altertumskunde*, vol. I, 1927 (ed. by Nielsen with coöperation of Hommel and Rhodokanakis), p. 241. It is expected that the future volumes will present all the important South-Arabian inscriptions in text and translation.

the Semites have preserved in the legends of the Patriarchs
and Moses a tradition of the earlier Bedawi life and of the
entrance into a land of civilization." And indeed to understand Israel's origin we can and must go back to Arabia, and
have to recognize in Israel's perennial consciousness of her
Arabian origins and relationships her most vital spiritual
force. To quote Nielsen again (p. 243): "The central nerve
of the Hebrew religion leads back to Old-Arabia," in which
statement the word 'religion,' be it observed, denotes the most
extensive and most important phase of Israel's history.

And how great a part does Arabia play in the pages of the
Old Testament! There is other scenery in its drama which is
more brilliant and theatrical, such as the stories of the Egyptian sojourn at the beginning of the history, or of the sumptuous Babylonian and Persian courts in Daniel, the youngest
book of the volume. But those acts are exotic to Israel's home
and nature. Also there are *fin de siècle* crimson spots in its
domestic history, the court life of David and Solomon, the
reign of Ahab and Jezebel; but these are foils to Israel's spirit,
ill humors of its existence against which its conscience re-
volted. For elaborate and spectacular history, for world-stir-
ring events, we must leave the palm to Egypt and Babylonia.

But there is a peculiar color and atmosphere to the biblical
life which gives it its special tone, so that it is not just another
'civilization,' another 'culture.' And that touch comes from
the expanses and the free-moving life of what we call Arabia
—a touch which can best be conjured up to us by travelers'
tales of that mysterious land. And this phase dominates the
most part of Israel's peculiar history.

That begins with the Garden of Eden, which literalists
transpose to some definite geographical spot; but its legendary

features presuppose the scenery of a desert oasis, with its rivers springing miraculously from nowhere and emptying themselves again perhaps in the desert sands, like the rivers Abana and Pharpar of Damascus—itself an oasis which Mohammad, true son of the desert, judged to be the likest to the celestial Paradise. There is the preference for the shepherd Abel over Cain, who raised fruits of the earth, and it was this fratricide Cain who built the first city (Gen. 4:17). Or in the mixture of themes in this history Cain was the first smith, as his name probably designates, and subsequently in the genealogy, vv. 20-22, we have the three classes that appear all through Arabian history: Jabal the father of such as dwell in tents and have flocks; his brother Jubal, the father of those who handle the harp and pipe; and Tubalcain the smith of every kind of brass and iron tool; i.e., the flock-grazer, the minstrel, and the artisan.[11] Lamech's taunt-song, vv. 23-24, is our earliest example of the Arabian Hijá or battle-satire.[12] Again at the Tower of Babel we see what becomes of men who build cities—a sentiment how unlike the sophisticated Babylonians who made the first thing in civilization their

11. *Kain,* 'smith' in Arabic, and so *kainaya* in Syriac, equaling exactly biblical 'Kenite,' which would then indicate a smith tribe or caste. For the peculiar social position of smiths in Arabia see Doughty, *Arabia Deserta,* Index *s.v.* 'Sany' (i.e., smith). For 'the dwellers in tents' cf. the identical phrase for the Arabs in the Akkadian Cyrus Cylinder. Professor Speiser calls my attention to the ancient Sumerian city Bad-Tibira, 'Center of Smiths.'

12. See G. A. Smith, *The Early Poetry of Israel,* pp. 37, 44; G. Jacob, *Das Leben der vorislamischen Beduinen* (1895), pp. 144 ff.; and for an extensive discussion of the satirical, practically curse-song, Goldziher's essay in his *Abhandlungen zur arab. Philologie,* vol. I, pp. 1–105, and for comparison of this *genre* with the Balaam episode and similar passages, e.g., Num. 21:27 ff., see pp. 42 ff. On the other hand Daiches, 'Balaam a Babylonian *baru*' in the *Hilprecht Anniversary Volume,* pp. 60–70, would explain these scenes from a Babylonian *milieu;* but as Goldziher shows, native Arabian modes are to be found in those ancient literary remains.

tower-temples. Then Israel's line of the Fathers troops across the stage. Abraham has long been envisaged by us as a Sheikh, and it matters not to our purpose whether the history is true, for its coloring is correct to finest details. He moves through the lands of civilization, on equal terms with kings like Abimelech of Gerar, or with burgher citizens like the Hittites at Hebron, not settling down except to buy a tomb, while the *razzia* he inflicted on Amraphel's host is entirely Arabian in conception and execution. He and his son Isaac have their disputes with the natives over rights to wells, the most precious of boons to the nomads, Gen. 21:22 ff., 26:15 ff. The feebler Isaac exhibits one of the ever-recurring phases of nomadic life; he enters temporarily into the life of the semi-nomad, settling down as an agriculturist, the one essay at this mode of life that appears in the nomadic existence of the Patriarchs (Gen. 26:12). The scenery of the desert wells is repeated in the stories of Jacob and Moses coming gallantly to the relief of the shepherdesses, whereon was to hang romance (Gen. 29: Ex. 2:15 ff.).[13]

Our first picture of a caravan is given in the scene of Joseph's sad fate when he is carried off, picked up out of the pit, by a troop of Midianites, or as another source has it, of Ishmaelites, with their camels bearing "the spicery and balm and ladanum" of Gilead, and incidentally, like true Arabs, doing a side-business in the slave-trade. Then the patriarchal family, now grown large, starts off on a great trek into Egypt, an example repeated innumerable times throughout the length of Arabia, for many of the wandering Arab tribes of today trace

13. The presence of bovine cattle (AV 'oxen') as in the Patriarchs' possession has seemed strange to the present writer; e.g., Gen. 12:16; 13:5; 18:7. But Moritz, *Arabien*, p. 46, proves that this animal once abounded in Arabia, although it has now well-nigh disappeared except in the Yemen; the species is of the buffalo order.

their lineage back to the civilized peoples of ancient Yemen or Hijáz. They settled down in the royal pasture-lands of Goshen, and when threatened with the servile labors of what their masters might style civilization, trekked forth again into the desert and found themselves at home. The color of that desert sojourn is true to life; and if any doubt its historic detail, still the story represents the vivid memory of the desert origins which Israel always cherished. The story is not a patchwork of details artificially amassed any more than are the Homeric rhapsodies a sophisticated product of the later Greek imagination. We follow the intermittent marches from oasis to oasis. There is the part that the sagacious Moses played in procuring water out of the stony rock, while the 'nobles of the people' delved with 'scepter and staves,' as in the Song of the Well, Num. 21:16–18.[14] They found miraculous food in the swarms of migratory quails, which still pass over the Sinai peninsula, and were fed with 'bread from heaven,' the manna which can be identified by scientists.[15] They encountered poisonous serpents, which later became in popular legend winged flying serpents, monsters similar to which the sober Assyrian records also report, while modern travelers record the horror of those vermin of the desert.[16] They wandered about seem-

14. The water of the desert often lies close beneath the surface and its presence can be detected by the keen Arab; indeed some profess the art of locating water by a hyper-sense. The water is then exposed by digging out the sand with a stick, exactly as is described in this song. See Lammens, *Le berceau de l'Islam*, pp. 34 f., and for the songs at the well, Musil, *Arabia Petraea*, vol. III, pp. 255 ff., Nicholson, *Literary History of the Arabs*, p. 73; cf. Smith, *Poetry*, pp. 63 f.

15. See *Enc. Bibl.*, *s.v.* 'Manna,' and for the most recent study of this tamarisk exudation Bodenheimer and Theodor, *Ergebnisse der Sinai-Expedition 1927*, Part 3.

16. Num. 21:24 ff., 'fiery serpent'; Is. 30:6, 'flying serpent'; 14:29, 'fiery flying serpent.' (The word for fiery is *sarap*, whence the Seraphs of Is. 6, that is, dragon-like creatures.) Esarhaddon reports on the march of his troops against Egypt across the

ingly without motive or object, and finally found an opportune conjunction of conditions to break into the lands of civilization. This history has been repeated time and time again through the ages by Arabian folk. Above all nothing is more plausible, although no point has been more disputed by critics, than the general religious picture of the Wilderness wanderings: their going on a pilgrimage to seek their God in the desert and finding him there on the Mount of God.[17] And in no respect is the story more true to life than in the picture of the leader Moses knitting the clans together into a nation, giving his decisions by oracle and the divine lot, Urim and Thummim, both institutions of the old Arabian religion, and so building up a body of law within a generation.[18] All this

Arabian desert ". . . serpents of two heads . . . died. I trampled on them," and there follows a reference to something "with wings," see Rogers, *Cuneiform Parallels to the Old Testament*, p. 359; Luckenbill, *Ancient Records of Assyria*, II, 229. Another text of Esarhaddon's describing a campaign in Arabian Bazu, the biblical Buz, tells of a district full of scorpions and serpents, "covering the plain like ants," Luckenbill, p. 209. And Colonel Lawrence in his *Revolt in the Desert*, p. 93, gives this account of a remarkable experience in the Wady Sirhan to the east of Trans-Jordan: "The plague of snakes which had been with us since our first entry into Sirhan, today rose to memorable height and became a terror. . . . This year the valley seemed creeping with horned vipers and puff-adders, cobras and black snakes. By night movement was dangerous; and at last we found it necessary to walk with sticks beating the bushes each side," etc. This tradition of fiery serpents survived in Arabic literature; see G. Jacob, *Studien in arab. Dichtern*, Heft 1, p. 93; Heft 4, p. 10. Also Herodotus tells about these winged serpents of Arabia, II, 75; III, 109.

17. Scholars dispute over the respective antiquity and the relation of the ark and the tent. With Arnold, *Ephod and Ark*, the former probably contained the apparatus of oracle-giving, the Urim and Thummim, and was therefore antique. For the primitive and Arabian character of the 'tent of meeting' (i.e., *rendezvous* with God) see the article by R. Hartmann, 'Zelt und Lade,' *Zeitschrift f. d. alttest. Wissenschaft*, 1918, p. 209. In addition to the well-known tent of the Carthaginians he gives evidence to show that the Arabians possessed this sacred institution, it being used as a place of communion with the Deity. For the primitive, nomadic nature of the biblical notion of 'the God of the fathers,' see Alt, *Der Gott der Väter* (1929).

18. See Wellhausen, *Reste arab. Heidentums*, pp. 130 ff.

seems impossible, but when we realize that Mohammad effected the same result in a shorter life and with a far more 'stiffnecked people'; that the founder of the reforming Wahhábi movement in the middle of the eighteenth century repeated this marvel with effects that shook Arabia to the core, and that Ibn Saúd is welding in our own day a nation on the simple elements of 'unitarianism' and a puritanic law like that of the Hebrews, the marvel of the story of Moses becomes reasonable.[19]

And all this history is not accidental or incidental. It is after all not what happens to an individual or a people but what it believes has happened that counts in its future, although always there must have been an initial basis for such belief. This experience in the desert was woven for Israel into the warp and woof of its consciousness. For the Prophets, who are the voice of that consciousness, both of its history and its ideals, that experience was the classic age of Israel's spiritual life. So Amos distinguishes it among the great act of Yhwh, 2:10: "I brought you up out of the land of Egypt and led you forty years in the wilderness;" and their religion in the wilderness was pure worship, 5:25. Hosea develops the theme romantically, 2:16 f.: "Therefore I will allure her, and will bring her [again] into the wilderness, and speak tenderly to her.

19. Notice that according to Ex. 18, Moses' father-in-law, the priest of Midian, is represented as instructing Moses in the art of managing a people; the tradition is not at all abashed at this affiliation with a desert people. The land of Midian, which stretched down the Red Sea coast, possessed a culture of which today it is entirely void; the remains, Arabian inscriptions, and the reports of the Græco-Roman geographers have much to tell about the country; see Chapters VI and VIII. We have to heed the warning insisted upon by Hartmann in the article cited in a preceding note that it is fallacious to regard those Hebrew tribes as 'primitives.' I shall not discuss the problem whether Moses adopted the God of the Midianites, answered in the affirmative by some eminent scholars; if he did, our respect for Midian must increase. But that is an explanation of *ignotum ab ignoto.*

And I will give her her vineyards from thence, and the vale of Achor for a door of hope. And she shall make response there, as in the days of her youth, and as in the day when she came up out of the land of Egypt." Cf. also 12:10, "Again will I make thee dwell in tents." And so Jeremiah, yet more idyllically (2:2):

> "I remember thee for thy youthful affection,
>   Thy bridal troth,
> How thou wentest after me in the wilderness,
>   In a land not sown."[20]

Ezekiel follows suit, although with his dour Calvinism, touched with morbidity, it is not the early love and troth of Israel, but her innate depravity from the beginning—her love was lust—that the desert tradition recalls to him (c. 16). Elijah, he of the broad steppes beyond the Jordan, fled to Mount Horeb to receive consolation and inspiration from the God of his fathers. The Rechabites and Nazirites, puritanical castes of desert heritage, like the modern Wahhábis, appear fitfully in the Bible pages, but they must have played a larger part in the spiritual history than appears on the surface, as Amos indicates (2:11).[21]

Again in the New Testament the Apostle Paul retires to

20. 'The Desert and the Sown' is still the Arabic distinction of the two kinds of region.

21. For the primitive abstinence of the desert Arabs from intoxicating liquors cf. Robertson Smith, *Prophets of Israel*, p. 388; this was a principle of the Essenes on the Dead Sea; and we possess a Palmyrene inscription, erected by Nabatæans, dedicated to the Nabatæan deity Shai-al-qaum ('Help-of-the-Folk') 'who does not drink wine'; Littmann, *Semitic Inscriptions*, 1904, pp. 70 ff., Cooke, *North-Semitic Inscriptions*, pp. 304 ff. Mohammad's prohibition of wine is based on primitive nomadic custom, but in the lands of settled civilization wine and spirituous liquors were early introduced. For this strain of primitive asceticism persisting through Israel's history see the writer's article, 'Ascetic Strains in Early Judaism,' *Journal Bibl. Lit.*, 1932, pp. 183–213.

'Arabia,' to some unknown solitude in its expanse. And the life of John Baptist in the Judæan Desert, and the temptation of Christ in the same wilderness were reversions to type, for the wilderness of Judah is a long projection north from the Arabian deserts to the gates of Jerusalem.

This classical tradition of the Patriarch and the Exodus was reinforced by the vital contact with the desert maintained through the ages. There is the patent fact of the wide-open back door of Arabia fronting the whole length of Palestine from the haze of antiquity down into the Roman-Byzantine empire, becoming at last the portal of the mightiest of conquests, spiritual as well as political, of Islam. It is only peculiar to Israel that they never forgot, never felt shame for, that origin in the desert. This appears in one significant fact. Israel's own name for itself—and for the Semite prevails the canon *nomen omen*—the Bnê Israel, Children, or rather, Sons of Israel, is redolent not only of its origin but also of its permanent self-consciousness; throughout its history it bore and emphasized this name of desert origin and flavor, still a standing name-formation of the nomad tribes of Arabia. To this day there roam in the desert the *Bnî* Sakhr, the *Bnî* Salim, the *Bnî* Amr, the *Bnî* Tamim, the *Bnî* Hajar, etc. The settlers in the lands of the Sown otherwise dropped this appellative out of affectation for their new culture; the Bnê Israel and the Bnê Ammon alone preserved it. The several tribes also maintained it, the Bnê Judah, the Bnê Joseph, etc., expressive of the slow development out of the primitive tribal constitution into the forms of a settled state.[22] In this connec-

22. Our English 'children' is a sentimental weakening of the original tribal term. And we have to remember that the term 'son' in such a connection means primarily an individual of the group, which group may be called Israel, Kelb, or what not. Such a

tion we may also note that the Hebrew word for home is the nomadic 'tent,' *ohel.* This use occurs not only frequently in the Arabizing poem of Job, but as a commonplace, e.g., 2 Sam. 20:1, "every man to his tent!" i.e., "go home!" cf. 1 Kings 12:16.[23]

But Israel's immigration is only one, a minor case, among many similar phenomena. In addition to Israel's own tradition of itself, there were the movements into Palestine of the vague Habiri, to whom most authorities believe the Hebrews to have belonged, and of the Aramæans from the east and the north. There is always the constant border warfare of the Midianites on the east and the Amalekites and other Arab peoples on the south, which could be repressed only by the strong hand of a David or Solomon, pacifying the desert borders. As soon as the resistance of the lands of civilization weakened, the incursions of the desert peoples were renewed. With the extinction of the Jewish state by Nebuchadnezzar there succeeded the invasion of its territories by Edomites and Arabs; and with the fall of the Persian empire, the Arab

phrase as we have in "Israel is my son, my first born," Ex. 4:22, is Arabian; South-Arabian peoples spoke of themselves as 'children' of their gods; and so a common name of the deity for Hebrews, Amorites, South-Arabians was 'father.' The Bnê Ammon were named after their god Amm ('uncle'), on which there is an etymological play in Gen. 19:38. Tribe-names identical with God-names, like God and Asher, are doubtless reductions from the fuller Bnê Gad, etc. In the 'civilized' states only kings might arrogate such names; cf. Ps. 2.

23. Another word of similar Arabic flavor appears in 1 Sam. 18:18, translated by the EVV: "who am I, and what is my life [or] my father's family in Israel?" The word for 'life,' *hai,* is to be understood from the still prevailing use of it by nomads as of the family (properly 'the life'), and so of the tent or home; and in this passage the asyndetic 'my father's family' is a gloss to explain what had become of an obsolete word. Moffatt's translation recognizes the true meaning. In the region called Havvoth-Jair in Gilead (Num. 32:41, etc.) the first element *haw* (Arabic) is identical with Hebrew *hai,* i.e., 'Encampments of Jair'; we may compare the development of *castra* in English place-names.

Arabia and the Bible

Nabatæans centering at Petra in the old land of Edom pressed northwards into Trans-Jordan and ultimately extended their power as far as Damascus in the early days of the Roman empire. There was the remarkable movement of the Arab Ituræans (the Jetur of Gen. 25:16) into Southern Lebanon about the turn of the era; and later that of the Ghassanids into Trans-Jordan, who served as a buffer state of Byzantium against the Sassanid empire.

The same phenomenon has been witnessed through the ages on the Mesopotamian border of the desert. Study of the Akkadian documents reveals the presence of nomad Arabian tribes, for instance the Aramæans to the east of the Euphrates and Tigris, whither they moved irresistibly in search of water and pasture, or pressed forward by stronger foes in the rear. The Arabs still claim the seasonal rights of occupying their ancient pasturages, whither they trek from the Syrian Desert. One of the pressing problems of the British Mandatory in Iraq, and now of the independent Kingdom, has been how to handle these floating tribes—not citizens of Iraq, yet possessing immemorial claims of occupation, involving the Mandatory in vexed disputes with Ibn Saúd, the potent ruler of all interior Arabia, over the question of control and citizenship of these Bedawin. There is no fixed delimitation of boundaries in the desert, and this the British Government has found to its cost in its efforts to define the line between its territories and those of the Nejd.[24]

24. See a general statement of the vexed problem and of the attempt to delimit boundaries between the Mandate and the Nejd in my paper 'Arabia To-day' (*Journ. Am. Or. Soc.*, 1927), pp. 124 ff. The subsequent fortification of posts by the British along the boundaries has been resented by Ibn Saúd as infraction of the treaty which proposed an unfortified border; he refused to submit to the British action, and an *impasse* has since prevailed. For the British statement of the case see the official *Report* for Iraq for

The Bible and Arabia

Even in the history of Israel 'civilized' and finally settled in its new home we find survivals of the old Arabian spirit, showing how easily Israel could 'revert to type.' Deborah, that Hebrew Joan of Arc, is an Arab woman, singing her challenge to her followers and taunting the foe, on the front line of the combat.[25] Jephthah the border chieftain is far more Arab than settled Israelite, his votive sacrifice of his daughter is paralleled in Arab traditions[26]—how unlike he is to the more sophisticated Samson on the Philistine border, the fringe of civilization. Gideon's slaying of the Midianites Zeba and Zalmunna (Jud. 8:18 ff.) and Samuel's hewing of Agag to pieces (1 Sam. 15:32 f.) are scenes out of Arab life. The easy change of morale is well pictured in the story of David. When driven out of Judah by Saul's enmity he betook himself into the desert of Paran (1 Sam. 25). Thence he levied tribute on a worthy citizen of the Judæan territory, one Nabal, on the downright plea that that wealthy proprietor should be grateful for the 'protection' granted him by the freebooter. The gentleman was 'fool' enough—as his name means in Hebrew (not in Arabic)—to refuse, and was saved only by the good sense of his comely wife Abigail. Nabal dies of fright when he learns what he had escaped. And David crowns his effort at 'protection' by marrying the widow.

To this panorama of ethnical movements and relations between Arabia and Palestine are to be added the picturesque

1928, p. 30. Palestine, it should be noted, has perforce been divided into two Mandatory states independent of each other; the Arab state of Trans-Jordan with an Arab Emir, Abdullah, brother of King Feisal of Iraq, having been established by Great Britain with the consent of the Powers. The terms of the Balfour Declaration do not hold across the Jordan.

25. Smith, *Poetry*, pp. 30, 80 ff., cf. Miriam 'the prophetess' at the Red Sea, Ex. 15.
26. Wellhausen, *Reste arab. Heidentums*, pp. 115 f.

scenes of the actual life of the desert, of its vast and terrible stretches, and yet of the oases, centers of simple but orderly human life, as in the stories of the homelands of Laban and Job. There are pictures of the caravans threading their way through those deserts depicting the illusions and disappointments that oppress the hardy wayfarer, e.g., Jer. 2:6; Job 6:15 ff.[27] But the objectives of those caravans were fertile oases and notable states in which was focused a lively civilization throughout the length and breadth of the peninsula. The book of Isaiah has its oracles concerning these oases. In 21: 11 f. is 'The Oracle (burden) of Dumah,' generally identified with the Akkadian Adummu, the modern Dumat al-Ghandal, an oasis far out in the Syrian Desert on the shortest road to Babylonia. In 21:13 ff. is given "the Oracle 'In Arabia.' " Here appears Teima, the well-known oasis on the ancient route between the head of the Red Sea and the upper Persian Gulf, whither the Dedanite caravans—from the land of Midian—are summoned to take refuge. The historical circumstances are doubtless those of the later Assyrian or the Neo-Babylonian empire, when those states attempted to gain control of the interior of Arabia.[28] But these routes also con-

27. We may note the item of the 'howling' wilderness, Dt. 32:10, expressive of the eerie, ghastly sounds in the desert due to contraction and expansion of the stones between the extremes of temperature (cf. Smith, *Poetry*, 31), which are pulverizing the larger rock into ever smaller fragments, producing the pebbled surface of the desert; also the *sharab*, Is. 35:7; 49:10, translated by the EVV 'parched land,' but rather to be understood with the same word in the Arabic as the mirage or *fata morgana*, common in the desert. Euting, *Tagbuch einer Reise in Inner-Arabien*, p. 98, gives his experience of this phenomenon; it occurred every morning for half an hour and held forth the prospect of a beautiful lake to thirsty mortals.

28. On Teima and these imperial ambitions, see Chapter IV. The reference here to 'the thickets,' v. 13, in the oasis is corroborated by travelers' observation of the thick undergrowth found where water appears. Moritz, *Arabien*, p. 35, would translate by 'forest' and uses this text as proof of the one-time forestation of the land.

nected with the distant land of gold-bearing Ophir, of Sheba
and Hadhramot famed for their incense-trade, and with the
Persian Gulf. The commerce of the desert is epically pictured
by Ezekiel in his description of the far-flung trade of Tyre,
'the merchant of the peoples unto many isles,' c. 27. Indeed
there are direct references to a life of opulence and culture in
those Arabian lands which we are wont to label as 'howling
wilderness.' Solomon's wisdom could be compared only with
that of the Sages of Egypt and the Sons of the East, some of
whom are individually named, i.e., the Arab folk to the east
of Palestine; that is, there was a wisdom of Arabia as well as
of Egypt and Babylonia. And the Queen of Sheba is type of
the wealth and culture of Arabia, for she came all her long
journey with rich gifts to hear the wisdom of Solomon.[29]

The Arabian background, or as some believe, origin of the
book of Job will concern us later (Chapter VIII). I may but
note here the brilliant pictures in c. 39 of the wild life of the
desert, 'the wild-goat of the rocks,' the wild-ass, the wild-ox,
the ostrich,[30] with finally the epic description of the horse, our
earliest description of the Arabian horse, still one of the finest
stocks for the racing-studs of Europe.[31]

29. These points will be developed in subsequent chapters.

30. For the wild-goat, *capra beden,* a chamois-like animal, see Tristram, *Fauna and
Flora of Palestine;* it is still found in Sinai. The wild-ass, *onager,* is now about extinct; Doughty reported its existence in the Palmyrene Hamad, *Arabia Deserta,* vol. I,
429; von Oppenheim reports in his *Tell Halaf* (Leipzig, 1931) that it had become
extinct in the region of his work by his second visit; for references to it in Arabic literature see Moritz, *Arabien,* p. 42. The wild-ox, *re'ém,* is the unicorn of AV, following
ancient Versions, but now generally recognized to be the *rîmu* or wild-ox of the Akkadian; the same word in the Arabic means the oryx. The wild-ox is the *bos primigenius,*
see Tristram, p. 7; Arabic references to it are given by Moritz, *loc. cit.* The ostrich is
still found in the northern deserts, Moritz, *ibid.* Bertram Thomas reports the ostrich as
existent in the Desert Quarter within the memory of Arab followers.

31. Jacob, *Studien,* Heft 3, 73, and Lammens, *Le berceau de l'Islam,* p. 139, have

Arabia and the Bible

To repeat an initial observation, we are wont to think of the relations of biblical Palestine by way of the north with the Babylonian civilization of the Euphrates valley, by the south with Egypt of the Nile. Probably as we look at the map and note the Palestinian ports of Jaffa and Haifa—by which some of us may have entered the Holy Land—we consider that sea frontage to be an essential part of Israel's geography. But Israel never possessed ports on the Mediterranean until down into the Hasmonæan age, and the littoral played almost no part whatsoever in Israel's history. Jonah thought that he could escape the hand of his God by taking ship on that sea.[32] The one line of maritime venture pursued by Judan policy was the development of the Red Sea routes (e.g., 1 Ki. 9:26 ff.); that is, the commercial prospects of the state looked towards Arabia; this will be considered in Chapter VIII.

But there remains, too little observed, the long borderland on the east and south of Palestine, fringing what we call the desert of Arabia, the Arabia Petræa of the Roman empire. Here there is no natural line of demarcation. It is the scene of the conflict between the Sown and the Unsown, between two civilizations. The culture of the settled land may push east and south and make the desert blossom as the rose by tapping

denied the early existence of the horse in Arabia; but in Arabian booty taken by Sargon horses are listed (Rogers, *Cuneiform Inscriptions*, p. 316); pictures of horses are found on South-Arabian monuments. See Moritz, pp. 43 ff., excursus on the horse. For the quest of the blooded stock see Lady Anne Blunt's *Pilgrimage to Nejd* (1881).

32. The one exception to the denial of Israelitish ports might be found in 1 Ki. 4:11, when one of Solomon's administrative districts is 'the coast land of Dor.' But there is no mention of commercial development of this ancient Phœnician port. According to the tradition in 2 Ch. 2:16 the Lebanon timber was floated in rafts to (Philistine) Joppa. Doubtless part of Solomon's compact with Hiram of Tyre was that he should 'keep hands off' the Mediterranean trade. The only advance Solomon made into the Philistine territory was through the capture and gift to him of Gezer by the Pharaoh, 1 Ki. 9:16.

the water springs at a distance, bringing them by long aqueducts, as at Palmyra, and so providing irrigation, if only a
proper policing system be established against the Arab Bedawin. In the days of the Hellenistic age, under the Roman
empire, on into the days of the Byzantine empire, and with a
revival in the Caliphate, the border of Trans-Jordan was
pushed far to the east and included flourishing and notable
cities and fertile lands, which have since lapsed into ruins and
reverted to desert, with only the wonderful monuments of
Greek and Roman and Byzantine and Arabian art to witness to
former glories. As a map of the civilization about the beginning of the era will show, the area of Trans-Jordan was well
nigh doubled over its present condition.[33] A similar condition existed in the country south of Judah, the Negeb or
Southland, where remain ruins of Roman and Byzantine
times, indicating a considerable and prosperous population,
whose means of subsistence we can hardly imagine today.[34]
One locality might especially be distinguished as known by
fame to all and visited by many travelers, namely Petra, tra-
ditionally identified as the biblical Sela,[35] ensconced in the
rocky deserts of Edom, once the proud capital of an important Arab kingdom, the center of the great highways between
South Arabia and the Indian Ocean on the south and Syria-
Palestine on the north, while east and west passed through
it caravan routes, connecting Egypt and the Mediterranean
world with ports on the Persian Gulf. Yet another queen of

33. See Smith and Bartholomew, *Historical Atlas of the Holy Land*; Smith, *Historical Geography of the Holy Land*, chaps. 27, 28; Brünnow and von Domaszewski, *Die
Provincia Arabia* (2 vols., 1904–5).

34. Cf. Woolley and Lawrence: *Wilderness of Zin* (1915).

35. E.g., 2 Ki. 14:7—so the Vulgate; the identification is based primarily on the
equation, *sela* = 'rock' = Petra.

Arabia and the Bible

the desert is Tadmor-Palmyra in the North-Syrian Desert, which in the third century shook the Roman and Persian empires and attempted an imperial dominion of its own; it has this interest to the Bible student that it is mentioned in the Textus Receptus of the Bible, but by a change of the Hebrew text which must have occurred in the third century B.C.[36] But human degeneracy has destroyed these marts and capitals of civilization, and the desert has taken them back into her bosom.

The point I desire to make is that there is no natural barrier, no Chinese Wall, to delimit the eastern and southern borders of Palestine from the desert lands of Arabia. That marge of the desert, pushing forward or receding as man or nature dominated, is a long open entry, where the two regions confront each other and intermingle. To this day the Arab tribes have been moving into Trans-Jordan and then across the river into Samaria and Upper Galilee, while in the south there is not even the barrier of the Jordan canyon to prevent now, as in ancient times, the free passage of desert tribes into Judah's land. We recall the conflicts of Saul and David with the Bedawi Amalekites,[37] and after the Exile Judah as far

36. On Tamar-Tadmor see Chapter IV, Note 17. For Petra and Palmyra and the intermediate metropolis Jerash and the part they played on the Græco-Roman frontier, see the delightful book by Rostovtzeff, *Caravan Cities* (Oxford, 1932).

37. According to Gen. 36:12, Amalek was a bastard Edomite stock, and for the Arab historians a primitive 'Cushite' race and then extinct; see Caussin de Perceval, *Histoire des Arabes*, I, 18 ff., E. Meyer, *Israel und ihre Nachbarstämme* (see Index). Amalek is the Arabic Amálik, an Arabic 'broken plural' (the Arab writers name as their father Amlak or Amlik), to be pronounced therefore Amálek, an extremely early instance of this formation in northern Arabia. (We may compare a probable similar form in the Akkadian *ahlame*, a designation of the Aramæans of the second millennium. The place-name Aroer in Moab is a similar broken plural.) The Arabs report an Amalekite king Samayda, a name of old-Semitic formation (see Chapter VII), Caussin de Perceval, vol. I, 18 f. Rekem, a king of Midian, Num. 31:8, Josh. 13:21, is given as

north as Bethlehem appears to have been occupied by the semi-Arabic Edomites, pushed northwards by movements from the south.[38] Indeed David himself when he was playing a lone hand in the Wilderness of Judah reverted to primitive type, as we have observed; he can best be compared with the semi-barbaric Lakhmid and Ghassanid Arab dynasts on the borderlands of northern Arabia, marching with the Byzantine and Persian empires.[39] Even the traditional poetic art of David has its complement in the early Arabic poets who sang and were patronized by those Arab princes, and some of whom themselves were kings, like the romantic Imrulkais; David's Lament over Jonathan is likest to Arabic poetry.

Now, given this open back door between the desert and the bordering land of civilization, Babylonia, Syria, Palestine, we have to note an ethnological fact of greatest moment. Arabia, as reservoir of the Semitic race, is ever refreshing and repleting those culture-lands with fresh Semitic blood. There is the moot question whether Arabia is the original home of the Semitic race, a question yet to be settled by philological and ethnological inductions; yet, wherever the Semitic headsprings may have lain, in the light of history Arabia has been the breeding-ground of the Semites. I would not allege with Winckler that there have been periodic movements, outbursts of population out of Arabia, as though when the reservoir was full there came a great spill over the brim of the vessel. But history and present experience prove the perennial infiltration of Arab blood into the lands of the Sown, the movements

the ancient name of Petra by Josephus, *Antiquities*, iv, 7, 1, while Amalekite kings were known in the plural form *arkam*, Caussin de Perceval, pp. 20, 22. Thus noteworthy historic traces survive in the Hebrew tradition.

38. See Meyer, *Entstehung des Judentums*, pp. 165 ff. and map at end of volume.

39. For a brief account of these states see Huart, *Histoire des Arabes*, vol. I, chap. 4.

varying with economic and political conditions on both sides of the border. Also, and this is of particular importance to the student of the history of religion, spiritual stimuli have had effect; long ago on a small scale in the Hebrew conquest of Palestine, in which Yahweh led his invading hosts; and again almost two millennia later over a vast theater in the torrent inspired by Mohammad in the name of Allah.[40]

Also the contrary process has acted, although its results are historically far more obscure, namely the reversion to original type of Arabic peoples which had entered the spheres of civilization, become domesticated, and assumed political forms of settled society. The wandering tribes of Arabia to-day have in their veins the blood of ancient proud centers of civilization, of Petra and Palmyra, of Teima and Dedan, of Nejd the mother-land of classic Arabic poetry, of South Arabia with its highly advanced civilization. Indeed this reversion to type appears most strikingly in the last-named quarter; with the fall of its commercial and political importance its population changed into the hordes which, for the centuries before Islam, invaded the north of the Peninsula, where as Yemenites, so called, they constituted a distinct segment of the population, playing its part as a divisive factor in the history of the Caliphate.[41]

40. Winckler has interpreted this movement from economic causes; but Lammens, *Le berceau de l'Islam*, rightly makes the spiritual factor of the religious and national unification of Arabia the predominant cause.

41. For this northern feud between the Yemenites, particularly the Bnî Kelb, and the 'Northerners,' the Bnî Keis, see Muir, *The Caliphate* (1915), Index, under 'Keis,' 'Kelb,' 'Yemenis.' For extensive discussions of this feud, which has lasted through history, see Goldziher, *Mohammedanische Studien*, vol. I, 78–98; R. Hartmann, *Die arabische Frage*, vol. II of his *Der islamische Orient*, 530–547. For the continuance of this line of migration see R. Graves, *Lawrence and the Arabs* (1927), p. 62, where, after describing the confinement of Yemen by the seas and the Hijáz, he remarks: "The

The Bible and Arabia

This infiltration has been, in the large, not by way of conquest, as in the two historical instances just cited. The nomads come into the lands of the Sown, peaceably and as of wonted right, to get water and supply themselves with provisions in exchange for their live stock and wool and hides; they may settle down for a few seasons tempted by the ease and food of settled life, and then decamp to parts unknown; or they may become settlers on the soil for good and disappear as a distinct social element. The pictures of the Patriarchs in Canaan run true to this normal form. Then comes the disappearance of the Patriarchal clan, because there was "a famine in all the earth," Gen. 41 ff., and its reappearance in Egypt, admitted over the Suez border by governmental permission and settling in the grazing lands of Goshen, after the fashion of Bedawi movements into Egypt recorded in the monuments.[42] Fleeing out of Egypt, they toilsomely return to their original haunts in Palestine. This constant seeping-in of desert wanderers still continues. It is only a step then to agricultural and settled life in village and city. Commerce and the native Semitic urge to sociability soon make a citizen of the one-time Bedu. Withal it is to be noted that there is no barrier of race or language or caste or religion to stamp the Arab as inferior in fact or in sensibility to that more polished environment. The upperclass Arabs, the sheikhs and their retinues, make their visits to the cities as gentlemen, and if there is any social con-

only way out is the east; so the weaker tribes on the Yemen border are constantly pushed out into the bad lands, where farming becomes less and less easy, and further out still until they become pastoral and are forced into the actual desert. There they work about from oasis to oasis perhaps for several generations until they may be strong enough to establish themselves again as agricultural Arabs, in Syria or Mesopotamia. This, writes Lawrence, is the natural circulation that keeps Arabia healthy."

42. Breasted, *Ancient Records of Egypt*, vol. III, nos. 11, 638.

trast it is they who look down upon the effete citizens, for the Arab has no 'inferiority complex.' As gentlemen free and unafraid they treat, as on the same footing, with pashas, kaimakams, effendis, European officials—all alike. The picture of Abraham's manners and dignity is exemplary of the courtesy and self-possession of the Arab sheikh.

The observation of this phenomenon explains one remarkable feature of the Semitic lands. They have remained Semitic to this day, and this despite powerful extraneous influences which challenge that ancient characteristic. After the fall of the ancient Semitic empires there entered Persia, Greece, Rome, Byzantium, Persia again, then the fitful rule of the Crusades—all of the Indo-European stock. But despite manifold varieties of intruding race and religion those lands are as Semitic as ever, with an Arabic-speaking population, with a specifically Arabian religion as the dominant faith.[43] It is symptomatic rather than accidental, that today king Feisal of Iraq (now deceased) and his brother Abdullah, emir of Trans-Jordan, are native-born Arabian princes, while the former once ruled as *fainéant* king of Syria, at Damascus, for a few months until dispossessed by the French in 1920.

It is known that the death-rate in Eastern cities habitually exceeds the birth-rate;[44] the balance is countered by influx from outside.[45] Probably the same ratio exists in the countryside under bad economic and political conditions, as under the

43. It is a mistake, producing unfortunate misconceptions, to speak of the Arab-speaking population of e.g., Palestine as Arabs, with the *nuance* of Bedawin and nothing better, as fallacious an error as to call ourselves Englishmen because we speak the English language. But as our country belongs to the Anglo-Saxon sphere of civilization, so Palestine in its roots and constant environment harks back to Arabia.

44. W. Robertson Smith, *Religion of the Semites,* ed. 1, pp. 12 ff.; G. A. Smith, *Historical Geography of the Holy Land,* p. 11.

45. Moral degeneracy of these centers of civilization was a potent element, recog-

Turkish empire. And the sources of replenishment have come perennially from Arabia.

Languages have indeed changed with kaleidoscopic succession and confusion. The original Hebrew of the land[46] was followed by Aramaic for the centuries before and after Christ, this again by Arabic, still the language of the land. But these are all Semitic dialects, whereas the invading foreign tongues, Greek, Roman, Frankish, Turkish, have disappeared, leaving but slight traces to be pursued by the philologist.[47]

Accordingly there exists a living blood-fellowship between Arabia and its contiguous lands, which implies a sense of spiritual unity, for the tradition of the desert is kept perennially fresh. Just as an Arab clan may settle down and its members become citizens, so those who belong to that civilized life have their social connections with the Arabs of the great out-of-doors, and the gentleman landowners of Syria and Palestine boast of their origin from famous Arab stocks.[48] If there are two kinds of civilization between the Sown and the Unsown— although their distinction was not emphasized as it is today with the highly artificial character of our Western civilization —yet the possibilities of social intermixture have always been

nized by Israel in its condemnation of 'the sins of the Amorites,' which are illustrated in the story of Sodom, Gen. cc. 18, 19.

46. The ancient Semitic language of Syria-Palestine was Hebraic, as geographical nomenclature, native epigraphical monuments (with now the newly discovered Ras Shamra texts), and Akkadian and Egyptian records prove.

47. The perpetual complexity of political and linguistic conditions in Palestine is now illustrated in its postage stamps, which are surcharged 'Palestine' in Arabic and English and Hebrew, an exact duplicate of Pilate's title on the cross of Jesus, 'in Hebrew, in Latin, in Greek,' John 19:20.

48. Observe that there is no sense of shame, but to the contrary one of pride in regard to this lineage, as also was the case in the old Hebrew tradition—unlike the shame that comes to possess immigrants into America, when they confront the program of 100% Americanism.

preserved, and the genuine, old-time citizen of Syria-Palestine knows that he is, in some part, of the Arabian Desert and that the Arab is of his kin.

And finally I make the following observation: Ancient Egypt and Babylon have disappeared, but Arabia still remains a static quantum on the Palestinian border. History proves the former to have been transitory, while Arabia is the permanent factor.[49]

49. Supplementarily I call attention to a section in Sir John Hope Simpson's recent Report on Palestine, October, 1930, bearing on the Beduin Population west of Jordan. They number over 100,000 souls, belonging to five main tribes. "One of the problems of land administration in Palestine lies in the indefinite rights of the Beduin population. . . . They claim rights of cultivation and grazing of an indefinite extent. . . . In any solution of the Palestine problem their existence cannot be overlooked" (p. 73).

II

ARABIA AND ARABS IN THE BIBLE

I CONFINE myself in this chapter to the occurrence in the Bible of the terms 'Arab,' 'Arabian,' 'Arabia.' The Arabic word from which these words are derived, *via* both the Hebrew and the Classical languages, is *'arab*. Its earliest datable occurrence is in an Assyrian inscription of the ninth century (see Chapter IV). The word is the same as that used by the Arabs for themselves throughout their folk-usage and literary tradition, the elder vocalization of the word, *'arib*,[1] being the same as that found in the Akkadian texts. The word *'arib* in a pluralized form, *a'ráb*, also occurs in South-Arabic inscriptions, denoting the Arabs as a distinct element of society,[2] and in an interesting way in two inscriptions celebrating repairs in the famous dam at Marib, the Sabæan capital (see Chapter VI), one of date 449 A.D., the other of 542, in which the royal dedicator of each of the inscriptions entitles himself as 'King of Sheba, Hadhramot, Yamnat (= Yemen),' etc., and then adds 'and of their Arabs';[3] i.e., the Arabs appear as feudal dependents of the states in question; they are referred to in the same way as Byzantium and Persia might have referred to 'their Arabs,' the vassal nations of the Ghassanids and Lachmids. This ancient name 'Arab,' thus appearing in all our sources, so

1. For *'arib, 'aribat*, as designating the oldest population of Arabia see Caussin de Perceval, *Histoire des Arabes*, I, 4 ff. Along with the Akkadian spelling *aribu* are found *arabu* and *urbi*. Delitzsch, *Paradies*, p. 305.

2. *Corpus inscriptionum semiticarum*, IV (Pars himyaritica), nos. 79, 343, 397.

3. E. Glaser, *Zwei Inschriften über den Dammbruch von Marib* (1897); and in the volume of the *Corpus* cited in Note 2, nos. 540, 541; the phrase occurs at the beginning of each inscription.

far defies interpretation. It is simplest to connect it with
'arābāh, generally translated 'wilderness' or 'desert,' occurring parallel with midbar (which latter means 'steppe' or
more exactly the Dutch South-African Veldt); while the
word is also the biblical designation of the Jordan-Dead Sea
canyon, e.g., Dt. 1:1, and hence the name Sea of the Arabah,
e.g., Dt. 3:17. The word by no means connotes a sandy 'desert'; the Jordan's banks have lush vegetation. In general the
original native use of the word 'Arab' applied it to the free-
moving sons of the desert, and then by proud tradition it is
preserved by the settled or half-settled Arabs, as in the lands
of the Nejd, where the citizens live in walled towns and
houses, and yet apart from the menial classes; these citizens
are still occupied with the life of the desert in caravans or
razzias. Ibn Saúd is Arab of the Arabs, although he lives in a
palace. They are Arabs in the same sense that the Breton folk
are sailors, to whom the sea is the first home.[4] The word itself
is, as also in biblical use, a collective noun, cf. 'Israel'; it
means the Arab people, not the geographic entity Arabia, for
which the Greeks first coined the word, and this has been fol-

4. The name, indefinite in its origin, has developed various *nuances* which render its
actual definition difficult. Thus Meyer, *Die Israeliten und ihre Nachbarstämme*, pp. 301 ff.,
claims, citing Schumacher, p. 303, note, that the Bedawin distinguish between themselves
and the Arabs whom they regard as the (partially) settled folk, tending towards agriculture. But Hartmann, *Die arabische Frage*, p. 113 ff., has a wider, more authentic
view of the name. *Arab* is confined, he holds, to the free-moving sons of the desert:
arab = bedu; and even the half-settled Arabs despise and never give themselves up to
labor on the soil. As a proud name of the race it appears throughout history. In the
earliest proto-North-Arabic inscription we possess, from en-Nemara in Trans-Jordan, of
date 328 A.D., the epitaph names Imrulkais king of all the Arabs (*'arab*). The text,
discovered by Dussaud, was published by him in *Rev. archéologique*, II (1902), 409 ff.;
and is given in his *Arabes en Syrie avant l'Islam*, p. 34 ff., and in Lidzbarski, *Ephemeris*,
II, 34 ff. The last one to assume this proud title was the arrogant and rash Husein, late
Sherif of Mecca along with the title of Caliph; see my 'Arabia To-day,' *Journ. Am. Or.
Soc.*, 1927, pp. 118 f. Ibn Saúd has been too politic to venture on this claim.

Arabia and Arabs in the Bible

lowed by the comparatively late Arabic name for the Peninsula, Jezírat (properly 'island' = peninsula) al-Arab.

In the Old Testament the collective noun *Arab* and its gentilic derivative *Arabi* are of comparatively late usage, corresponding to the late appearance of the word in the Akkadian.[5] The two earliest instances of the word give a picture of the nomadic Bedu: Is. 13:20 (if pre-exilic), "the Arab shall not tent there," and Jer. 3:2 in an address to whorish Judah, "thou hast sat [lurking] for them like an Arab in the wilderness." An individual Arab appears for the first time, in the rôle of the inveterate enemy of Nehemiah, Geshem the Arab, as he is called in Neh. 2:19; 4:7, playing politics along with the Arabs, Tobiah the Ammonite, and the Ashdodites, the cabal having Sanballat as leader (4:1). It is of interest that in the occurrence of the name in 6:6 it is spelled after Old-Arabic fashion, as in Nabatæan and Palmyrene names, Gashmu, with the original Arabic noun-formation and the final case-vowel. The form is paralleled by the good Arabian

5. A differently vocalized noun, *'ereb,* is generally translated, e.g., Ex. 12:38, 'mixed multitude,' as of the miscellaneous horde that accompanied Israel at the Exodus. This meaning may be appropriate at Jer. 50:37. But in other places it can better be vocalized as *'arab,* 'Arabs.' So at Eze. 30:5, where the old Jewish translators Aquila and Symmachus along with the Syriac and Vulgate, as also in the parallel at 2 Ch. 9:14, have 'Arabs,' while Solomon's commercial relations with Arabia corroborate this rendering (see Chap. VIII); also at Jer. 25:20; *ibid.,* v. 24, where there is apparently a doublet between *'arab* and *'ereb;* at Eze. 30:5, with Aquila, Symmachus, Syriac; possibly at Neh. 13:3, where Meyer, *Entstehung des Judentums,* p. 130, prefers so to vocalize it. Is it so to be understood at Ex. 12:38, which would then give the earliest occurrence of the word? Intentional change of vocalization to produce another is a common trick in the Semitic. The accompanying adjective 'great' militates against the supposition here; however Meyer, *Israel u. ihre Nachbarstämme,* p. 80, inclines to this change except for doubt as to such high antiquity for the name 'Arab.' Hartmann (reference in Note 4) derives the latter word from the root 'mix,' but without reference to the biblical *'ereb;* and in this he follows Lane, *Dictionary,* p. 1993, col. 3, who directly identifies *'arab* and *'ereb.*

name of Moses' father-in-law, Jethro, which indeed once appears in Hebraized form as Jether, Ex. 4:18.[6]

The remaining specific references are mostly of uncertain date on critical grounds. In the Jeremianic list of the nations which are to drink of the reeking-cup of the Lord, Jer. 25, appear, v. 24, "all the kings of Arabia[7] and all the kings of the mingled people that dwell in the wilderness," these being preceded by a list of known Arabian regions, v. 23, Dedan and Teima and Buz, with a reference, v. 24, to "all that have the corners of their hair polled," a custom of Arabian tribes, otherwise vouched for.[8] In a similar list of peoples, the tributaries to the wealth of Tyre, in Eze. 27, there are recorded, v. 21, "Arabia (*Arab*) and all the princes of Kedar," accompanied (vv. 20, 22) with reference to North-Arabian Dedan and South-Arabian Sheba and Raamah (Raghamah). The remaining references are in Chronicles, a composition of the end of the fourth century, where the Arabs are named four times along with the Philistines as enemies or tributaries of Judæan kings.[9] These passages are illuminative of conditions in that

6. This name, properly Yatr, appears in South-Arabic, Watr.

7. 'Arab,' name of the folk, is used, without the article, of their domain, just as 'Philistines' means 'Philistia'; cf. Gen. 10:14; similarly 'Libyans,' 'Ethiopians,' Dan. 11:43, etc. The Greeks also used the ethnic plural for the country.

8. The same phrase in 9:26, as descriptive of the Arabs, and at 49:32. Herodotus refers to the custom as a religious practice, iii, 8, and hence the Jewish prohibition of it, Lev. 19:27; see W. Robertson Smith, *Religion of the Semites*, ed. 1, p. 305 ff. The usage expressed by the same root is vouched for in Arabic literature, Moritz, *Arabien*, p. 19.

9. Of these passages, in addition to 2 Ch. 17:11, c. 22:1 has an obscure text; 26:7 refers to Arabs in Gur-baal, for which the Greek has 'on the rock (*petra*),' while the oldest text of the Vulgate (Code Amiatinus) reads Turbaal, i.e., 'Rock of Baal,' and hence some would find here a reference to Petra. In 21:16 "the Lord raised up the spirit of the Philistines and the Arabians from the quarter of Ethiopia (Kushim)," i.e., Egypt. This is one of several references to Cush (e.g., Moses' Cushite wife, Num. 12:1) which have induced some scholars to find an extensive Cush in NW Arabia, e.g., Hom-

later period which we know of from South-Arabian sources, informing us of Arab control of trade routes towards the Mediterranean, centering upon Gaza, the ancient Philistine port. Whatever the age of the Chronicler's references may be, they exhibit the conditions of sharp competition for those southern avenues of commerce, which Judah wished to secure and which the Arab peoples contested against her.[10]

The references to Arabia and the Arabs in the Apocryphal books can be fairly well precised; they concern mostly the Nabatæans, coming in out of Arabia in or even before the Hellenistic age, to enter the lists for possession of the trade routes encircling Palestine, towards Damascus and Gaza and Egypt.[11] These references excellently illustrate the constant pressure of the Arabs upon the lands of the Sown and of their consummate political art in controlling the trade routes of

mel in Hilprecht, *Excavations*, p. 742, Cheyne in *Enc. Bibl.*, *s.v.* 'Cushan'; Hab. 3:7, parallel to Midian, is brought into the argument. But see Meyer's vigorous criticism of this theory, *Israel und ihre Nachbarstämme*, pp. 315 ff. It is to be noted that the land west of a line from the Wady of Egypt to the Elanitic Gulf has always belonged to the Egyptian political sphere, and actually that is the present boundary of Egypt. As we shall see later the South-Arabians called the same region *Msr*, i.e., Misraim, Egypt.

10. See further Chapter VIII, and *ibid.* for the Meúnim of 1 Ch. 4:41, etc.

11. They are not the Nebaioth, brother of Kedar, Gen. 25:13, Is. 60:7, although the identification has been proposed (so still Luckenbill and Musil) on the basis of the conjunction of the Nabatæi and the Cedrei in Pliny, *Hist. nat.*, v, 12. The etymological connection is impossible. For the history of the Nabatæan state see Schürer, *Geschichte des jüdischen Volkes* (1901), Excursus at end of vol. I (also in Eng. tr. from an early edition). For recent literature may be named A. B. W. Kennedy, *Petra, its History and Monuments*, 1925 (richly illustrated); A. Kammerer, *Pétra et la Nabatène* (1930), and the excellent volume by Prof. George L. Robinson of Chicago, *The Sarcophagus of an Ancient Civilization* (New York, 1930). For the political background of the remarkable development of Petra and Palmyra see Burkitt's chapter in the recent Schweich Lectures by T. H. Robinson and others, *Palestine in Ancient History*, and Rostovtzeff's book cited in Chapter I, Note 36. J. Cantineau has published in his *Le Nabatéen* (1930–1932) a most useful manual of the Nabatæan inscriptions with grammar, lexicon, etc.

the Peninsula from sea to sea. The Nabatæans first appear in conflict with Antigonus, one of the Successors of Alexander the Great, and his son Demetrius; the latter about 311 B.C. waged a punitive expedition against them, without much success. Arabia now meant primarily what the Romans later officially constituted as a province, Arabia Petræa, i.e., the Arabia of Petra, practically the modern Trans-Jordan, extending to the Red Sea. History repeats itself, for again today that same region is an Arab state with an Arab emir from the heart of Arabia.

The Nabatæans and their Arabian confederates appear fitfully as friends and enemies of the powers in Syria-Palestine. The upstart Syrian king Alexander Balas took refuge from Ptolemy Philometor in Arabia, where a certain Arabian Zabdiel cut off his head and sent it to Ptolemy II, 165 B.C. (1 Mac. 11:16, 17). The unfortunate prince left behind him in that alien land a son, Antiochus, in charge of an Arab, Imalkue (11:39), a name identical with the good Nabatæan (and Arabic) name Yamliku, famous later in its Græcized form Yamblichus; the child was later raised to the throne by his father's field-marshal Lysias, who appears in the Maccabean history. Also a notorious Jewish refugee took asylum in Arabia, Jason, the whilom high priest, who having dispossessed the pious Onias was ousted by his brother Menelaus; he fled to the court of Aretas, 'tyrant'[12] of the Arabs, and thence was expelled to Egypt; 2 Mac. 5:5 ff. This Aretas (= Harîthat) was doubtless of the line of the Nabatæan dynasty, of which four at least bore this name. There are also two specific references to the Nabatæans, in 1 Mac. 5:25[13] and 9:35, where

12. For this use of the word see the writer's *Daniel*, p. 125.
13. By a reconstruction of the text here Winckler, in Schrader's *Keilinschriften u.*

they appear as allies of the Maccabean brothers Judas and Jonathan, although the enemies of Judas could "hire Arabs" against him, 5:39—typical Arabian folk! In the parallel 2 Mac. 12:10 ff. they are also called the 'nomads.' Of the Maccabean prince Jonathan, 1 Mac. 12:31 relates that he "smote the Arabs who are called Zabadæans" near Damascus on his return from a campaign in Syria. Thus these semi-settled Arabs, potent in means, astute in politics, played an important part in those turbulent days. The Greek cities of Across-Jordan protected themselves against these volatile enemies by the famous league of the Decapolis.

The strength and wiles of Herod brought standing to the Jewish state, whose king he was. Of his origin we know nothing with certainty; the Jews made of him an Edomite, i.e., an Idumæan, of the land south of Palestine, and he may well have been of Arab blood; his brother's name Phasael is found among the Arab Palmyrenes. This would be one of many instances, continuing into contemporary history, of the native political ability of the Arabs in finding place for themselves among the notables of the world; their parallel in the West is found in the sea-roving Normans.[14]

The apogee of the Nabatæan power came under its most distinguished ruler, Aretas IV, 9 B.C.–39 A.D., when in the supine days of the emperors Caius and Claudius he was able to seize and control Damascus while his domain stretched as far south as Madáin-Salih in the northwest of the Peninsula. It

das Alte Testament, p. 152, discovers the Salamians, an early segment of the Nabatæan group. And this people is found by Wellhausen and others (see Gesenius-Buhl, Handwörterbuch, p. 838) in Song of Songs 1:5, reading 'Salamians' for the 'Solomon' of the text.

14. In Judith 2:25 there is an indefinite reference to Arabia; 2 Esdras 15:29, "the nations of the dragons of Arabia," is reminiscent of Is. 30:6.

was from the governor, 'ethnarch,' of this Aretas that the Apostle Paul made his escape out of Damascus, 2 Cor. 11:32. But Trajan finally put an end to this troublesome border state and constituted its territory into the province of Arabia Petræa, 105 A.D.

This experience of St. Paul with the Nabatæan government of Damascus was preceded by his retirement into Arabia immediately after his conversion, as he briefly relates in Gal. 1:17. The region no doubt was what the Romans came to call Arabia Petræa, Trans-Jordan; he returned thence to Damascus. There were 'desert' districts there in plenty to gratify his desire for solitude; again one of the great souls of the True Religion started his career from the desert. That this Arabian experience of the Apostle brought him actually to Sinai, in the footsteps of Moses and Elijah, has been advanced by some scholars,[15] in view of his subsequent reference, in the same Epistle, to Sinai and Hagar, 4:24, 25. The *textus receptus* of the Greek is represented by the American Standard Version: "Which things contain an allegory; for these women are two covenants; one from Mount Sinai, bearing children unto bondage, which is Hagar. Now this Hagar is Mount Sinai in Arabia and answereth to the Jerusalem that now is." But the second 'Hagar' is now generally admitted to be a gloss, and there remains the question how to interpret the sentence with the excision. I suggest that the meaning is: "This is Mount Sinai in Arabia (then the gloss) that is, Hagar," i.e. the land of the Hagarenes; and so the gloss is interpretatively correct, although out of place. The Arabians are called 'Sons of Hagar' in Baruch 3:23, while the Hagarenes (or Hagarites—

---

15. E.g., Dean Stanley, *Sinai and Palestina*, p. 50.

both in AV) are frequently mentioned in connection with the Arab peoples to the east and south of Palestine.[16] However, St. Paul need not have experienced the sight of Sinai to make this allusion; the identification of Hagar and Sinai may already have been made by Jewish midrash or developed by Paul himself on those lines.

A suggestive reference to Arabia is found in Acts 2:11, where among the Jews and proselytes from many lands present at the spectacle of Pentecost are listed Arabs. These may have been merely pilgrims from nearby Arabia Petræa. Or in view of the conjunction of Arabs with the distant Cretans we may have here a rhetorical polarization of the peoples of the Mediterranean and the waters of the Arabian (Indian) Sea, and we are intrigued to think that colonies of the Jews had already pushed into the recesses of Arabia. In the subsequent centuries we find the Jews as an active proselytizing and political power in South Arabia engaged in mortal combat with the Christians, entailing crusades from Christian Abyssinia for the relief of the latter; while large colonies of the Jews in and about the Holy Cities of Arabia for Mohammad's day are well attested by tradition. The Jews of the Yemen still sur-

---

16. E.g., Ps. 83:6, 7, "Edom and Israel, Moab and the Hagarenes, Gebal [= the Arabic plural *jibál*, 'mountains,' still the name of the mountainous region south of the Dead Sea], and Ammon and Amalek." 'Hagarene' may have served as a general name of the Arabs for the Jews with reminiscence of the concubine Hagar; cf. the medieval 'Saracen,' of disputed etymology; the Syriac 'Tay' = 'wanderer' of the Syriac. Identification of Hagar and Hagarenes has been made with the Agraioi of Ptolemy, of Strabo, etc., in NW Arabia; but this important people must be connected with al-Hijr in the Thamudene Country, the region of el-Ula; the *h* differs in the two Semitic words. For Egra = al-Hijr see Sprenger, *Alte Geographie Arabiens*, p. 21; Musil, *Oriental Explorations*, vol. I, pp. 299 ff. For the text in Gal. and its interpretations see Lightfoot's two excursus in his *Commentary*, pp. 192 ff. For variations in the rendering cf. the differing translations by Moffatt in his *Historical New Testament*, and his more recent *Holy Bible . . . A New Translation*.

vive, a depressed but sturdy class in that far end of the Peninsula.[17]

17. At the rise of Islam, Medina was dominated by the Jews, and the neighboring fertile oasis of Khaibar was in their possession, until the policy of Islam expelled them. Margoliouth in Lecture 3 of his *Relations between Arabs and Israelites* takes a strongly skeptical attitude towards the common Mohammadan and Christian traditions concerning the Jews in Arabia. The Jewish literature gives no data on the early beginnings of the Jewish settlement in the Yemen; see Schürer, *Geschichte*, vol. III, 11. S. Reinach, art. 'Diaspora' in *Jewish Enc.*, would carry the colonization back to the second century after Christ; according to Arabic tradition they had become a political power in the land early in the third century, and the king Abu-kariba accepted their religion, see Caussin de Perceval, vol. I, 90 ff., and Hartmann, *Die arabische Frage*, pp. 45 ff., 49 ff. For the Jews now in the Yemen see art. 'Yemen' in *Jewish Enc.* According to W. Schmidt, *Das südwestliche Arabien* (1913), pp. 66 ff., they number 60,000 out of a population estimated from a half to three quarters of a million. For the most complete collection of data on early Christianity in Arabia see Agrain, art. 'Arabie' in *Dict. de l'histoire et de la géographie ecclésiastiques*, vol. III, col. 1158–1339. For a lively view of the Jewish Ghetto in Sanaá, the capital of the Yemen, see Rihani, *Arabian Peak and Desert* (New York, 1930), c. 17. I add supplementarily that C. C. Torrey in his recent notable volume, *The Jewish Foundation of Islam* (New York, 1933), insists upon the early origin of this Jewish dispersion in Arabia, going back possibly to the age of the Exile.

III

THE HEBREWS AND THEIR COUSINS
THE ARABS

THE preceding chapter recalled the occurrence of the words 'Arab,' 'Arabia,' in the Bible. We will now consider the several genealogies which report the close kinship of the Hebrews with the Arabian peoples. In the Table of Nations in Gen. 10 two such genealogies are presented, one of the descendants of Shem, vv. 21 ff., the other of the Hamites, vv. 6 ff., which in part, v. 7, pairs with the Shemite pedigree. The former is regarded by scholars as the older document, belonging to the ancient Yahwistic source of the Pentateuch.

Here we are given the line Shem-Arpachshad-Shelah-Eber, the latter the father of two sons, Peleg and Yoktan (EVV Joktan). Through the elder son Peleg is derived in another and later genealogy, 11:10 ff., the line Reu-Serug-Nahor-Terah-Abraham.[1] Thus the patronymic ancestor of Abraham and the biblical Hebrews was Eber, which name should rather be pronounced Heber as in the Vulgate, to express the relation of the word with its derivative 'Hebrew.'[2] Now of Heber-Eber's two sons, according to the Yahwist, the elder Peleg is the ancestor of Abraham in c. 11; from the younger, Yoktan, descended a swarm of Arabian peoples, re-

1. Doubtless some similar pedigree connecting Shem with Abraham was given in the Yahwistic genealogy; but this was omitted by the editor in favor of the pedigree in c. 11, assigned to the Priest Code.

2. The root of the words is 'br, the inverted upper comma representing a peculiar Semitic guttural, which was pronounced by the Greeks with an aspirate and so passed over into Latin as h, producing Heber and Hebræus. But AV dropped the h in the Patriarch's name and so obscured the etymological identity.

37

corded immediately, as we shall see, in c. 10. That is, they too were 'Hebrews.' And it is to be noticed that the Yahwist makes this relationship of the Hebrews with Arabs closer than with many other Semitic peoples with whom history associates the Hebrews; for according to v. 22 the Assyrians (Asshur), and the Aramæans (Aram), were only great-uncles of Eber.[3]

The name of Eber's elder son, Peleg, means 'division,' used *par excellence*, 'the Division,' even as Shem may mean 'the Name,' i.e., the people of renown. His younger brother's name, Yoktan, means 'little,' i.e., younger brother.[4] Muslim-Arab genealogists identify Yoktan with Kahtan, their assumed ancestor of the South-Arabian peoples, an identification still widely accepted, but the combination is etymologically impossible. However, our genealogy deduces mainly South-Arabian peoples from Yoktan, and their names can in almost every case be identified as Arabian geographically or by etymology.

We find in this genealogy the well-known Arabian lands of Sheba (which we shall have constantly to discuss), Ophir,[5]

3. The brothers of Asshur and Aram are Elam, Arpachshad (cuneiform Arapcha, Greek Arrapachitis, modern Kirkuk), Lud (Lydia ?), all comprehended in this Semitic list on grounds of culture, not of race.

4. The name is vocalized in the Greek and Latin as Yektan, the correct verbal form, i.e., 'who-is-little.' The name-form is primitive, and may well have been used of a younger tribal division.

5. Ophir has been located in all regions of the Indian Ocean, even in far South Africa and India. But we need not go away from Arabia to seek the gold of Ophir; reports of gold deposits in the Peninsula extend from the Greek geographers down to the Arab writers of the Middle Ages; see the encyclopedic treatment by Sprenger, *Die alte Geographie Arabiens*, pp. 53–59. Cf. Moritz, *Arabien*, p. 7: "The granite formation of the land has shown itself in its whole extent from the extreme northwest, Midian, to the little-known southeast, as gold-bearing, with sole exception, as it appears, of the Shammar region [the northern Nejd]." Moritz, in an excursus to the same volume entitled 'Das Land Ophir,' considers at length the ancient and modern authorities, and

and Hazarmaveth, the latter the great frankincense country east of Sheba-Yemen, the modern Wady Hadhramot, running parallel with the coast for some two hundred miles.[6] With Sheba and Ophir is aligned Havilah (so also Seba and Havilah in v. 7), and this land appears in the Garden of Eden story, c. 3, as the source of gold and bdellium (?) and onyx (?). Its location is disputed. Hommel, Glaser, and others would find it in northeastern Arabia in connection with the rivers of Eden; others identify it with Haulan on the west side of Arabia, known in a South-Arabic inscription, which reports an attack made by Sheba and Haulan upon a Minæan caravan.[7]

would locate Ophir in Asír, the territory between the Hijáz and the Yemen. For the claims of the land Midian see Burton, *The Gold Mines of Midian*. Glaser finds Ophir in Yamama, SE of the Nejd, making combination with the Pishon and Havilah, the land of gold, Gen. 2:11; *Skizze*, pp. 347 ff. (He finds in this region the gold land of Parvaim, mentioned in 2 Ch. 3:6, identifying it with a locality Farwain, p. 347). But the western coast of Arabia is more likely for the origin of the biblical gold. All biblical references pertain to Arabian gold except Job 37:22. Sprenger and others identify the word *ophir* with the *apyron*-gold found in Arabia according to the Greek geographers and popularly etymologized as 'fireless,' as being found in pure grains or nuggets. For the exhaustion of once rich alluvial gold deposits we may compare the working-out of the gold fields of Indian Dardistan, which once paid Darius annual tribute of 360 talents; see H. G. Rawlinson, *Intercourse between India and the Western World*, pp. 18, 102. It may be observed that the Hebrew word for gold, *zahab*, is also used in South-Arabic for a running stream; i.e., the metal was a river gold.

6. The consonants of the name are identical in Hebrew and Arabic. The Hebrew has broken the last vowel and produced the dissyllable *maweth*, 'death.' Cf. the development of *salmuth*, 'darkness,' into *sal-maweth*, 'shadow of death,' and so all subsequent Versions, e.g., Ps. 23:4. The name thus is made to mean 'enclosure (or oasis) of death.' Pliny, *Hist. nat.*, xii, 30, reports the restrictions laid upon the cultivation and harvesting of the frankincense, amounting to strict taboos (tr. in Schoff, *Periplus of the Erythræan Sea*, p. 124), and it has been suggested that the element 'death' is reminiscent of these restrictions. According to Van den Berg, *Le Hadhramout et les colonies arabes* (Batavia, 1886), p. 9, the native pronunciation is Hadhramut, not Hadhramot, as generally received.

7. Halévy, no. 535, in Hommel, *Südarabische Chrestomathie*, p. 103, Rossini, *Chrestomathia arabica meridionalis* (1931), no. 71. The affair occurred near Raghamah, which

Arabia and the Bible

Of the remaining names in this genealogy, Diklah is Arabic (also Aramaic) for palm tree, probably name of an oasis (cf. Tamar in Judah with the same signification); Almodad, to be read with the Greek Elmodad, the second element coming from the Arabic root *wadada*, 'love,' and the name meaning 'God is a friend' by good Old-Semitic name formation;[8] Abimael composed after fashion of Amoritic-Babylonian and South-Arabic names, meaning 'God is father,' and identical with Hebrew Abiel;[9] Yerah (Jerah) i.e., Moon, the moon being the chief deity of the South-Arabic pantheon;[10] Hadoram, a name occurring in the South-Arabic, probably = Haddu-ram, Haddu-Adad being a North-Semitic deity. Of the remaining names Uzal[11] is claimed by Arabian tradition to have been the ancient name of Sanaá, the modern capital of the Yemen;[12] while Sheleph, Obal, and Yobab escape identification.[13]

At the conclusion of this Arabian genealogy derived from

is connected with Sheba in another biblical reference to be considered below. The land of Haulan can be identified as to the north of the Yemen; see Sprenger, pp. 49 ff., Moritz, p. 91. As the biblical Arabian pedigrees run north and south, it is preferable to place Havilah in the west of Arabia.

8. *Modad* means 'acquaintance, friend' (cf. development of Hebrew *moda'*); so Mudadu as Amoritic-Babylonian name, Ranke, *Early Babylonian Personal Names*, p. 30. For these 'Amoritic' names see further Chapter 7. In the recently discovered North-Syrian Ras Shamra texts of the fourteenth century Modad-El appears as title of a minor deity. For the literature see Chapter VIII, Note 1.

9. Cf. South-Arabic Abi-ma-Athtar and similar names (Hommel, *Chrestomathie*, p. 16); Babylonian Abi-ma-Ishtar (identical with the preceding), Ili-ma-abi.

10. Hebrew *yerah*, 'month,' *yareh*, 'moon'; the tribal name has been abbreviated to the divine element, as in the case of the Hebrew tribes Gad and Asher, and the personal name Jehu. This word for moon appears in South-Arabic, has disappeared in modern Arabic except in a derivative verb, 'to date,' i.e., by the moons.

11. Read by some into the text of Eze. 27:19; see SV margin.

12. In the form Auzal; see Caussin de Perceval, *Histoire des Arabes*, vol. I, 40.

13. For Sheleph cf. Arabic *silf*, 'brother-in-law,' such terms of relationship are common in name-compounds.

Yoktan is given an interesting geographical note, v. 30: "their domain extends from Mesha, as one goes to Sephar, the Mount of the East." The Greek vocalizes the first name Massae, which suggests identity with Massa in the family-tree of Ishmael, to be considered below.[14] Separ, Greek Sopher, has been most extravagantly identified with Zafar, ancient metropolis of Hadhramot;[15] but the initial sibilants of the two words defy assimilation. The Mount of the East ('Kedem') must be paralleled with the frequent Bnê Kedem, AV Children of the East, and so refers to peoples of North Arabia in the Syrian Desert; cf. Jer. 49:28; Eze. 25:4, 10; Job, 1:3, etc. This mountain land has not been certainly identified.[16] But if in Num. 23:7 in Balaam's word, "from Aram Balak bringeth me," 'Edom' is to be read for 'Aram,' then the following parallel "from the Mountains of the East" would identify the latter with the mountain range of Seir or Edom, and so the term would have arisen in the land south of Judah.[17]

In the younger genealogy in 10:6 ff. some of these Arabian tribal names reappear, but as of Hamitic-Cushite stock,

14. Probably to be found in Prov. 31:1, where read "Lemuel king of Massa," see Chapter VIII.

15. E.g., Hommel, *Ethnologie und Geographie des alten Orients*, pp. 653, 710; the name also occurs in the Yemen, with which Moritz, *Arabien*, p. 84, would identify our locality. For denial of a South-Arabian identification see Meyer, *Israel und ihre Nachbarstämme*, p. 244.

16. We might think of the Jebel Hauran, or Druse Mountain to the NE of Trans-Jordan. Some find it in the lofty mountain peaks near Hail in northern Nejd, reaching in Jebel Aja 5,500 feet. Glaser, *Skizze*, p. 419, identifies it with the mountain range from Medina to the northern Nejd. Delitzsch connects it with the Akkadian Mash near Iraq, *Paradies*, p. 242. The northern Nejd is called 'the Mountain,' el-Jebel; see Euting, *Tagbuch einer Reise in Inner-Arabien*, p. 154, and Doughty, *Arabia Deserta*, vol. I, c. 21.

17. See Chapter II, Note 16; also below in this chapter; and for the Balaam episode, Chapter VIII.

and so are summarily dismissed from close kinship with the Hebrews. The nearest explanation of this scheme is that it is based on historical and political motives, although some scholars would find here a reliable tradition of an original Cushite (African) element that once pervaded Arabia.[18] Here among the descendants of Cush, son of Ham, appear Seba and Havilah, and farther down Sheba and Dedan; Seba is a dialectic variation of Sheba, giving the Arabic pronunciation, and with Havilah is found in the earlier genealogy.[19] Dedan appears again as grandson of Abraham's concubine Keturah (see below). As we shall observe in Chapter IV, Sheba-Seba had its abode both in the north and the south. Raamah, or with the Arabic Raghamah, identified in a South-Arabic inscription cited above (Note 7), is here made the father of Sheba, and the two are connected in Eze. 27:22 as engaged in the typical Arabian trade of spices, precious stones, and gold. Of the two remaining names, Sabtah and Sabteca (the latter a variant?) the former has generally been identified with Shabwat, the ancient metropolis of Hadhramot.

More closely affiliated with Arabian groups appear the genealogies of Abraham's descendants by his concubines, in Gen. 25. The more diffuse of these is the line by Keturah, vv. 1–4, in part repeating far-flung tribes appearing in the earlier genealogies. Keturah itself may be etymologically connected with the Hebrew *ketoreth*, 'frankincense,' and

18. Without doubt there was early exchange of populations between Arabia and Africa, especially across the strait of Bab-el-mandeb, a close relation, illustrated in later political history, which may well have suggested the African origin of South-Arabian peoples.

19. In Ps. 72:10, "the kings of Sheba and Seba," the two peoples are sharply distinguished; if this is more than an archaic reminiscence, it may distinguish South Arabia and Abyssinia.

breathe of the South-Arabian trade routes. By this union there were six sons, eleven grandsons and great-grandsons. Of the sons Midian is best known; his territory can be definitely located as along the upper stretch of the Red Sea littoral, upon data furnished by the Classical and Arab geographers.[20] The Midianites appear as raiders in the Palestinian lands, as in Gideon's day, Jud. cc. 7, 8, but also as caravan merchants, e.g., Gen. 37 (exchanging with Ishmaelites), and as spiritually related to Israel through Reuel-Jethro, priest of Midian, Moses' father-in-law, Ex. 2:16; 3:1; 18:1 ff., etc. In Is. 60:6 we read of "the camels of Midian and Ephah, all coming from Sheba, bringing gold and frankincense"—a passage which helps to explain the artificially constructed genealogical schemes. Indeed Sheba appears also in Gen. 25, as Midian's nephew, along with Dedan, who is coupled with Sheba in 10:7. The Ephah (Eypah) of the Isaianic passage occurs also here as son of Midian; the name is doubtless, with false vocalization in the Hebrew, the same as the Haiapa, one of the tribes listed in the Assyrian inscriptions along with Teima, Massa, and the Sabæans (see Chapter IV). Two of Ephah's brothers, Abida and Eldaah, have names actually borne by South-Arabian kings, Abiyada and Yadail. The other sons of Midian, Hanoch (or rather in English Enoch—the same as the antediluvian patriarch's name in Gen. 4 and 5)[21] and Epher cannot be identified. Medan, a brother of Midian, if not a sheer variant to the latter name, may appear in a South-

20. The Arabic name remains as Madyan, as the Greeks also pronounced it. For the region see Doughty, vol. I, chaps. 14 ff.; Burton, *Gold Mines of Midian;* Musil, *Topographical Itineraries,* vol. I, chap. 9.

21. Also an Enoch in the Reuben tribe, Gen. 46:9. The name has religious significance, 'initiated'; there is no reason, as has been proposed by some scholars, to identify the name etymologically with that of the Babylonian sage Enmeduranki.

Arabic inscription as the homeland of a hierodule.[22] Another brother Zimran, with name of Arabic root, is not otherwise known; but compare the gentilic formation Zimri, possibly Arabian, Jer. 25:25. Another brother Yishbak has been identified with Yashbuk in the far north mentioned by Shalmaneser II for the year 859, and his brother Shuh may belong to the same region on cuneiform evidence.[23] Yokshan has been identified by some with Yoktan, the Arabian progenitor at 10:25, and so here the Greek Yektan, but the identification is not supported etymologically. His sons are Sheba (again!) and Dedan, as they also appear in the Cushite genealogy in Gen. 10. Dedan is found in the South-Arabic inscriptions; its caravans are recorded in Is. 21:13, associated with Teima; it trafficked in valuable riding cloths, Eze. 27:20;[24] it is listed with Sheba and the merchants of Tarshish as representatives of cosmopolitan trading in Eze. 38:13, and mentioned with Teima and Buz and all the kings of Arabia in Jer. 25:23 f. In Eze. 25:13 a territorial limitation appears in the delimitation of Edom as lying from mid-Arabian Teima to Dedan. Dedan has now been identified topographically as the modern el-Ula in the land of Midian in the northwest of the Peninsula. For the South-Arabian Minæan colony located there see Chapter VIII. Dedan's sons have names in plural formation (cf. Pelishtim = Philistia): Asshurim, which probably appears in a South-Arabic text as lying in northwest Arabia;[25]

22. Glaser, no. 1238; see Gesenius-Buhl, *Handwörterbuch.* Or it may be the Badana of an Akkadian text (see Chapter IV, Note 7), even as Mecca was once Becca.

23. Schiffer, *Die Aramäer,* p. 89.

24. Dedan in v. 15 is a corruption for Rhodes; also Rhodes is found in Gen. 10:4, correcting 'Dodanim' to 'Rodanim' after the parallel text in 1 Ch. 1:7.

25. Halévy, no. 535 (cf. above, Note 7). The word may be an Arabic broken plural, represented in the Hebrew by the plural in -*im.* For identification of the word with

Letushim;[26] and Leummim, which however is a generic term meaning hordes.

Closer geographically to Palestine are the Ishmaelite tribes through Hagar, 25:12 ff. She is eponymous mother of the Hagarenes, who appear as constant foes of Israel in Trans-Jordan, e.g., 1 Ch. 5:10, 19 f., Ps. 83:6.[27] Two of her twelve 'sons' are recorded by Tiglath-pileser as submitting to him:[28] Adbeel (Akkadian Idibail) and Massa, for which latter see above in the genealogy of Shem. Two others, Nebaioth and Kedar, coupled again in Is. 60:7 ("the flocks of Kedar and the rams of Nebaioth," cf. Eze. 27:21), appear together in a campaign of Ashurbanipal's about 660. The Nebaioth were closely related to the Edomites, Gen. 28:9. One oracle at end of Is. 21 aligns Kedar with Teima; Is. 42:11 combines "the oases of Kedar" with Sela, i.e., Petra; a doom of "Kedar and the kingdoms of Hazor [itself an Arabic word] which Nebuchadnezzar smote" is given in Jer. 49:28 ff. Another son Dumah is with little doubt Adummatu of the Akkadian texts, which is generally identified with the oasis of Dumat el-Ghandel, now known as the Jauf or Hollow, lying in the Syrian Desert due east of Petra and the only important stopping-place between Syria and the Nejd.[29] Yet another son is

Asshur in the Balaam prophecy, Num. 24:22, and translation of the text in question, see Hommel, *Ancient Hebrew Tradition*, chap. 8.

26. The root suggests the meaning 'smiths,' and we recall the Kenites, the Smith-tribe.

27. For Hagar in Gal. 4 see Chapter II, Note 16. The attractive identification with al-Hijra of the Greek geographers (Sprenger, pp. 20 ff., 146 ff.), in the oasis of modern Madáin-Salih (for description see Doughty, vol. I, chaps. 4, 5, 13) shatters on the difference of the initial gutturals.

28. For the references to the Assyrian campaigns see Chapter IV.

29. See Wallin, *Geographical Journal*, vol. XXIV, 138–158; Euting, *Tagbuch*, chap. 5; Lady Anne Blunt, *Pilgrimage to Nejd*, vol. I, chaps. 6, 7; Musil, *Oriental Explorations*, vol. II, 160 ff., 470 ff. See more at length Chapter IV for Duma and Teima.

Teima, which is a great oasis and the ancient nucleus of desert routes in the north of the Peninsula between the Nejd and the head of the Dead Sea. Jetur, Naphish, and Kedemah form a group together, the latter being the land of the Bnê Kedem, the Children of the East (see above); Jetur, Naphish, and the Hagarenes are located by 1 Ch. 5:19 in Trans-Jordan. Jetur (properly Yetur) is the people of the Ituræans, mentioned in Luke 3:1, by which age they had established themselves in the southern Anti-Lebanon district, an interesting case of the permanence of an ancient stock and illustrative of the mobility of Arabian tribes.[30] The remaining sons, Mibsam, Mishma,[31] Hadad,[32] cannot further be identified except that the first two appear also as Simeonite clans in 1 Ch. 4: 24 f., probably affiliated Arab clans.

Thus the Ishmaelite stocks are represented as quartered in general to the east of Palestine in the Syrian Desert, as is expressed in a statement appended to the Keturah line, Gen..25: 6, but which applies rather to that of Hagar: "Abraham sent away the sons of his concubines eastward to the Land of the East." With these far-flung tribes the Assyrian empire came into collision in all quarters of the northern desert about which their domains extended. The Keturah stocks on the other hand lie rather to the south, in the land of Midian and beyond. It represents the tradition of the movement of the He-

---

30. For the Ituræans see Schürer, *Geschichte des jüdischen Volkes* (1901), vol. I, 707 ff.; G. A. Smith, *Hist. Geog. of the Holy Land*, pp. 544 ff.; Dussaud, *Les Arabes en Syrie avant l'Islam*, pp. 10 ff.

31. The word, from *shama'*, 'hear,' means 'subjects,' cf. Is. 11:14, or loyal bodyguard, e.g., 1 Sam. 22:14 (SV 'into thy council'), originally a name like Mishma-el, 'the god's subject'; cf. the Mohammadan term *Islam*.

32. The name of the Syrian deity; cf. Hadoram occurring in the Yoktanid genealogy, Gen. 10:27.

brew tribes from the south, and indeed it is Midian, rather than the present Sinai, that the most ancient traditions record for the desert habitat of the Hebrews, as in Deborah's Song: "O Lord, when thou wentest forth out of Seir, when thou marchedst out of Edom," Jud. 5:4;[33] and in the Song of Habakkuk: "God came from Teman [in the south of Edom], and the Holy One from Mount Paran [location?] . . . I saw the tents of Cushan in affliction, the [tent] curtains of the land of Midian did tremble," Hab. 3:3, 7. And we recall the traditions of the social and religious relations of Moses with the priest of Midian, Ex. 3:17.[34]

A further prospect of the contacts of Palestine with Arabia appears in the genealogies of Esau-Edom-Seir and the Horites in that land in Gen. 36. The nomenclature is largely un-Hebraic, with peculiar antique formations in -an, -on, and in some cases of particular Arabian origin, e.g., Yeush, v. 5, which is the well-known name of an Old-Arabian deity (in the Koran, etc.).[35] The lively interrelations of these Edomite peoples with the Israelites and their seeping into the territories of the latter is evidenced by history from the earliest

33. "Even you Sinai," v. 5, is a gloss.

34. We have to note the position taken by Musil that Sinai is to be located in the volcanic *harra* of Midian east of the Red Sea, the hypothesis explaining the tradition of the fiery phenomena at the scene of the giving of the Law; this view is still maintained by him in his *Topographical Itineraries*, vol. I, chap. 9, and it has been accepted by a number of scholars; see for example the argument by Phythian-Adams, 'The Mount of God,' *Quarterly Statement* of the Palestine Exploration Fund, 1930, pp. 135 ff., 192 ff. The same writer also identifies Kadesh-barnea of the Wanderings with Petra; *Quart. Statement*, 1933, pp. 137 ff.

35. Arabic *Yaghuth*, 'he-helps'; for the formation from the imperfect cf. Yhwh, the biblical treatment of which as an imperfect, Ex. 3:14, is thereby corroborated. The name Esau occurs in a South-Arabic epitaph, and the word-play in Gen. 25:30 is Arabian; see Chapter VIII.

to the latest ages, in the Post-Exilic Edomite intrusions into Judah and in the northern advance of the Nabatæans.[36]

There is yet another relationship with the quarter of Arabia, namely that with the Aramæans, who appear about the middle of the second millennium on the borders of the Mesopotamian countries, and then are found pressing into the land of the Sown to the north and the west, a movement like that of the 'Amorites' in the preceding millennium.[37] They are ultimately connected with Abraham through his brother Nahor by the biblical genealogy, but a closer affiliation is expressed in the tradition of Abraham's son Isaac marrying Rebekah, granddaughter of Nahor in Abraham's 'homeland,'[38] and of his grandson Jacob obtaining two wives and two concubines from the same quarter, Gen. cc. 29–30. Rebekah's father Bethuel and her brother Laban, the father-in-law of Jacob, appear with the cognomen 'the Aramæan' (Gen. 25:20; 28:5; 31:20, 24), while the linguistic distinction of dialects is marked by the different names given to the Cairn of Witness, 31:46 ff., which Jacob and Laban erected in the land of Gilead to mark the bounds of their respective territories; Jacob called it Gal-ed (an artificial etymology for

36. See the full discussion of the Edomite genealogies in Meyer, *Israel u. ihre Nachbarstämme*, pp. 328–363. For these name-formations as distinctively Arabic see Moritz, *Zeits. f. d. alttest. Wiss.*, 1926, pp. 81 ff.

37. See Schiffer, *Die Aramäer*; Meyer, *op. cit.*, pp. 235–249; E. G. H. Kraeling, *Aram and Israel* (New York, 1918). The origin of the Aramæans is most obscure. Moritz has shown that the names listed in the Akkadian references to the Aramu include a large proportion of philologically Arabic names, so that the distinction between the two elements was not yet precised; see his paper, 'Die Nationalität der Aramu-Stämme in Südost-Babylonien,' in *Oriental Studies ded. to Paul Haupt* (1926), pp. 184–211.

38. Gen. 24; n.b. v. 7, 'land of my nativity,' in contradiction to the origin in Ur of the Chaldees.

Gilead), and Laban, in equally good Aramaic, Yegar-saha-dutha—the first literary witness we have for that dialect.

Now the tradition in the Yahwist places the Patriarchal Aramæans in the neighborhood of Harran in northern Syria, and beyond 'the River,' i.e., the Euphrates, 31:21. But according to 31:23 Laban overtook the fugitive Jacob in Gilead after only seven days' journey, which would not at all suffice for the distance from Harran; and indeed, as the notice of the Aramaic dialect in Gilead shows, the Aramæan territory was not far distant. The Aramæan Patriarchal family appear as semi-nomadic, with their flocks scattered over a wide area; Jacob separated his flocks from Laban's by a three days' journey, 30:36. Jacob's objective in starting from home was the Land of the East, 29:1, that is, to the east of Palestine, as observed above.[39] The story of his meeting Rachel at the well is a typical 'desert' scene, similar to the anecdote of Moses at the well of Midian, Ex. 2:16 ff.

A genealogical scheme is given of the Aramæans in Gen. 22:20 ff. The first-born is Uz, to which people or land the patriarchal Job belonged, himself a son of the East, Job 1:1, 3. Another son is Chesed, and this represents the Chasdim who despoiled the camel troops of his sons, v. 17.[40] Another

39. This ancient name for that country appears in the story of the Egyptian Sinuhe, who on his flight across Sinai came to Kedemi, the biblical Kedemah; for this story see Erman, *Literature of the Ancient Egyptians* (1927), pp. 14 ff., or Barton, *Archaeology and the Bible* (ed. 6, 1933), pp. 371 ff.

40. AV 'Chaldeans'; the Hebrew is Chasdim, the word which the Greeks knew as Chaldæans (by a well-known phonetic change within the Akkadian language), unfortunately the Græcized rendering is kept here in the English versions. Here we meet the desert aborigines from whom proceeded the Chaldæan element in Babylonia—yet another instance of the mobility and surprising historical fates of the Arabian tribes. The Sabæans in v. 15 are to be explained in the same way, as of the stock which came to people the Yemen, Sheba; see Chapter IV.

son, Buz, gives name to the clan of Elihu, the later speaker in the book of Job (32:2); it is aligned with Dedan, Tema, and all the kings of Arabia in Jer. 25:23 f., while Buz and his brother Hazo are doubtless to be identified with Bazu and its mountain land Hazu, a people whom Esarhaddon boasts of reaching and chastising, after a 180-mile march ("140 double hours"), "a district located afar off, a desert stretch of alkali, a thirsty region—of sand, thorn-brush and 'gazelle-mouth' stones, 20 double-hours of serpents and scorpions, with which the plain was covered as with ants."[41]

By this Aramaic affiliation, ultimately akin, the Abrahamic Hebrews renewed their contact and relations with fresh peoples of the desert. The relations of these various Arabian groups still remains phantasmagoric to our view. The Amoritic stocks to which Abraham and the folk of the First Dynasty of Babylon belonged are generally regarded as Semites of the West-land, the land of Amurru, as the late Professor Clay so strenuously argued. The Aramæans came along the length of the Mesopotamian valley, and indeed we find them early to the east of both Euphrates and Tigris. Here in contact with a high civilization they became semi-cultured and ambitious, and were ultimately established as the political power in the upper Euphrates valley (the original Mesopotamia), and then through the length of what we are accustomed to call Syria. But the Hebrew stock had its original kinship with the tribes to the east and south of Palestine-Syria, and especially southwards; and as we shall see later (Chapter VII) these traditions of relationship with far South Arabia are confirmed by archæology. If the Aramæans may be placed in the north-

41. See Luckenbill, *Ancient Records of Assyria and Babylonia*, vol. II, 214; for the pest of serpents see above, Chapter I.

east of the desert, and the Amorite-Hebrews on the western quarter, then those whom we come to distinguish as Arabs, in view of dialectic differences which produced the far later classical Arabic, may hail from the interior oases and plateaus like Nejd, and so have had immediate racial contacts particularly with the Hebraic stock to the west, as is shown by the technically 'Arabic' traces in that region at an early date.[42]

The above exposition of Israel's traditions of race and affiliations thus reveals most intimate relations with Arabia, both on the eastern frontier of the sown-land and to the south through Midian, along with knowledge of the trade routes that spread across the Peninsula, even to distant Hadhramot. Indeed the knowledge of Arabia contrasts in a surprising way with that of the culture-lands of Syria, Egypt, and Babylonia-Assyria. What few geographical identifications are offered for those lands by the Bible, what limited ethnical knowledge is displayed! To the contrary, what abundant information is presented for the inner life of the Arabian Desert, what specific knowledge of its peoples and localities! This knowledge is ethnical rather than geographical, and yet no less vague than the Assyrian reports. And the vagueness is due to the fact of the mobility of the Arabian peoples, their location over wide districts, their long treks in seeking new homes, their appearance as traders in far-flung caravans. We think of the land of Israel from the point of view of the Mediterranean littoral, which the Israelites never developed for themselves, or of Egypt and Babylonia, lands which have been opened up amazingly to our knowledge. These brilliant centers have confused our historical perspective. But Israel held itself in

42. See R. Hartmann, *Die arabische Frage*, pp. 115 ff., 462 ff., for an essay at precising the various groups within Arabia.

defense and offense towards those lands of 'culture.' It looked
to the desert. There alone commercially were its possible prof-
its, by way of the great trade routes which swept up through
Trans-Jordan to Syria or forking through the Negeb (the
South-land of EVV, e.g., Gen. 12:9) to the Mediterranean
and Egypt, or by the east and west roads by way of Dumah
and Teima to the Euphrates and the Persian Gulf. To the
west it was blocked off by the Egyptians, Philistines, Phœnicians, Syrians, cleverer traders than the Hebrews. The one
great enterprise in national trade undertaken by Israel was
Solomon's venture on the Red Sea; if it did not succeed, the
effort is symbolic of the quarter to which Israel's star beck-
oned, to the trade of Arabia.[43] For the desert highways were
open for the exploitation of those who sat across them. And
the internal economic development of Israel must have had
its basis chiefly from this overland trade, which flowed about
and across its territory.

Of far greater importance for permanent results was this
contact with the Arabian peoples in keeping fresh and potent
the desert traditions of the Hebrews. The Arabian sheikh that
Abraham was, the Bedawi Aramæans that their progenitors
were, such reminiscences were kept alive by the movements of
the same age-long Arabian life on their borders, by the infiltration of the desert peoples into the steppes of Judah and
the plateaus of Trans-Jordan. Out there in the desert, in Sinai
or the land of Midian, their national life with its religion had
been born. Cultured and civilized as the Israelites became,
that country in the rear was not merely a back door but a front
portal out of which they looked and from which they received

43. See Chapter VIII.

52

fresh supplies of the spirit and vitality of the desert. Of a truth:

God came from Teiman: and the Holy One from Mount Paran.

To conclude this chapter, there may be noted the influence of Arabist scholars in the interpretation of the Bible, primarily in the field of philology, but as well, and with more striking effect, in the presentation of the spirit and *mis-en-scène* of innumerable biblical passages and portrayals, on which no light is thrown by the literature of the great lands of culture. We may think of the great Arabists Pococke in the seventeenth century and Schultens in the eighteenth century, and for names epochal in our own day, of W. Robertson Smith and Julius Wellhausen, who have illuminated the Bible from the Arabian point of view. And our own greatest American Arabist, Professor Duncan B. Macdonald, has just published a volume on *The Hebrew Literary Genius* (Princeton, 1933), in which he masterfully shows the kinship of Hebrews and Arabs. "The Hebrews," he says, pp. xxvi, xxvii, "remained Arabs. . . . Their literature, throughout all their history, and to this day, in its method of production and in its recorded forms, is of Arab scheme and type. . . . When the literature of the Hebrews is to be considered as to the literary types which it contains, the key is to be found in the far wider Arabic literature." This brilliant book confirms the title of the present chapter.

IV

ANCIENT EXTRA-BIBLICAL REFERENCES TO ARABIA

THE Semitic lands of ancient civilization, the Tigris-Euphrates valley (Mesopotamia, as it is commonly designated, the modern Kingdom of Iraq) and Syria-Palestine, lie in a great arc of a full half-circle about the desert of North Arabia. From earliest times we learn of the movements of the peoples of Arabia along and into this fringe of civilization. If we may accept their Arabian origin, the Semitic or Akkadian inhabitants of Babylonia came in from that desert. A later movement is that which occurred towards the end of the third millennium producing the First Dynasty of Babylon, and which, especially through the sixth king of that dynasty, Hammurabi, created Babylon as political and spiritual capital of the Orient for two millennia. The fresh Semitic stock which this dynasty represents, as is universally recognized from its vocabulary, has close connections with the people of the Westland, as the Babylonians called Syria-Palestine, and to the dynasty of its period there are currently given the titles Amorite, Canaanite, or West Semitic. This racial trek has so impressed historical students that some have imagined an 'empire of Amurru' located somewhere in Northern Syria, of which the biblical Amorites would be the southern representatives. How these tribes moved we do not know, but their center appears to have been the North Arabian desert from which as a central fulcrum they could enter the lands east and north and west, the central desert homeland maintaining a steady relation with its offshoots.

Ancient Extra-Biblical References

A picture of one of these migrations is given by the Bible in the story of the Patriarch Abraham, whose family migrated from Ur of the Chaldees, on the southern edge of Babylonia, and trekked north to Harran in the upper Euphrates valley, whence Abraham wandered south until he found a home in Palestine. The picture is doubtless true in its representation of the free and far-reaching movements of these nomads and their ventures at finding settlement.

In the second millennium appears another movement, vaster in its extent and more enduring; at least we know more of its history and its results. This is the expansion of Aram, the Aramæans, or Syrians, as the English Bible is generally wont to call them. We have seen how they enter into the Patriarchal tradition in the generations after Abraham. In the later political development, the Aramæan states formed in Syria are generally considered to be the result of a southward movement from North Syria, Eber-naharaim (Across-the-River); but there is better reason to hold that this Aramæan 'push' moved in from Arabia on the exposed frontiers of the inlands of the Sown. The Aramæans founded their first political states in the north occupying the lands of the Mitanni and Hittites after their downfall, and actually later this region appears as the heart of the Aramaic culture.

The Aramæans appear first under that name in the Assyrian inscriptions, when Tiglath-pileser I, towards 1100 B.C., records his campaigns against the northern Aramæans.[1] But there was an extensive Aramæan immigration eastward, into Babylonia, which found its particular settlement in the lands east of the Tigris. The people are found there from the ninth

1. Luckenbill, *Ancient Records of Assyria and Babylonia*, vol. I, 83; see at length, Schiffer, *Die Aramäer*; Kraeling, *Aram and Israel*.

century and on, and proved so great a thorn in the flesh of the growing empire of Assyria that Tiglath-pileser IV had to wage a war with them that lasted seventeen years (from 745 on) before he subjugated them.[2] With this Aramæan migration must be associated that of the Kasdim, i.e., Chaldæans, who appeared in the Sea-lands of Babylonia about the eleventh century, and who ultimately developed into the dominant political stock of that land, so that the Neo-Babylonian empire of Nebuchadnezzar was really that of a Chaldæan dynasty. The eponymous ancestor of these Kasdæans, or Chaldæans, is given by the Bible as Kesed, Gen. 22:20 ff., where he appears as a son of Nahor, brother of Abraham, and an uncle of Aram through his brother Kemuel. These early Aramaic Chaldæans appear, in parallelism with the Sabæans, as one of the predatory bands which contributed to the destruction of the patriarch Job's wealth, Job 1:17. These antique elements of the Job story are entirely true to the facts of the second millennium; the Chaldæans whom we later find in control of South Babylonia were once, centuries earlier, for part of their stock at least, roaming the deserts east of Syria-Palestine.

This last biblical reference discovers Aramæan tribes in the desert east of Syria-Palestine. As we saw in Chapter III, Job is placed in the land of the Children of the East; and when Jacob fared forth to visit his father's relatives and to find a wife, he comes upon them in the land of the same Bnê Kedem. This name Kedem, i.e., East, can only be explained from the Palestinian point of view and the region must have lain east of Palestine. And it lay in the so-called desert, the Roman Ara-

---

2. Schiffer, *op. cit.*, pp. 1 ff., cf. 44 ff. Ultimately these Babylonian Aramæans imposed their language upon the whole country.

bia Deserta, as all the scenery in both the Jacob story and that of Job demonstrates, for it is a land where the flocks pasture over a wide extent of territory (cf. Gen. 30:36; Job 1:3), where the wells must be carefully guarded against Bedu depredators (Gen. 29:2 ff.), and where there is the constant danger from the nomadic tribes of the steppes (Job 1:15, 17).

"A wandering [nomad] Aramæan was my father," is the profession put in the mouth of the offerer of first fruits in the ritual prescribed in Dt. 26:1 ff. Jacob represents, as the Bible distinctly indicates in its record of his Aramæan wives, the Aramaic element in the composition of Israel. That element came from the east of Palestine, settlers in the land of the Sown out of the nomadic hordes of the desert, which were pressing in from Arabia Deserta into the culture lands east and north and west. The Jacob-tradition presents the racial relations of Israel with the deserts of North Arabia, even as the Exodus story relates Israel's history with the land of Midian and southerly Arabia.

These early hordes out of the desert, by whatever name they are called—Amorites, Hebrews, Aramæans, Chaldæans —are Arabian, although it is not till a later age that the word 'Arab' actually occurs. The meaning and original application of the name, as remarked above, is not known, nor why it appears not earlier than the ninth century.[3] It must have been an autochthonous word, as it is applied to them equally by the Assyrians and Hebrews, while the word occurs in South-Arabian inscriptions. As a general ethnic designation it does not occur in the Arabic languages until the proto-Arabic inscription of Imrulkais, 'king of all the Arabs,' dated in 326 A.D.[4]

3. Unless it is to be recognized in the word *ereb*, 'mixed multitude,' of the Exodus story, see Chapter II, Note 5.

4. See Chapter II, Note 4.

Arabia and the Bible

The first mention of an 'Arab' is that of 'Gindibu the Arab' in Shalmaneser III's campaign of 854 B.C., when this desert-chief brought 1000 camels to the support of Damascus and its allies, among whom were included 'Ahab the Israelite' and 'Baasa the Ammonite.'[5]

In 738 Tiglath-pileser IV received as a tributary, along with Israel, Damascus and others, 'Zabibe queen of the Arabs,' or 'Arabia';[6] she concludes the list, which is followed by a fulsome record of the rich spoils obtained from the humbled foes, recalling the commodities trafficked in by Dedan, Arabia, Kedar, Sheba, Raghamah, in Eze. 27:20 ff. The same monarch in his campaign of 732–1, after recording the conquest of Damascus, registers the tribute of another Arabian queen, Samsi, as also of a number of Arabian tribes "in the land of the West, whose dwelling is far off," among them names we can identify in the Bible, Massa, Tema, Sheba,

5. See for the Assyrian records Luckenbill, *Ancient Records of Assyria and Babylonia*, vol. I (and for this reference, p. 223); Rogers, *Cuneiform Parallels to the Old Testament* (ditto, p. 296); Barton, *Archaeology and the Bible*, ed. 6, 1933 (ditto, p. 457). The first named work contains all the Assyrian inscriptions, but the Babylonian historical texts have not yet appeared; the others present only the texts that bear upon the Bible; Rogers alone gives the Akkadian in transliteration. All the Assyrian and Babylonian references to Arabia and the Arabs are now most conveniently presented by T. W. Rosmarin, 'Aribi und Arabien in den Ass.-Bab. Quellen,' *Journ. Soc. Or. Research*, 1932, pp. 1–37. For essays at precising the geography of the Assyrian campaigns in Arabia see Friedr. Delitzsch, *Paradies* (1881); Glaser, *Skizze der Geschichte und Geographie Arabiens* (published as vol. II, 1890, vol. I never appeared), chap. 22; Hommel, *Ethnologie und Geographie des alten Orients* (completed in 1926), pp. 557 ff., 578 ff., 597 ff.; Musil, *Topographical Itineraries of Explorations in Arabia and Mesopotamia 1908–1915* (the series published by the New York Geographical Society, 1926–28), vol. II, 477 ff. A new chapter in the sources of early Arabian history was opened up by R. P. Dougherty in his article, 'The Sealand of Arabia,' *Journ. Am. Or. Soc.*, 1930, pp. 1–25, which he has greatly enlarged upon in his notable volume, *The Sealand of Ancient Arabia* (New Haven, 1932); in his chapters 6 and 7 he gives a most useful survey of relations of Arabia with Assyria, Babylonia and Persia.

6. Luckenbill, *op. cit.*, I, 276; for these 'queens of Arabia' see Chapter VIII.

Haiapa = Ephah, Idibail = Adbeel, Badana = possibly Medan (Gen. 25:2).[7] The presence of Sheba in this list of tribes of northwestern Arabia is noticeable, and it occurs again in the next Assyrian reference. In 717 Sargon made a campaign against the Egyptian border, including the adjacent lands of the desert; he reports that he conquered the tribes of Thamud,[8] Ibadid, Marsimanu, Haiapa, 'distant Arabs,' whom he deported and settled in Samaria (cf. 2 Ki. 17:24 ff.), and then, to cite directly: "From Pharaoh king of Egypt, Samsi queen of the Arabs, It'iamara the Sabæan, the kings of the seacoast and the desert I received gold, . . . of the mountains, precious stones, ivory, seed of . . ., all kinds of herbs, horses, and camels, as tribute."[9]

Here we have for the first time the name of a Sabæan king. And we may pursue this Sabæan dynasty farther. In a building-inscription of Sennacherib's recently published, probably belonging towards the end of his reign (705–681 B.C.), we read:[10] "At the laying of the foundation of the Temple of the New Year's Feast, the treasure which Karibi-ilu, king of Saba . . ? . . precious stones, choice herbs ordered to be

---

7. Luckenbill, *op. cit.*, p. 287, cf. p. 279; Rogers, *op. cit.*, p. 318. For the identifications see Chapter III. In a broken line Rogers reads "Aribi in the land of Sa[ba]."

8. The occupants of the el-Ula oasis in northwest Arabia, with whose inscriptions we are acquainted and whose traditional fame is cited in the Koran.

9. Luckenbill, *op. cit.*, vol. II, 7; Rogers, *op. cit.*, p. 331; Barton, *op. cit.*, p. 463. Hommel, in Nielsen's *Handbuch*, p. 75, translates the word represented by the first lacuna 'sweet-smelling spices,' which would refer to the South-Arabian trade. With this interpretation Dougherty agrees, *The Sealand of Ancient Arabia*, p. 4, note 20, in discussing a text of Tiglath-pileser recording a very similar list of booty taken from Merodach-baladan of the Sealand, Luckenbill, p. 285. For this earliest reference to the Arabian horse cf. Chapter I, Note 31. With this is to be compared Sargon's booty of 2500 horses taken from the same Merodach-baladan, Dougherty, p. 6, text in Luckenbill, II, 20.

10. Luckenbill, II, 185; the text was published by Schroeder in 1922. Cf. Hommel's discussion of it in Nielsen's *Handbuch*, p. 76.

brought,—from that treasure, stones and herbs I laid down in the heart of the foundation of that Temple of the New Year's Feast; . . . silver, gold, lapis-lazuli [and a list of obscure precious stones], all kinds of choice herbs. . . ."

We may suppose that this Karibil, king of Saba, was son and successor of Itiamara of Saba in Sargon's day. Now there is this surprising coincidence with data of South-Arabic inscriptions: both of those names are frequent in those texts, being of good South-Arabic formation; and, further, in the oldest dynasties of Saba, of the so-called *Mukarribs*—probably priest-kings, like the Sumerian *patesis* who preceded the kings,—we find two cases of father and son named Yathi-amara and Kariba-il. Hommel pertinently remarks that we have herewith gained a foundation for South-Arabian history we could never have surmised. What its interpretation is awaits solution. The royal names indicate that the Sabæans of the northwest of Arabia are identical with those of the South. Are we to suppose that the northern Sabæans had already migrated into South Arabia and taken possession of their future holdings there? In this case we would have the earliest dates in South-Arabian chronology. If then the Minæans preceded the Sabæans, as is generally maintained, the Minæan period must be placed very early, to the support of the early chronology held by many South-Arabists for the South-Arabian civilization. Or have we in the Assyrian data references to the Sabæans of the north, whose successors migrated south and settled in their new lands, continuing their dynasty and its hereditary names? It must be admitted that the items in the 'gift' of Karibil to Sennacherib with its gold, silver, precious stones, and, above all, choice herbs, i.e., frankincense and the like, point to the Yemen. But the similar tribute given by Merodach-baladan

Ancient Extra-Biblical References

of the Sealand in northeast Arabia (the Berodach-baladan of
2 Ki. 20:12 ff.) rather indicates that in like manner the northern Sabæans imported from the southern spice-lands, even as
did the later Nabatæans; then they would subsequently have
seized control of the sources of supply and transferred themselves and their dynastic names to the far south. In any case
the Arabian background to the Old Testament for *circa* 700
B.C. is brilliantly illuminated for imagination and hypothesis.[11]

A reference in an inscription of Sennacherib's casts interesting light upon inner affairs in Judah. In the famous Prism
Inscription describing his campaign against Syria and Palestine in 701 B.C., he tells (col. iii, lines 30 ff.) how "as for
Hezekiah the fear of my dominion overwhelmed him, and
the Urbi and his regular troops whom he had brought into
Jerusalem his royal city, deserted." It is now coming to be recognized that by the obscure Urbi are meant Arabs, who would
then have been mercenaries serving the Judan king, even as
David had his Pelethites and Cerethites, Philistines and Cre-

11. See further Chapter VI. The movements of the Sabæans like those of other Arab
peoples, as has been elsewhere noted, are to be compared with those of the Normans of
the sea, carrying with them their dynasties, civilization, etc. It is to be observed that
early biblical references know only of Sheba, those instancing the Minæans are late (see
Chapter VIII); the Queen of Sheba in the story of Solomon is one of numerous queens
of northern Arabia, but her gifts are those of the far south. It may be recalled that J. H.
Mordtmann in his *Beiträge zur minäischen Epigraphik* (Supplement 12 to *Zeitsch. f.
Ass.*, 1897, pp. 105–116) held for the priority of the elder Sabæan inscriptions over the
Minæan on epigraphic and linguistic grounds; see Hartmann's counter-arguments, *Die
arabische Frage*, pp. 130 ff. But the former view is still maintained by scholars, e.g.,
Dussaud, *Les Arabes en Syrie*, p. 73, cf. Rossini, *Storia d'Etiopia*, I (1928), 98. The
new datum offers a problem equally with the longer and shorter chronologies claimed for
South-Arabian history.—Saba and Sabum appear in Sumerian texts of the third millennium (Barton, *Royal Inscriptions of Sumer and Akkad* (1929), pp. 115, 299) and have
suggested identification with South-Arabian Sheba; but these would be then the northern
Sabæans.

tans. We also have the coincidence, noted at the beginning of Chapter II, of 'their Arabs' whom South-Arabian kings claimed among their subjects.[12]

The opposition which the Arabs made against the advance of the Assyrian empire in the reigns of Tiglath-pileser and his successors, and then with the conquest of Egypt by Esarhaddon and its reconquest by Asshurbanipal, involving the policy of maintaining a direct trans-desert route to the imperial possessions in the West, led the last-named monarchs to the attempt to conquer Arabia. To these moments of general policy was added the support of the Arab tribes rendered to Asshurbanipal's rebel brother Shamash-shum-ukin, who, in the king's own words, "had stirred to revolt against me the people of Akkad, Chaldæa, the Aramæans, the Sealand (in Arabia) from Akaba to Bab-Salimeti," in which Akaba may be the same as the present name of the northeast arm of the Red Sea and the town at its head.[13]

There are repeated references to conquests undertaken in the land from both the eastern and the western front, in which Kedar in particular and 'the Arabs' in general are the objectives, and Adumu or Adummatu, the biblical Dumah (Is. 21:11), appears as 'the fortress of Arabia'; this oasis was cap-

12. For the passage see Luckenbill, II, 120 f.; Rogers, p. 344; Barton, p. 471. The identification suggested by Delitzsch, *Paradies*, p. 305, is accepted by Luckenbill, Sidney Smith, Ebeling, Speiser, and is corroborated by Sennacherib's listing in another place of "Urbi, Aramæans, Chaldæans" (Luckenbill, p. 132). For the vocalization the classical Arabic knows 'urub as a plural of 'arab (Lane, *Dictionary*, p. 1993, col. 3), and 'urban (De Goeje, in *Enc. of Islam*, vol. I, 373, col. 1).

13. Luckenbill, *op. cit.*, p. 301. The word means 'steep' and is applied to the great sandstone bluff which marks the division between the western part of the Syrian Desert and the lower Peninsula; see Doughty, *Arabia Deserta*, vol. I, 51: Moritz, *Arabien*, p. 8. From it is taken the modern application to the gulf and its port. See Dougherty, *The Sealand of Ancient Arabia*, pp. 99 ff., etc., for the implications of these geographical references.

tured and destroyed by Sennacherib and again by Esarhaddon.[14] For two extensive campaigns, that of Esarhaddon against Bazu, the biblical Buz, and in particular Asshurbanipal's ninth campaign against Uaite 'king of the Arabs,' we have vivid details of the desert marches of the Assyrian troops, the distances and terrors of the way, the horrible ravaging of the subjugated territories. But for the collapse of the Assyrian empire Arabia Deserta might have been for once 'pacified.'[15]

At the end of the seventh century, we come upon the first recorded crossing of the northern or Syrian Desert of Arabia. The hero of this feat is no less a person than the great Nebuchadnezzar, who, according to a fragment of Berossus, after crushing Pharaoh Necho at the battle of Carchemish in 605 and reincorporating Syria into his father Nabopolassar's kingdom, upon learning of the latter's death, pushed straight through the desert to Babylon to secure the succession for himself. Josephus adds to this the information that he pressed on "and took all Syria as far as Pelusium except Judaea."[16] What route the Babylonian prince followed we know not. If he was in northern Syria he may have pushed across the desert *via* Tadmor-Palmyra, the desert city that leaped into im-

---

14. See Luckenbill, vol. II, 158, 214; for the place cf. Chapter III.

15. For the Bazu campaign see Luckenbill, p. 209; for that of Asshurbanipal, pp. 313–319. In the latter passage the Arabian national god is named Atar-Samain, i.e., Athtar of the heavens, Athtar being a chief South-Arabian deity. (Athtar is the feminized Babylonian Ishtar.) For other references to these Arabian campaigns see *ibid.*, pp. 207, 214, 218, 220, 337, 364, 365, 367. Moritz, *Arabien*, p. 19, locates Buz in the el-Ula oasis, but Musil, *Topographical Itineraries*, vol. II, 484, in the Sirhan depression, southeast of Trans-Jordan.

16. Berossus, in Müller, *Fragm. hist. graec.*, fragm. 14; Josephus, *Ant.*, x, 6, 1; cf. Jer. 46:2. The same fragment of Berossus reports that Nebuchadnezzar conquered Arabia; but this may not mean more than Josephus's statement, x, 9, 7, that he subjected Ammon and Moab.

perial fame in the third century of our era, but of whose existence in the second millennium B.C. we now know from Akkadian records.[17] But as Nebuchadnezzar was of the Chaldæan stock which had employed the Arabs as allies in the earlier revolt against Assyria, he may have pushed east by a more southerly route, and so possibly *via* Teima, of whose importance as a key-point in the Neo-Babylonian empire we learn from the records of the last Babylonian king, Nabonidus, the father of the prince Belshazzar, king Belshazzar of the Book of Daniel. Of a campaign of Nebuchadnezzar into Arabia we have a memorandum with accompanying oracle in Jer. 49: 28–33: "Of Kedar and of the kingdoms of Hasor, which Nebuchadnezzar king of Babylon smote"; here Hasor probably represents an Arabic word signifying the settled Arabian oases.[18]

Prof. R. P. Dougherty, of Yale, has opened up fascinating vistas of the Arabian relations of this Neo-Babylonian empire in some recent publications.[19] Reference should be made to c.

17. Dhorme, *Revue biblique,* 1924, p. 106; the Akkadian name is Tadmar. The next witness to this oasis center is 1 Ki. 9:17, where 'Tamar in the wilderness' (doubtless the Judæan wilderness is meant) is ordered by the Masorah to be read 'Tadmor in the wilderness,' and this *Krê* ('reading') has become the actual text in the parallel 2 Ch. 8:3. The *Krê* 'Tadmor' appears in the Greek translation, so that this tradition of Solomon's 'building of Tadmor' goes back at least to the third century; or if we may regard 'Tadmor' in 1 Chron. as original, to the fourth century. According to Caetani, *Annali,* II, 2, 392 ff., it was this same route that was taken by Khálid ibn Walíd in his dash across the desert, in the thirteenth year of the Hijra; but Musil, vol. II, App. 8, argues for the route *via* Dumah, Dumat el-Ghandel.

18. Other marches of early record across Arabia are those of the Egyptian king Zeher-Tachos, who fled for help to the Persian court at Susa, 362 B.C. (Diodorus Siculus, xv, 92, cf. Petrie, *History of Egypt,* vol. III, 384); and Seleucus Nicator, who returned from Egypt to seize his kingdom in Babylon in 311, making his march through waterless and desert country (Arrian, *Indica,* §43).

19. 'Nabonidus in Arabia,' *Journ. Am. Or. Soc.,* 1922, pp. 305–316 (cf. an earlier note, *ibid.,* 1921, p. 458); "Nabonidus and Belshazzar," in *Yale Oriental Series, Researches,* 1929. Add now his last volume noticed at end of Note 5.

10 of his volume for the facts developed by Dr. Dougherty and here only briefly summarized. According to a recently published Akkadian inscription[20] Nabonidus divided his power with his eldest son (Belshazzar) and entrusted the kingship to him,[21] and "he himself undertook a distant campaign; the power of the land of Akkad advanced with him; towards Teima in the midst of the Westland (*Amurru*) he set his face. He undertook a distant campaign on a road not within reach of old. He slew the prince [*malku* = Heb. 'king'] of Tema with [sword]; the dwellers in his city [and] country, all of them he slaughtered. Then he established his dwelling [in Teima]. . . . That city he made glorious; . . . They made it like the palace of Babylon." Further, from the so-called Nabonidus Chronicle, col. 1, we learn of a campaign into Arabia by the same king, which apparently proceeded from the north through Syria (Amurru) and Adummu, i.e., the oasis Dumah,[22] and which may have been the expedition which conquered Teima. The same Chronicle gives an annual diary of Nabonidus's reign for seventeen years, and records that for his seventh, ninth, tenth, eleventh years he was in Teima and did not come to the New Year feast at Babylon. For the remaining years of the reign the Chronicle text is mutilated and we are left in doubt as to the king's subsequent whereabouts. But Dougherty has amassed evidence (c. 10) to show that for a large part of the reign his son Belshazzar was

20. The so-called 'Persian Verse Account of Nabonidus,' published by Sidney Smith in his *Babylonian Historical Texts* (1924).

21. This statement is interesting as a unique corroboration of the biblical description of Belshazzar as king; for the passage see Smith, pp. 84, 88; Dougherty, *Nab. and Belsh.*, p. 106.

22. Hardly, as Smith prefers, Edom, which is spelled Udume in an inscription of Asshurbanipal, listed with Ammon, Hauran, Moab, Seir; see Luckenbill, II, 314.

actual regent in Babylonia and that accordingly the father must have spent much of his time in Teima. In c. 11 the same scholar discusses at length the reasons that may be conjectured for this prolonged absence of the king from his kingdom. Three points of especial interest to our present discussion may be observed. First, the central position of Teima made it a strategic fulcrum whence rapidly moving forces might be thrown out to protect the far-flung empire against the threatening conquest by Persia, while the position offered a natural liaison with Egypt for effecting a combination of the two ancient empires against the new Iranian foe. In the second place, with his provinces threatened and largely detached, Nabonidus may have desired to tap and control the wealth of the trade northwards from the lands of spice and gold of inner and southern Arabia. Finally it is to be observed that Teima was found or made to be a place fit for a king to live in, a position Teima has never since enjoyed, but which for a few years placed it in the rank of ancient Petra and Palmyra, of modern Háil and Riád; "that city he made glorious . . . like the palace of Babylon." The district of Teima is one of the most attractive oases in Arabia, as it still remains one of the main trade centers of the land.[23] Thus twenty-five hundred years ago Nabonidus for once developed the potentialities of the region. Were conditions, climatic, economical, racial, different then from what they have been in later times?

The Bible contains two references (already noted) to the metropolitan position of Teima in the trans-desert trade: Is.

23. For descriptions see Doughty, *Arabia Deserta*, vol. I, chaps. 10, 19; Jaussen and Savignac, *Mission archéologique en Arabie*, vol. II, part 1, chap. 4. The oasis was once the site of seven cities, Doughty, p. 151. For its history see Musil, *Oriental Explorations*, V, 224–229.

21:13 ff., where the inhabitants of the land of Teima offer refuge and hospitality to Dedanite caravans fleeing from hostile invasion—the Arabian campaigns of the Assyrian monarchs or of Nebuchadnezzar and Nabonidus?—and Job 6:19, where "the caravans of Teima and the companies of Sheba" are presented in a picture of the desert.

These external references to Teima are brilliantly illustrated by an inscribed early-Aramaic monument, the Teima Stele, possibly to be dated in the sixth century B.C.[24] The inscription records the fee-simple grant of specified palm lands and perpetual right in the priesthood of the local god, Salm, to a certain priest Salm-shezib. The cosmopolitan connections of Teima are interestingly indicated. The name of the priest for this title—the Aramaic word *kumra* is used—is either Akkadian, or, more likely, Aramaic; his father's name is Petosiri, which is Egyptian. The name of the deity Salm means 'image,' 'idol'; that is, he is the personification of the stone or pillar, probably roughly sculptured; the word in various forms is found over the later Semitic world and is of Aramaic distribution.[25] With this local deity Salm, who is under the patronage of another Salm, deity of Mahram (an Arabic word = 'sanctuary'), are associated two deities Shingala (Singala?) and Ashera, of which the former may be of Akkadian origin (composed from Sin), the latter is the *Ashera* of the Hebrew, generally translated 'grove' or 'groves' in AV,

---

24. First seen by Doughty in 1878, copied by Huber, and subsequently through the latter's efforts, in which he lost his life, transported to the Louvre; see Hogarth, *Penetration of Arabia*, pp. 280 ff., and for the inscription and its translation, Cooke, *North Semitic Inscriptions*, pp. 195 ff.

25. E.g., 1 Sam. 6:5, Amos 5:26, etc.; in Phœnician and also occasionally in the Old Testament the word appears as *semel* (with a different *s*), e.g., Dt. 4:16, and in Arabic, as *sanam*, which is the usual Islamic word for idol. Cf. the biblical name Ebenezer, '(the) Stone is help,' and 'Rock' (*sur*) as epithet of Deity.

but correctly as a proper name in SV (e.g., 2 Ki. 21:7)—herself probably the personification of the tree as symbol of fertility. Other terms of the text are also variously explained from various origins. It appears thus that Teima was a cosmopolitan center in which a hybrid stranger was able to attain for himself priestly rights and where the gods were equally of diverse origin. Part of the priestly income is to be given from 'the estate of the king'; if this be a local prince, it corroborates that title given by the Assyrians to the Arabian chiefs with whom they came in contact.[26]

Dr. Dougherty presses a statement in Xenophon's *Cyropaedia* (the 'Cyrus Romance') to the effect that Cyrus "subjected the Arabians,"[27] but Xenophon's authority and the statement are too uncertain for any inductions. However, the conquest of Egypt by Cambyses was in part effected by cooperation with the Arabians of the desert, and Herodotus's description of the campaign implies that it was made across the desert, under the security of a certain 'Arab'; the Greek historian pauses to describe how the latter provided water for the desert march, and also indulges in an excursus on Arabian religion and ethics.[28] The conquest of Egypt having been accomplished by Cambyses, his successor Darius took the next great step towards consolidation of his wide-flung western domains, the control of the sea-approach towards the West by way of the Indian Ocean (Arabian Sea) and the Red Sea. According to Herodotus[29] he sent a Greek adventurer, a certain

26. For the pervasive expansion of the Aramæans in North Arabia in this age see the interesting discussion by M. Hartmann, *Die arabische Frage*, pp. 35 ff.

27. Chap. 12 of his *Nabonidus and Belshazzar*, entitled 'The Conquest of Arabia by Cyrus'; see note above on Berossus's statement that Nebuchadnezzar conquered Arabia.

28. iii, 7 ff.

29. iv, 44, cf. 42.

Ancient Extra-Biblical References

Skylax, on a voyage from the mouth of the Indus to the head of the Red Sea; "he was the first Greek to visit India and make the Red Sea voyage,"[30] and this statement might be made more inclusive by claiming Skylax as the first known circumnavigator of Arabia. This feat of Darius's policy was followed by the opening up of the freshwater canal which ran from the Pelusiac branch of the Nile to the Red Sea, attributed by the Greeks to Sesostris of the Middle Kingdom, the reopening of which was attempted by Necho, *c.* 600.[31] Had these attempts permanently succeeded, the story of the Suez Canal would have been anticipated by two millennia and Arabia would have been made accessible to an extent not known in history.

This reference to Skylax's circumnavigation of Arabia brings up the whole problem of early maritime transportation by way of the coasts of Arabia. Voyaging on the Red Sea to the land of Punt, probably the biblical Put (Gen. 10:6), and generally regarded as Somali Land opposite the southern end of Arabia, had been undertaken by the Egyptians from the time of the pyramid-builders; the expedition ordered by queen Hatshepsut of the XVIIIth Dynasty is classical because of the detailed description given of it in her famous in-

30. H. G. Rawlinson, *Intercourse between India and the Ancient World*, ed. 2 (1926), p. 17. For other works on the fascinating topic of ancient Oriental trade may be named E. H. Warmington, *The Commerce between the Roman Empire and India* (ed. 2, 1928); M. Cary and E. H. Warmington, *The Ancient Explorers* (1929); Arnold Wilson, *The Persian Gulf* (1928); S. B. Miles, *The Countries and Tribes of the Persian Gulf* (2 vols., 1919).

31. See R. W. Rogers, *A History of Ancient Persia* (1929), pp. 119 ff. Darius records in his Suez Inscription, *ibid.*: "So was this canal built, as I had commanded, and ships passed through this canal from Egypt to Persia." Cf. Breasted, *History of Egypt*, pp. 276, 584. Darius refers to Arabia, Arabaya, as among his dominions; Behistun Inscr., I, 15; Naks-i-Rustum Inscr., A, 27 (in Tolman's edition).

scription at Deir el-Bahri.[32] It was with similar purpose that Solomon attempted to open up the Red Sea trade with a navy (see Chapter VIII). Of the approach towards circumnavigation of Arabia from the other side we know little. From earliest ages the inhabitants of Babylonia had maritime connections with the sacred island of Dilmun in the Gulf, with which the pearl islands of Bahrein are now generally identified.[33] Recent evidence indicates that Sumerian copper was brought to Babylonia from Jebel Akhdar in Oman, which may involve maritime connections.[34]

I may not enter upon the vexed problem of Magan and Meluhha which have been placed in regions of the Arabian coast as well as in the Nile valley, Egypt and Ethiopia. If indeed there was no early continuous circumnavigation of the Peninsula, there must have been an early coasting trade along its shores, whereby commodities were passed on from hand to hand. The riches of South Arabia, Somali Land, India, and the insatiable desire for them on the part of the imperial civilizations must have early developed and constantly stimu-

32. Breasted, *Ancient Records of Egypt*, vol. II, nos. 252–295; *History*, pp. 127, 274 ff.; Flinders Petrie, *History of Egypt*, II, 80 ff.

33. Only at this point in Arabia have archæological excavations been made, in the very ancient tomb-tumuli. (But see now Chapter V, Note 4.) Following attempts made by Theodore Bent (see his *Southern Arabia*) and Prideaux, a scientific exploration has now been accomplished by the British School of Archæology in Egypt, the results published in its *Publications* by Mackay, Harding, and Petrie, *Bahrein and Hemamieh* (1929). The minimum date of the tumuli is placed at 1500–1200 B.C. The translation 'pearl' in AV at Job 28:18 is incorrect; the word *peninim*, *ibid.*, translated 'rubies' by AV RV, is held by some to mean pearls, which then would have come from Bahrein. Professor Dougherty informs me that the name of a jewel in Sumerian, in a text from Ur, may mean pearl; Professor Legrain renders the word by 'fish-eye.'

34. On basis of chemical analysis; see H. Peakes, *Antiquity*, II (1928), 452 ff. In a monograph by A. Hertz, 'Die Kultur um den Persischen Golf' (*Klio*, Beiheft xx, 1930), p. 99, evidence is offered for trade intercourse between the earliest civilization in Babylonia and Upper Egypt, which must then have gone by sea.

lated such trading ventures. From an early date the island of Sokotra, 130 miles south of Arabia, appears to have been known in Indian literature, while the island, itself desirable for its production of "gum and resin-producing plants and aloes" was a convenient central position for the trade in the Arabian Sea.[35] It is to be observed that the southern coasts of Arabia have admirable harbors; the Sultans of Oman were rulers of Zanzibar until the middle of the last century, a Hadhramotic sheikh held Sokotra as his fief until the British occupation in 1886.[36] There were two policies struggling over Arabia: that of the Yemen which was determined to keep in its own hands the frankincense of Hadhramot and remain the depot for the Indian trade, and so possess the lucrative monopoly of the transport through the length of Arabia; the other that of the rival states, Egypt, Israel and the Phœnicians under Solomon, the Persians, Greeks, Romans, who plied the sea-routes to destroy the Arabian monopoly. The success of the Greeks and Romans destroyed the Sabæan state and its civilization.

Alexander pushed his conquests far to the Orient into the Indian Punjab and so brought the Greeks into touch with the Indian Ocean on its farther side. He commissioned his ad-

35. See Schoff, *The Periplus of the Erythræan Sea*, pp. 133 ff.; Rawlinson, *India and the Western World*, p. 113. For the occurrence of the Sabæan dynastic name Du-Raidan in the Indian epic of the Mahabharata, see Nielsen's *Handbuch*, p. 107.

36. The regular occurrence of the monsoon winds in the Indian Ocean, blowing southerly in summer and northerly in winter, by which the run between Arabia and India is immensely facilitated, was first discovered, according to the Greeks, by Hippalus, *circa* 45 A.D. But this discovery was one for the Greeks, the secret must have been early known to the coastwise inhabitants of the Indian Ocean. See Schoff, *op. cit.*, pp. 45, 227–230, in which latter place he gives strong evidence for the antiquity of this sea-trade; for the monsoons see Warmington, *op. cit.*, pp. 48 f., Rawlinson, *op. cit.*, p. 109.

miral Nearchus to prospect the maritime route westward to the Persian Gulf, which this doughty sailor effected. Alexander also attempted the circumnavigation of Arabia from both the Gulf and the Red Sea.[37] Seleucus Nicator sent Megasthenes to India, and a certain Eudoxus sailed thither from Egypt under Ptolemy Euergetes II (146–117).[38] Thus the Greeks promptly visualized the prospect of control of the trade of the Indian Ocean and its arms, the Red Sea and the Persian Gulf, and the opportunity so offered of gaining access to the frankincense lands of South Arabia and the still more exotic products of eastern Africa and India. This development took place under the Ptolemies, whose Egyptian kingdom was naturally the nucleus of the Mediterranean and the Indian Ocean. The more evident route from the head of the Red Sea at Suez with its possible canal connections with the Nile Delta was actually replaced by ports lower down the Gulf, first Berenike, later Myos-Hermos, with which access was had by a well-regulated road from Koptos, modern Kart on the Nile, not far south of Luxor. This routing of commerce gradually increased, until in the early days of the Roman empire the value of its goods reached a fabulous sum annually, so great was the demand of the rich and luxurious West for the incense, spices, jewels and precious metals, *objets d'art* and

37. Cary and Warmington, *op. cit.*, p. 61.

38. Rawlinson, *op. cit.*, pp. 40 ff., 96 ff. Another prospect of ancient trade is opened up by the narratives of circumnavigation of Africa; see Cary and Warmington, chap. V. The spread of Greek influence in South Arabia is seen in its coinage of Hellenic type; see G. F. Hill, *Catalogue of Greek Coins of Arabia, Mesopotamia and Persia* (Brit. Museum, 1922), and his earlier monograph, 'The Ancient Coinage of Southern Arabia,' in *Proceedings of the British Academy*, vol. VII; while the spread of Arabian trading colonies appears from the South-Arabic inscriptions found in Egypt and Delphi. Glaser offers evidence for Greek colonies in Arabia, *Skizze*, chap. 12, pp. 152 ff., and so he explains the appearance of Yavan in Eze. 27:19 as an Arabian group.

curiosities of the inexhaustible East.[39] This overseas route was in competition with the ancient land routes across Arabia, the one running north from the Yemen, which was the nucleus of the Oriental trade for the riches of South Arabia, Africa, and India; the other running across the neck of the Peninsula between the land of Edom and the gulf ports of Babylonia or the more southerly Gerrhae, in the neighborhood of the Bahrein islands, which was a trans-shipping point for the Gulf trade. These routes made the ancient land of Edom, thus centrally placed between the seas and the continents, an international emporium, and produced the potent trading state of the Nabatæans, with their capital Petra. These Nabatæans, an Arabic people which had adopted Aramaic language and letters, were able to hold their own and increase their monopolies of trade, until the powerful empire of Rome undertook the control and development of Oriental trade. Its forcible grasping of the Red Sea route—which included an abortive attempt at conquest of Sheba by Augustus's general Gallius in 26 B.C.[40]—ultimately spelled the ruin of the Nabatæan kingdom, which was finally incorporated in the Roman empire by Trajan in 106 A.D. Also the conflict between Rome and the Oriental empire which centered in Persia, the Parthians earlier and the Sassanians from the third century after Christ, rendered the overland trade with the East more difficult and encouraged the all-sea route to India.

39. See Rawlinson, chaps. 5, 6; Schoff, *passim.* The drainage on the gold coinage of Rome was enormous: Mommsen has calculated on the basis of Pliny's figures that the Orient absorbed annually $5,500,000 of gold. "Even as early as the days of Sulla we hear of two hundred and ten talents weight [of spices] being used at his obsequies. The climax was of course reached by Nero, who at the funeral of Poppaea, in 66 A.D., burnt more aromatics on her bier than Arabia produced in a year"; Rawlinson, *op. cit.,* p. 103.

40. For this expedition, which started in the Nabatæan land and reached, or nearly so, the Sabæan capital, see Glaser, chaps. 3, 4.

Arabia and the Bible

This commercial circumnavigation of Arabia, which traded at the Arabian ports but which upset the immemorial privilege of the Arabs in control of the overland trade to all points on the periphery of the Peninsula, brought on the degradation of the economics of Arabia. But on the historical side this interest of the West in the East produced and has left for us, unfortunately often only in fragments, a number of invaluable geographical memoirs, which reveal the inner history of Arabia and map out its trade routes in a brilliant fashion that is not equaled until we have the similar literature of Islamic origin, which had its origin not earlier than the end of the eighth century. This literature of the Hellenic-Roman empire grew to comparatively great proportions. We may only record the names of the writers: the botanist Theophrastus (*c.* 312 B.C.); Eratosthenes, the head of the Alexandrian library (died 1·96 B.C.), cited by Strabo; Agatharcides (*c.* 120 B.C.); the *Periplus of the Red Sea*, written about 60 A.D.;[41] Strabo the geographer and historian of the Augustan Age; Pliny the Younger (*c.* 79 A.D.); and the great geographer Claudius Ptolemæus of Alexandria, who flourished in the reigns of Hadrian and Antoninus (writing between 138 and 165).[42] Study of the latter's work, as interpreted by Sprenger, reveals in the West for the second century a knowledge of

41. See the valuable volume under the same title, giving translation and full notes, by W. H. Schoff, 1912. Agatharcides's description of Arabia, cited by Diodorus, iii, 38–48, it has been remarked, is a commentary on Eze. 27.

42. This geographical material bearing on Arabia is admirably summarized by Tkatsch, art. 'Saba' in *Enc. of Islam*; the Greek geography for Arabia Deserta is studied by Musil, *Topogr. Itineraries*, II, App. 3. The most extensive treatment is given by Glaser, *Skizze*, cc. 1–23. Sprenger's classic volume, *Die alte Geographie Arabiens*, 1875, is a discussion of Ptolemy's work; it is accompanied with a map representing Ptolemy's notions of Arabian geography (conveniently reproduced in Zwemer's *Arabia, the Cradle of Islam*, p. 75).

the unknown Peninsula which is in some respects not matched by modern map-makers. The trade routes crisscross the Peninsula and are dotted with emporia, so that there appears little left of the inaccessible desert, even in the south. Indeed Sprenger remarks, p. 7, that "in general Ptolemy knows of no desert." This is information for the beginning of the era, it is of value for centuries earlier; indeed, the importance of Arabia was waning in Ptolemy's day. And these Greek geographers are invaluable, for they inform us for the first time of the Arab peoples and their relative locations, and this enables us to obtain a view of tribal movements and dislocations, so dominating a feature in Arabian history.[43]

43. The remarkable discovery of texts written in a cuneiform script but in a Hebraic dialect has been made at Ras Shamra in North Syria; see Chapter VIII, Note 1, for the literature. The texts belong to the fourteenth century B.C. In the latest of the texts published, by Virolleaud in *Syria*, 1833, pp. 128 ff., occurs, dubiously, the word 'Arabs.' If this be the case, it is the earliest occurrence of the word. For discussion of the ethnical and geographical possibilities of this text see Dussaud, 'Les Phéniciens au Negeb et en Arabia,' *Revue de l'Histoire des Religions*, 1933, pp. 1 ff.

V

ARABIA DESERTA

The Land of Arabia

ARABIA is a land that in the past has defied, while it still challenges exploration. Few Westerners have crossed it between east and west, none has traveled it from north to south, the nearest to this accomplishment having been made by Philby.[1] Many of its great trade routes have never been pursued by the foreigner. The mapping out of its great features, like the watersheds, is still in process; and vast stretches of historical interest, like Yamáma and Oman, remain *terrae incognitae*.[2]

1. The crossing has been accomplished by Sadlier in 1819; Wallin in 1848; Palgrave in 1862; Capt. W. H. I. Shakespear in 1913–14; Miss Gertrude Bell in 1914; Musil in 1914–15; Philby in 1917–18.

2. See D. C. Hogarth, *The Penetration of Arabia* (1906), for the story of exploration to the beginning of this century. For more recent literature see my article 'Arabia To-day,' in *Journ. Am. Or. Soc.*, 1927, pp. 97 ff. A notable series of volumes of adventurous exploration have been published in the last decade, among which I note: St. J. B. Philby, *The Heart of Arabia*, 2 vols. (1922); R. E. Cheesman, *In Unknown Arabia* (1926); Bertram Thomas, *Alarms and Excursions in Arabia* (1931), and *Arabia Felix* (1932); Philby, *The Empty Quarter* (1933). All these explorers have visited parts hitherto unknown, Thomas reporting that he explored "five hundred miles untrodden by a European," and finally Philby effecting for the first time the crossing of the Desert Quarter.

To the great credit of the American Geographical Society is the publication in six sumptuous volumes along with atlas of maps, of the distinguished explorer A. Musil's *Topographical Itineraries of Explorations in Arabia and Mesopotamia 1908–1915*. A one-volume abridgment of this work has been published by the editor, Mr. Wright, entitled *In the Arabian Desert* (1930).

For the very recent political history of Arabia are to be noted: Philby, *Arabia of the Wahhabis* (1928), and *Arabia* (1930); A. Rihani, *Maker of Modern Arabia* (1928), and *Around the Coasts of Arabia* (1930), along with a valuable book in Arabic with title *History of the New Nejd* (1928); E. Topf, *Die Staatenbildungen in den arabischen Teilen der Türkei seit dem Weltkriege* (1929). The British Government's Man-

Arabia Deserta

Its Two Holy Cities, the Haramein, Mecca and Medina, may not be visited by the infidel on pain of death, and two explorers, Rathjens and v. Wissmann, were refused the privilege of exploring the Hijáz in 1927.[3] The dangers and hazards of a strange life confront the western traveler; and a dour fanaticism closes the door to investigation. Archæological exploration has been confined to narrow quarters, to the western fringe of the Syrian Desert in the northwest of the Peninsula with the adjacent land of Midian and to the Yemen in the far south and the neighboring land of mystery, Hadhramot, in which regions the chief results have been gained only by the hardiest of adventurers, such as Halévy and Glaser. Of excavation, which is often naïvely identified with exploration, there has been naught; only within a few years indeed have the French begun to clear out Palmyra, and Petra has not yet been touched with the spade. Of the ethnology of the Peninsula we are ill informed, being still dependent upon the traditional family trees of the Arab tribes. In the field of anthropology, the study of the vestiges of primitive man, almost nothing has been learned.[4]

date Reports, published annually since 1920, are invaluable for the political relations of Arabia northwards.

An air-reconnaissance of Shibam and other cities in the heart of the Hadhramot valley has been recently made by R. A. Cochrane and associates; his account has been published in the *Geographical Journal*, March 1931, and some of the air-views in the *Ill. London News* of April 1, 1931. These illustrations of crowded 'sky-scraper' mansions reveal the survival of a rich ancient civilization.

3. The most recent European visitor to Mecca is Eldon Rutter, going with the profession of Islam; he has published a fascinating work, *The Holy Cities of Arabia*, in two volumes (1928). For visits of Christians to these holy cities see A. Jefferys, under that title, in *The Moslem World*, July 1929. I have not seen a book by A. Ralli, *Christians at Mecca* (1909).

4. Some qualifications may now be made of the above statements. Rathjens and v. Wissmann in vol. II of their *Südarabien-Reise* (1932), report their excavation of the temple at Hugga in the Yemen under the interested patronage of the Imam himself—a

Arabia and the Bible

While any survey of the biblical data, such as we have superficially pursued, informs us of the intimate relations of the Bible peoples with Arabia, the impression is fugitive, we do not easily realize it in imagination. To us of the comfortable life of the one 'civilization' as we boastfully think, that desert land is physically repellent, its unsettled state of society morally unsympathetic. It is difficult for us to realize that the Arabs, the Bedawin as we picture them, have affected the lands of culture that fringe Arabia more than the Indians have influenced our American civilization. Yet the Bible constantly defies this obstinacy of ours, while growing archæological science, insufficient as has been its opportunity, more than corroborates the Bible. We may proceed now to examine that 'Arabian Desert.'[5]

Arabia as mere peninsula, measured from the line between the heads of the Red Sea and the Persian Gulf is the largest peninsula in the world, measuring some 1,000,000 square miles, or about a third of the area of the United States exclusive of Alaska; to this should be added, for the full measure

cheering prospect for the archæologist. The beginning of anthropological survey of the Syrian Desert has been made most fortunately by the Field Museum North Arabian Desert Expeditions of 1927-28 under the charge of Mr. Henry Field; reports of the results may be found in his article, 'The Ancient and Modern Inhabitants of Arabia,' *The Open Court*, December 1932; 'The Antiquity of Man in Southwestern Asia,' *American Anthropologist*, 1933, pp. 51 ff. Remarkable discoveries of the remains of primitive man have now been made, in 1932, in the form of pictographs at Kilwa, to the southeast of Palestine, on the line between Akaba and the interior oasis of the Jauf; this brilliant discovery is due to Mr. Horsfield, Director of Antiquities in Trans-Jordan, and Prof. N. Glueck, at the time Director of the American School of Oriental Studies in Jerusalem. See their beautifully illustrated article in *American Journal of Archaeology*, 1933, pp. 381 ff.; also Dr. Glueck's articles in the *Bulletin* of the Schools, September 1933. These discoveries are to be immediately further pursued.

5. For a convenient summary of the physical features (in addition to excellent articles in the several encyclopædias), see *Handbook of Arabia* (published by the British Admiralty since the War, without date), chap. 1.

of the connotation of the term, the great extension northwards of the characteristic Arabian features, inserted like a wedge between Syria-Palestine and the Euphrates basin, the so-called Syrian Desert. The common features of this great region are generally summed up for popular thought in the one word 'desert.' And by this word we generally think of a sandy and sand-blown waste, recognizing withal the presence of an occasional oasis with feeble water supply.

'Desert' and 'wilderness' are the usual translations in the English Bible for the Hebrew words *arabah* and *midbar*. In Chapter II we noticed the former word in connection with its congener 'Arab'; we recall that it is used of the Jordan-Dead Sea valley, in which the Jordan stretch has a luxuriant low vegetation on its banks.[6] Hence the word does not imply a waterless region, certainly not at all a sandy waste. The other and more usual word *midbar* (also Akkadian *madbaru*, while the word also occurs in the North-Arabian Safaitic texts), does include the notion of the desert in the strict sense, waterless, uninhabited, e.g., Is. 35:6; 41:18; and Jer. 2:6: "through the wilderness (*midbar*), through a land of deserts and pits, through a land of drought and gloom (AV 'shadow of death'), through a land that no man passed through and where no man dwelt"—speaking of Israel's experiences in the desert. But it is used equally of good grazing grounds for sheep, e.g., hard by Dothan in the center of Palestine, Gen. 37:22, near Bethlehem where David kept his flocks, 1 Sam. 17:28, and we constantly read of "the pastures of the wilderness," e.g., Jer. 9:10. The word actually appears to mean a region where flocks are *driven*, and can best be translated by 'steppe' or perhaps the Dutch 'Veldt,' as it appears to be used

6. See Smith, *Hist. Geography of the Holy Land*, bk. 2, chap. 22.

in South Africa. Another, rarer word, is more specifically 'desert' in our sense, namely *yeshîmôn*, e.g., Dt. 32:10, "he found him in a desert (*midbar*) land, in a waste,[7] a howling wilderness"; the word is connected with a root which implies the psychological effect of the real desert, its terrifying, confusing, unnatural character. Another synonym, *sîyah*, means 'dryness,'[8] e.g., Is. 41:18 "in the land of drought springs of water." There are no references to the sand of the desert, as we generally visualize such a region, and sand is only connected with the seashore (e.g., Dt. 33:19), for sandy wastes are remote from Palestine.[9] Another word, translated 'parched places' in AV, JV, *harêrîm*, occurs in Jer. 17:6; it is the same as the common Arabic *harra*, designation of volcanic lands of lava, such as surround Palestine; these will be considered below.

Now actually Arabia is by no means the sandy waste, the 'howling wilderness' of monotonous characteristic, as our imagination visualizes it. There does exist such a region, with its offsets, in the southeastern part of the Peninsula, the so-called Ruba el-Khali (= English *alkali*), the Desert Quarter, covering about a fourth of the area of the Peninsula which

7. So JV: 'waste' = *tohu* the word for 'chaos,' e.g., Gen. 1:2; the following phrase is strictly 'howling of desert,' which, if text be correct, refers to the uncanny noises of the desert. See Chapter I, Note 27.

8. The related Ethiopic word means 'salt'; as we shall note, alkaline and salty stretches of land abound in Arabia.

9. In Is. 21:1 ff. is given "the Oracle of the Wilderness of the Sea," followed by the clause, "as whirlwinds in the Southland sweep through, it cometh from the wilderness, from a terrible land." 'Sea' here may be metonymy for sandy wastes. Cf. Dougherty's similar interpretation of the Akkadian term 'sealand' used for regions of Arabia, *Journ. Am. Or. Soc.* 1930, pp. 15 ff. I may add that the Arabic has from the root of the Hebrew word for 'sea' (*yam*) a verbal form *tayammama*, used of sanding one's self in lieu of water for ritual ablutions.

has been crossed by only one European, Mr. Philby, and which has generally been supposed to be intraversable.[10] It shuts off contact with lands of the Persian Gulf, which accordingly have lain apart from the usual currents of Arabian history, having their connections by sea with Iraq and the lands of the Indian Ocean, especially India and its archipelagos, with which Hadhramot also has its ancient associations that are still maintained.[11] From the solid Desert Quarter of driven sand there stretches northward a great arm consisting of series of sandy strips, running parallel to the Persian Gulf encircling the inner plateau of Nejd to about Lat. 29°, when it makes a sweep westward and enlarges into an area of some 4° east and west and 2° north and south. The long arm northward is called the Dahna, and its bulb-like projection at the north the Nafúd. This projection has played its part in protecting Nejd, the veritable homeland of the genuine Arab race and spirit especially against influences from the east, from the civilizations that encircled the Persian Gulf; while to the west the interior is protected by the high range of mountain land running parallel and near to the Red Sea, marking off the Hijáz, from which range the Peninsula slopes to the northeast. An excellent description and explanation of this

10. But see Philby, *Heart of Arabia*, II, 216 ff. Philby in his route through the Wady Dawásir approached the northern fringe of this desert and was able to secure information concerning its inhabitants and settlements; he met members of al-Muna, one of its tribes, who had crossed the desert from north to south, which Philby holds is not an exceptional feat. This information agrees with reports gained by Bertram Thomas, as also by Glaser; the latter after listing the desert tribes east of Sabæan Marib states that they travel with their camel herds over the whole of the Desert Quarter as far as Oman; *Reise nach Marib*, p. 33. And Hommel knows of ancient routes through this desert, *Ethnologie*, p. 549.

11. See Van den Berg, *Le Hadhramout et les colonies arabes dans l'Archipel Indien* (Batavia, 1886).

Arabia and the Bible

Dahna-Nafúd phenomenon is given by B. Moritz.[12] This desert of sand dunes is produced by the action of the north and northwest winds blowing the sand into hollows which mark the base of the great arm of sand. In the northern Nafúd the phenomenon assumes the form of monstrous cup-like formations, called 'hoofs' by the Arabs, from their likeness to the impression of a horse's foot; this is caused by some original projection, a rock, even a lowly bush, which stems the wind and piles up the sand in circular formation about it, just as we may see the effect of an obstacle in the formation of snow-drifts. The sand itself is the result of the disintegration not only of the sandstone basis of the land, but also of the actual materials of the surface of the land, the result (*Verwitterungsprodukt*) of the action of sun and change of temperature. It is to be noticed accordingly that this sanding-up of the desert is a progressive process, and one that can be artificially restrained by the erection of barriers, an art that is practised to-day in protecting the plantings by hedges against the sand drifts.[13] Further, these sandy stretches are not the wastes we should expect. To quote Moritz, p. 16: "After winters of

12. *Arabien*, pp. 15 ff.; cf. Euting, *Tagbuch einer Reise in Inner-Arabien*, chap. 6, and Doughty, *Arabia Deserta*, see Index.

13. Cf. Philby's description of his view of the site and remains of ancient Yamáma in the Wady Dawásir, once capital of a powerful Arabian group, vol. II, 32 f.: "What remains of it to-day is but a solid block of palm on the side of the Nisah, perhaps a mile square with four small hamlets embedded in its midst. The rest is choked with sand, whose rolling billows extending southwards from the edge of Wady Hanifa are only prevented from engulfing the modern settlement by a slender barrier of palm-fronds set about its northern flanks. Here and there from beneath the sea of sand to the northward peep perished ruins of palaces and often tenements." An accompanying picture illustrates the scene. These barriers of vegetation are often referred to by Philby as defenses against the encroachment of the sands. With regard to the destruction of Yamáma he holds that "the theory of desiccation falls to the ground when we remember that we are dealing with the very core of the drainage system of Arabia; there remains therefore naught but the assumption of a great flood," the site lying in the great drainage valley.

plentiful rain there develops in it within a few days a varied vegetation of fodder plants, so that in the spring the Nafúd is the paradise of the Bedawin. There are even some species of trees, two or three species of acacia and of tamarisk of 2–3 metres in height." The former phenomenon, remarked by many travelers, gives the naturalistic basis to the poetical idea of 'the desert blossoming like the rose,' Is. 35:1. Moritz proceeds to remark that the undergrowth constitutes the forest for the Bedawin, who burn the wood into charcoal. The statement illustrates the reference to 'the thickets in Arabia' where Dedan is to lodge, Is. 21:13. Moritz is abundantly corroborated by other travelers, for example Euting, *Tagbuch*, p. 146: "As soon as the first rain falls, the Nafúd begins to rouse; the tender fodder-grass springs up out of the ground, and in a moment the Bedawin and their herds of camels and sheep are on the spot. Now begins the time of carefree luxury for these desert-folk; they move whither they will; the disturbing care for water has disappeared; they live on the milk of the suddenly revived camels." Similarly Lammens, *Le berceau de l'Islam*, p. 104: The Nafúd "constitutes still a valuable pastoral reserve for the immense flocks of the nomads."

Another remarkable formation in Arabia is that of the volcanic lands which are overstrewn with the missiles of ancient eruptions or actually covered with beds of lava. These are the *harras*, which have already been mentioned, the same word appearing in the Hebrew. They lie mostly on the western marge of Arabia from the latitude of Damascus to the neighborhood of Mecca.[14] The best known of these is the Lejá-Trachonitis, by which latter name it appears as an administra-

14. See Moritz, *Arabien*, pp. 11 ff., with map indicating the *harras* in the central west of Arabia, and Doughty, vol. II, chapter 15, with similar map.

tive district in the New Testament, Luke 3:1. To the east of this, northeast of Mount Hauran, the present Druse Mountain, is a similar district, which shared with the Lejá in the Roman empire the name of one of the two Trachones.[15] In the land of Midian there are extensive *harra*-districts, and to the northeast of Medina lies that of Khaibar,[16] famous as an oasis in pre-Muslim times, the glory of which departed with the expulsion of its Jewish citizenry by the Caliphs. What has taken place in these lava-beds and made them possible for human settlement is that in process of time the lava has broken up, allowing the reappearance of the water springs, while the lava itself furnishes rich chemical elements to the soil which nature gradually superimposes upon it. Hence the Lejá and its volcanic neighbor Es-Safa grow a good vegetation for the flocks in the time of the rains, and the ability of such lands to support man and flock was increased by the aqueducts reared in the Græco-Roman age. Khaibar indeed appears to have too much water, from lack of drainage, and the oasis became malarial.

These volcanic deposits raise the question whether the biblical language has not been inspired in some of its descriptions by actual volcanic outbursts. Moritz records (p. 13) the account of such phenomena by the Arabic historians, occurring near Medina in the time of the Caliph Omar, again in 1256, and in the same century similar outbursts near Aden and on the margin of North Syria; and he would illustrate from Is. 34:9–10, in the judgment upon Edom, whose southern bounds ran into the lava-region of Midian: "The streams

15. See Smith, *Hist. Geography*, pp. 543 ff.; Dussaud, *Les Arabes en Syrie avant l'Islam*, 1907, pp. 24 ff.; and the brilliant pen-picture of the Lejá in Syria, *Publications of the Princeton Archaeological Expeditions*, Division I (1930), p. 97.

16. See Doughty, vol. II, chapters 4–8.

thereof shall be turned into pitch, and the dust thereof into brimstone, and the land thereof shall become burning pitch." These volcanic phenomena have indeed induced some scholars to place the fiery and smoking Sinai of biblical legend in the *harras* of Midian.

Other 'bad lands' are the scarred and bare mountains which run parallel to the west coast of Arabia, giving the name Hijáz to the west of that watershed from its nature as a 'barrier.' The rainstorms break against this long ridge and produce almost in a moment raging torrents—the Arabic *sail*, spate—which sweep away all obstacles without warning and with loss of life of man and cattle, leaving the countryside barer than ever with the destruction of vegetation and the removal of the surface soil. This phenomenon illustrates the many references in the Bible, as in Psalms and Job, to 'waters' as symbol of overpouring troubles, dangers, enemies, e.g., Job 27:20; Ps. 124:4, 5. We may indeed have a technical word for this inundating spate in Is. 28:15, translated in our Versions 'overflowing scourge,' in which the noun (*shot*) means a torrent.[17] The Arabic poetry has constant references to this phenomenon, its terrors and dangers. And modern travelers give anecdotes of its instantaneous and destructive character.[18] In fact too much water is periodically one of the greatest of Nature's destructive agents in Arabia. Yet these waters

17. So a verse in the Koran proves, Surah 89:12, and cf. the Ethiopic verb *sota* with the same meaning. This avoids emendations that have been offered to remove the absurd 'overflowing scourge.'

18. Cf. G. Jacob, *Das Leben der vorislamischen Beduinen*, p. 23, for literary references. E.g., an anecdote to the point in Doughty, II, 29. Glaser, *Reise nach Marib*, pp. 12 f., tells a striking story of a *sail* he encountered on his visit to Marib in 1888, of such force that he had to improvise a detour through a hostile district. The Arabs of his caravan had already "smelt the *sail*" (cf. Job 14:9), while the traveler skeptically observed their attitude. But they were in the right; "the flood, broad and majestic, rolled

can be handled by human art through reservoirs in the mountain slopes and with irrigation. As will be noticed below, Mecca and Medina were garden spots in the age of the Omayyads. Mecca, which started about its insufficient spring of Zemzem, still draws its water from an ancient dam up in the hills; the city itself suffers from periodic inundations of the *sail* with loss of life and destruction of property and especially of the buildings within the low-lying area of the mosque.

Another geological formation, due to chemical processes, is the salination of the Peninsula, especially in bottoms whither the salts are brought down by the torrents to sour the springs and to deposit salty layers on the surface, in lack of constant rains to dissolve the salts and carry them off to the sea. Thus a salination is proceeding in such lands similar to the process which has caused the saline character of the ocean and land-locked seas. Akkadian references given in Chapter IV mention such lands, and the Bible refers three times to this 'salt land.'[19] A word of the same root, translated by 'mallows' in AV, and 'salt-wort' in RV, JV, occurs in Job 30:4, as the kind of food which the most miserable eat; the species grow by the seaside and in salty districts.[20]

To the far south lies 'Araby the Blest,' the Yemen as it is now called and its eastern appendage, economically speaking, Hadhramot. These lands are blessed with a rich soil and with vegetable species coveted by the world, ranging from frankincense to coffee. Their inhabitants early learned to impound

on with its waters; there was no doubting of the *sail.*" It was impossible to cross the torrent with its metre-deep of water and another equal depth of mud. Jaussen and Savignac detail a similar experience near Madain-Salih and give photographs of the sudden flood, 200 metres broad; *Mission archéologique*, I, 89 f.

19. Jer. 17:6; Ps. 107:34; Job 39:6; AV translates correctly only in the first case.
20. AV's 'mallow' is etymologically correct; it is the actual Hebrew word *malluh.*

the waters of the rainy seasons and to canalize them with the greatest waterworks known in antiquity, so that in that region arose one of the most remarkable and yet least known of ancient civilizations. To this region we must devote a separate chapter.

Of the far distant land of Oman in the southeast of the Peninsula, almost unknown to the Westerner as far as the interior is concerned, we need not speak, as it lies beyond the ken of the biblical student. It is a fertile land with a population given almost wholly to agriculture, of which the date is the chief product, but where various grains and fruits are also produced. All cultivation is dependent on irrigation, that lost art for most of the Peninsula.[21]

Outside of these peculiar geological formations Arabia consists of a pebbly, arid soil. However, this soil bursts into grass and flower upon the spring rains, and upon it the Bedawin and their flocks exist, apparent deserts being in season covered with idyllic scenes of human and animal life. The Arabs wander to and fro, pasturing their flocks, moving great distances in the course of the year, trekking south in the winter, then northward in summer and on the Iraq quarter entering within its borders for water and pasture. They follow exact lines of movement, for they claim, tribe by tribe, their hereditary rights to pasturage.[22]

21. See *Handbook of Arabia*, p. 241. Oman doubtless played an important part in the civilization of the Persian Gulf; some regard it as the Magan of Akkadian texts. It has recently been proved by chemical analysis that the copper of the Sumerian civilization came from Oman.

22. For the territories and seasonal movements of the tribes in the Syrian Desert at the present day see the valuable paper by C. R. Raswan, 'Tribal Areas and Migration Lines of the North Arabian Bedouins,' in the *Geographical Review* (New York), July 1930, pp. 495 ff. Mr. Raswan had spent some seven years among the Bedawin, engaged in the study of Arab horse-breeding.

Arabia and the Bible

Spotted over this vast area are the water-springs which have been tapped and built up by human labor. These create the oases, small or large, measured by the number of palm trees, e.g., the twelve springs and seventy palms at Elim (Ex. 15:27). Around these springs and wells grow up settlements, primarily the centers of the Bedawin, then becoming emporia for the neighborhood with its citizenry of a village folk to minister to the needs of the nomadic Arabs, and if the settlement be on the line of a caravan route and offer a sufficiency of water and food and accommodation, it becomes a walled town with a developed civic life. And so in the course of history it happens that in consequence of commercial opportunity or political possibility some compact tribe, as likely as not of outside origin, will take the leadership of the community for its own as well as for the common good, as in the case of the Kureish at Mecca. Or some strong-minded and strong-armed sheikh will arise who will demand and command the loyalty of his tribe and of the mixed town-folk and the country about, until a hereditary principality is founded. All this goes quietly on in a quarter screened from the world, until a favorable opportunity arises, and therewith a great commander to exploit it, and then the world of a sudden witnesses the existence of a new power with which it has to reckon, and cannot easily cope, since it lies entrenched in the desert. And often there bursts forth an explosive movement. We think for ancient times of Petra and Palmyra, both defying Rome, the latter boldly establishing an empire carved out of Roman territory; of Mecca with its convulsion of Islam; of the sudden explosion of the Karmatians who harried all Arabia and desecrated Mecca at the end of the ninth century; of the Wahhábi movement in the latter part of the eighteenth century and the beginning of

88

the nineteenth, which the Turk could not repress and to which job he had to urge on the ambitious Khedive of Egypt, the latter achieving his end only by costly expeditions; the continuance of this movement into our own times with the rise of the Shammar state at Háil in northern Nejd and then the passing of its imperium into the hands of the elder Wahhábi line of the Ibn Saúd dynasty, with its center at Riyád. The contemporary Ibn Saúd is the ruler of Arabia, even as he calls himself Emir of the Arabs, controlling the whole of Arabia except the Yemen, which remains independent, and the coast lands of the Indian Ocean and the Persian Gulf, which are protectorates of Great Britain; while the extension of his power to the north is hampered only by the British Mandates for Palestine and Iraq and the artificial corridor run east and west by the British to connect the mandated territories for imperial purposes.[23]

This geographical survey and its political postscript accordingly forbid us to think of Arabia as a sheer desert, a howling wilderness, and of its history as a monotonous stretch of Bedawi life. There are inner resources in that inscrutable Peninsula and its people which cannot be precalculated. And some light may be thrown by these observations upon Israel's rise and advance. From Arabian lands came Yahweh, from the desert of Sinai according to one tradition, according to another from Seir and Edom, from Teman and Paran, from Cushan and Midian, i.e., the mountains and *harras* of northwest Arabia. The conquest of Palestine by the Hebrews is illustrated by many similar phenomena in the same quarters throughout history. We may think of the Amorite Sihon's conquest of the

23. For the history see Hogarth, *History of Arabia,* and the present writer's paper cited in Note 2.

lands of Moab and Ammon, Num. 21:21 ff.; of the movement of the Ituræans into the Lebanons at the turn of the era;
of the trekking of the Druses, perhaps of the old Ituræan
blood, from the Lebanon into the inaccessible fastnesses of
their Mountain in recent times.[24] What appears marvelous in
the eyes of the critical student of history, so marvelous that its
tradition might be rejected along with the miracles the tradition enshrines, is not unbelievable to him who focuses his attention on the physical and spiritual characteristics of Arabia.

The Problem of Physical Change in Arabia

The large part which Arabia played in ancient history, the
story of the caravans navigating the deserts with rich traffic in
precious metals and still more precious incense and spices, the
campaigns conducted by Assyrian and Babylonian monarchs
in the heart of the Peninsula where they encountered 'kings'
and peoples of rich possessions, especially the amazing revela-
tion of South-Arabian archæology, have suggested to some
historians that the physical conditions of Arabia were once
vastly different from those that prevail today. The hydrog-
raphy of such a land would have been far different, with
larger rainfall, with actual rivers coursing through the land,
settled populations forming considerable states. The deserts
of Turkestan, in which have been discovered some of the most
interesting remains of lost civilization of the early centuries of
our era, would offer a corroborative parallel to this hypothesis. Further, both native tradition and archæology reveal to us
the existence of ancient important settlements at points where
now exist but scanty waters and the most wretched and de-

24. See Hitti, *Origin of the Druze People and their Religion* (1928).

graded of populations. There are the Koranic traditions of the tribes of Ad and Thamud, which were destroyed by divine judgments for their wickedness, of a class of legend comparable to the biblical one of Sodom and Gomorrah; and this latter doubtless presents a true tradition of the overthrow of an ancient flourishing settlement at the south of the Dead Sea where now is a dreary, unhabited wilderness.[25] Thamud was well known to the Greek geographers, and its center can be located at Madáin-Salih, where a peculiar and much discussed special type of Arabic inscriptions, the Thamudene, has been discovered, revealing an ancient settlement of considerable civilization; the neighboring el-Ula was a settlement where South-Arabic inscriptions have been discovered.[26] Description has been given in Chapter IV of the flourishing condition of the oasis of Teima, a nucleus of the trade routes across Arabia, which the Babylonian Nabonidus made his residence for many years, where he built his temples and palaces, and which has now become an insignificant place, a watering station for the perennial caravans.[27] Petra and Palmyra, ancient populous cities of political importance, centers of trade empire, recur at once to mind. In Mohammad's day there existed flourishing settlements in the great oases of Khaibar, to the northeast of Medina, and Nejran, to the north of the Yemen, the former inhabited by a prosperous colony of Jews, the latter by a nota-

25. See the results of the expedition to the south of the Dead Sea by President M. G. Kyle and Director W. F. Albright as published in the latter's article, 'The Jordan Valley in the Bronze Age,' *Annual* of Am. Schools of Or. Research, vol. VI (1926), and the former's *Exploration at Sodom* (1928). They hold that Sodom is now submerged by the Dead Sea. This is corroborated by the accompanying place-name 'Gomorrah,' which means 'sunken,' according to the Arabic root.

26. For the present condition of this territory see Doughty, *Arabia Deserta*, vol. I, chaps. 4 ff., etc. For these inscriptions see Chapter VIII.

27. Doughty, *op. cit.*, chaps. X, XIX.

ble Christian community, which suffered under Persian perse-
cutions. Both communities were exterminated or forcibly
absorbed by Islam. South Arabia proper, the Yemen and
Hadhramot, still reveals the fertility of its soil in patches of
cultivation, a reminiscence of its former agricultural wealth.
But its peoples today are barbarous, degraded, hostile to for-
eigners to an extent that makes almost unbelievable the civilization, political and economical, of those lands as revealed by
their inscriptions and reported by the Greek and Roman
geographers.

Accordingly at first we are driven almost logically to accept the hypothesis put forward by some physical geographers
and accepted by at least a small group of historians that Arabia
once enjoyed a far greater rainfall, that it belongs to a vast
belt extending from the east in Turkestan to the west across
the north of Africa, where the Sahara has been pushing its
seas of sand northwards so as to engulf the lands of civilization, those of Phœnicians, Greeks, Romans, on the shores of
the Mediterranean. This theory has been presented in a field
of special interest to the Bible student by Ellsworth Huntington in his book, *Palestine and its Transformation* (1911). Professor Huntington has based his studies for the Semitic world
largely upon the assumption of certain historians that Arabia,
as the home of the Semites, has been subject to a change of climate, an increasing diminution of the rainfall and corresponding desiccation of the Peninsula.[28] This ultimate deterioration
of climate, marked indeed by periodic changes of greater and
less rainfall, he argues, has been the cause of the periodic outbursts of the population of Arabia as emigrants and conquer-
ors into the fertile lands of the civilization to the north. In

28. See his chap. XII, 'Climate and History.'

Arabia Deserta

this Huntington claims the support of a theory invented and pressed by the distinguished German scholar Hugo Winckler on historical grounds. According to this theory we may discover almost a rhythmic movement of such disturbance of the population of Arabia with corresponding potent effect upon universal history: the invasion of the Amorites in the third millennium B.C., of the Aramæans in the second, of the Nabatæans in the first, and then the mightiest of all these swarms, that of Islam, a century after the middle of the first Christian millennium, these waves then occurring at about 1000 years' intervals.

Another German scholar, Fritz Hommel, has still more persistently addressed himself to the subject of a vast change of climate, in regard to water supply and desiccation in Arabia within historic times. In his recently completed *opus magnum, Ethnologie und Geographie des alten Orients* (1926), he makes constant reference[29] to the three or four great Arabian streams which, as he holds, the Paradise myth associates with the Euphrates to water the Garden of Eden; of these important rivers ('wichtige Ströme') one is the great Wady ed-Dawásir, which runs northeast from the confines of the Yemen into the Persian Gulf; another the Wady er-Rumma which flows east from the Hijáz range near Medina into the Persian Gulf in the land of modern Kuweit; and two wadys, one of them the Sirhan depression east of Palestine, the other the Wady Hauran, the ancient drainage bed from the Jebel-ed-Drus, both of which he supposes to drain into the Euphrates. To be sure, as Hommel admits, these mighty rivers belong to prehistoric times, but he claims that the sanding-up ('Versandung') of their beds came only gradually and was

29. E.g., pp. 11, 271 f., 508 ff., 547 ff.

not so far advanced in historic times; at all events human memory in one form of mythical story goes back to vastly different physical conditions of Arabia, while the present map of Arabia presents a very different aspect from that of ancient history (p. 548). Similarly Glaser, the eminent South-Arabian explorer and archæologist, finds two of the Paradise streams, Gihon and Pishon, in Arabian wadys.[30]

With closer bearing upon biblical history is a hypothesis which presupposes a condition of a part of Arabia in the age of the late Assyrian empire entirely different from any conditions known ever since; it is that proposed by Winckler, who would find in the northwest of the Peninsula, in Sinai and the land of Midian to the east, an important and almost imperial kingdom which he names Musri.[31] Accordingly the references in the late Assyrian inscriptions to Musri, which had always been identified with biblical Mizraim, Egypt, would refer, along with a large number of biblical references involving Mizraim, to this Arabian land. A land of today sheer desert would then have been the home of a powerful and aggressive kingdom which potent Assyria found difficult to subdue, and whose existence presupposes very different physical conditions from those of the present.

This extreme view of a very different kind of Arabia from that we know today has not been accepted by Arabists in general outside of a small school of followers of Winckler, Glaser, and Hommel. Only one of the ranking Arabist scholars has given adherence to this theory, namely Caetani, the author of the monumental *Annals of Islam,* who devotes a long chap-

30. *Skizze,* 314 ff.
31. *Mitth. d. Vorderasiat. Gesellschaft,* 1898, no. 1; and in Schrader's *Die Keilinschriften und das Alte Testament,* ed. 3 (1903), 143 ff.

ter of his work to an argument in favor of it.[32] He holds, similarly with Winckler and Hommel, to the one-time physically luxuriant condition of Arabia, the change from which he dates at about 10,000 B.C., but it would not have been until about 5,000 B.C. that conditions came to vary so far as to oppress the inhabitants and to drive them forth to new lands in search of food; hence the historic migrations of the Arabs, or rather of the Semites at large, whose primitive seat he would find in Arabia. By this theory he believes he is able to controvert the theories which would place their original abode elsewhere, e.g., in Mesopotamia, as with Guidi.[33] Arabia would have been possible as the true culture-home of all subsequent Semitic civilization as represented in language and tradition, and the outburst of Islam was then primarily an economic problem with proportional reduction of religious and national factors.

But in the association of the historians who refer to physicists for support and of the physicists who depend upon the views, often the assumptions, of historians, there appears too much of the logical fallacy of *argumentum in circulo*. The one draws from the other so much as countenances his theory, and either party assumes the statements of the other as definitive, although physicists and historians may be respectively at odds among themselves, while their theories are too often more than vague. Reference may be made to a recent work, *Climate through the Ages*, by C. E. P. Brooks,[34] in which the author has accumulated the physical and historical data for the earth's climate with greatest painstaking, along with most cautious expression of judgment. His reserve may be an ex-

32. *Annali dell' Islam*, II, part 2 (1907), 831 ff.

33. 'Della sede primitiva dei peopli semitici,' in *Atti dell' Academia dei Lincei di Roma*, Class of Moral Sciences, series III, vol. 3.

34. English, with American reprint of no date; preface dated 1926.

ample to historians. He is slow in postulating general changes in climate, although admitting its possibility in cases that cannot otherwise be explained; in his last chapter, 'Climate through the Ages,' he essays a synthetical theory on the subject at large. His data appear often to demand not so much a deterioration of climate, e.g., decrease of rainfall, as a pulsation between recurrent extremes. A study of this kind to point concerns the famous African oasis of Khargeh to the west of Egypt,[35] for which the table constructed shows alternating conditions of water supply between 500 B.C. and 1300 A.D.; here the fluctuations of the water may depend upon the distant water levels of the Nile and so upon the latter's headwaters in Abyssinia and the Soudan. Unfortunately he avoids treatment of Arabia with exception of the Sinai peninsula, and this is doubtless due to the fact that that great peninsula has hardly been touched as yet by scientists in meteorology and climatology. It is avoided even in Walther's notable work, *The Law of the Formation of Deserts*,[36] which contains data so far as Arabia is concerned, only from the small Sinaitic peninsula, all which proves that Arabia still remains for science one of the least known of lands.

To the general body of historians of the Semitic world the argument of a change of climate as affecting historical conditions in Arabia, and so by impulses therefrom in the environing lands, does not make much appeal. The pictures in the Egyptian, biblical, Akkadian accounts of Arabian scenery and life are almost exactly the same as the traveler sees today. As

35. Pp. 374 ff.; based on H. J. L. Beadnell, *An Egyptian Oasis* (1909); cf. Huntington, 'The Libyan Oasis of Kharga,' *Bull. Am. Geog. Soc.*, 42 (1910), pp. 641 ff.

36. *Das Gesetz der Wüstenbildung in Gegenwart und Vorzeit* (1924), fully and admirably illustrated with pictures of desert formations.

the Shashu harried the Egyptian frontiers; as 'the homeless' Aramæan or Arab wandered in the desert lurking for his prey, and the caravans pursued their weary road on search for water or deceived by mirage, in the scenes of Job; as the Assyrian inscriptions picture the terrible desert, and even as the troops of Esarhaddon and Nebuchadnezzar and Cambyses made their arduous campaigns across it—it cannot be said that in general the scene of the ancient desert differs much from that of the present day with the wandering Bedu. The historian is equally aware of certain facts and conditions of the ancient history of Arabia that have long since passed away; of perished prosperous communities like those of Khaibar or the Nejran, el-Ula and Teima and Petra and Palmyra, or the later Arab nations of the Ghassanids and Lachmids on the marches of Byzantium and Persia, with their marvelous architectural remains like those of Petra and Palmyra in the Moabite land, or Ukheidir in the desert west of old Babylonia.[37] But he would desire first to explain these manifestations of civilized life and energy and their final extinction from human factors before resorting to climatological explanations.[38]

To give the usual point of view of the Oriental historian citation may be made from two historical scholars of distinction. Professor A. T. Olmstead, now of the University of Chi-

37. For Meshetta see Tristram, *Land of Moab*, chap. 11, and a supplementary chapter in the former's *Land of Israel*, and Kammerer, *Pétra*, pp. 337 ff.; for Ukheidir, Gertrude Bell, *Amurath to Amurath*, pp. 140 ff.

38. I emphasize here historical conditions, which alone concern my subject. For the prehistoric period such theories must be accepted and some historians of antiquity are inclined to bring down the earlier climatological conditions into the historical field; see V. G. Child's recent volume, *The Most Ancient East* (1929), chap. I, and Myres in the *Cambridge Ancient History*, vol. I, chap. I. But caution should be observed in applying broad physical generalizations to particular fields for which we possess historical data with definite contributions.

cago, has severely challenged Winckler's theory of a Musri kingdom in the territories of the Negeb (the 'South' of EVV, rather Southland, e.g., Gen. 12:9) and Sinai.[39] From the archæological observations made in that region by a party of which he was a member, from the American School in Jerusalem, with Professor Nathaniel Schmidt as Director, in 1904, Olmstead points out that there is no evidence of early settlement of man in that region; and then he appeals to Esarhaddon's account of his campaign through the same region.[40] In this record that monarch speaks of "the wady of Egypt [Musur, i.e., the biblical Brook of Egypt], where there is no river," of "making my troops drink well water from jugs,"— i.e., the water had to be transported from a distance—and of encountering "serpents with two heads," a marvelous phenomenon which we have noticed earlier. We may compare the vivid picture of the desert given by Ashurbanipal in his campaign against the Arabs, even to the minute detail of the fugitives ripping up their camels' bellies for drink;[41] and the story which Herodotus takes great pains to tell (iii, 7), how Cambyses negotiated with the Arab sheikh who controlled the Syrian Desert for the transport and watering of his expedition against Egypt, the conditions being just such as exist today.

A distinguished French Arabist, M. Lammens, one-time professor at the University of St. Joseph in Beirut, now at the Jesuit Pontifical Biblical Institute in Rome, has dealt at length with the question of climate as a factor in Arabian history in

39. *Western Asia in the Days of Sargon*, a long note, pp. 56–71; cf. his review of Huntington's *Palestine and its Transformation*, in *Bull. Am. Geog. Soc.* (45), June, 1912. Cf. also Hartmann's criticism, *Arabische Frage*, pp. 93–100.

40. 670 B.C.; text and translation in Rogers, *Cuneiform Parallels to the O.T.*, pp. 357 ff.; Luckenbill, *Ancient Records*, vol. II, 220.

41. Luckenbill, *op. cit.*, 316 ff.

his work *The Cradle of Islam*.[42] Lammens confines his study to the Hijáz, the western littoral of Arabia, in which lie the holy cities of Mecca and Medina, and to the age of Mohammad and the empire of the Omayyads, into the eighth century. Directly in opposition to the views of Winckler and Caetani he demonstrates that the Hijáz was by no means the famine-stricken, climate-cursed land that it has been pictured for Mohammad's time. The economic importance of the land had been fast increasing, this due in considerable measure to the large Jewish settlements as at Medina and Khaibar,[43] and, it may be added, to the decay of the Yemen, Mecca now replacing the South-Arabian cities. Not deterioration of climate produced the irresistible flooding of Arabic hosts upon the world, but the spiritual impulses of a people which now found itself a church-nation with a grand unifying principle. And the author describes at length the prosperity of the Hijáz as it came to be under the fostering care of the Omayyad Caliphs (pp. 178 ff.). Dams were built in the mountains, aqueducts conducted, wells sunk,[44] so that according to the authorities cited for economic details the now dreary and God-forsaken land must

42. *Le berceau de l'Islam, l'Arabie occidentale à la veille de l'Hégira*, vol. I (1914); see especially part 2, pp. 113 ff., but the subject is one the author constantly recurs to.

43. The Jews were largely the possessors of the wells, an indication of the real source of wealth.

44. Such waterworks may well have included engineering on a large scale to avoid the *sails* described in Part 1 of this Chapter. These floods have been especially disastrous in Mecca; in January 1910, the water reached the Black Stone; in 1913 several hundred pilgrims were drowned; the rains sometimes last for fifteen days; and on authority of Snouck-Hurgronje, the inhabitants count on a flood every quarter of a century. The practical problem of the climate is therefore not so much lack of water as of its proper distribution, in which the human factor may have its part. Compare Philby's theory of the destruction of Yamáma by a flood, *supra*, Note 13, and the dam outburst at Marib which, according to universal Arab tradition, destroyed the prosperity of the Yemen; see Chapter VI.

have been a garden of the Lord with its rich domains enriching both tenants and suzerain. The end of this came with the Abbasids, who on principled policy neglected the cultivation of the possibilities of the land, so that it has become a desert. As we shall see, South Arabia, the Yemen, has likewise decayed, although not to the same extent; but as in South Arabia, the uninviting Hijáz can be made a prosperous country by the ingenuity and industry of man. Lammens cites a report made to him by a Muslim engineer in the Turkish administration of the railroad to Medina concerning the present desolation (p. 153): "They have let all the works of the ancients fall in ruins. At Medina industry and agriculture are reduced to nothing. The inhabitants live on alms and extortions and on the pilgrims." For the part human art can play in the struggle with the fierce elements of Arabia's nature, Lammens remarks on the tenacity of the vegetable kingdom in employing to the utmost the secret nerve of the water supply, and adds (p. 149): "It needs only the intervention of human industry to give it the most beneficent extension. This is proved by the history of the oases and of the centers of culture in the Hijáz, above all at every place where man interests himself to second the latent resources of the Arabian soil and climate." In another passage he remarks: "As far back as we are able to pursue the pre-Islamic annals we come upon the same succession of meteorological phenomena, upon the continuity of the physical laws regulating the seasons of Arabia. Between the ancient and the contemporary period, there is affirmed not a lacuna but continuance." The distinguished Arabist Martin Hartmann takes similar position in denying Winckler's and Caetani's theory of a change of climate; thus he says (*Ara-*

bische Frage, p. 112): "In the time for which we possess records, or for which the records at hand give us a clear view, changes in climate and soil have not occurred to an extent that conditions the possibilities of development." To this dictum may be added the judgment expressed by W. Schmidt in his *Das südwestliche Arabien*, pp. 40 f., the first part of which carefully compiled work deals with the physical nature of the Yemen. He finds in the Yemen abundant and sufficient rainfall, and explains the deterioration of the land from the debasement of its cultivation: "As soon as the rainwater is again caught, collected, and evenly distributed, the ancient fertility will blossom once more, in my opinion." There is further an interesting statement from Glaser, who generally is grouped with the school of Winckler, but who, so far as I know, has never committed himself upon the question of climatic change; he observes in his travel-diary, *Reise nach Marib*, p. 19, that the underground water supply was the same in antiquity as now, and acknowledges that the cataclysmic rainfalls need only to be husbanded to restore the ancient fertility. Indeed one of Glaser's practical purposes was an engineering survey upon which to memorialize the Ottoman government to undertake the scientific irrigation of the Yemen.

There is, however, one variable phase in the condition of Arabia which is not due to a change in climate. This is the increasing growth of the desert, the continued process of disintegration of rock and other surface materials through sun and changes of temperature and the spreading of the sand over the contiguous lands by the violent winds. This process has been described above, on the authority of Moritz, and is fully substantiated by Lammens, who adds the element of increasing salination of the soil, the surface water being insufficient to carry off the deposits of salts and alkali. These results have been taking place steadily in historic times, and thus the desert has been slowly growing, amassing in depth above the natural level, and spreading out laterally under the fierce-blowing winds. The phenomenon appears to have been more clearly noted and diagnosed by those who have studied the great desert of the Sahara. Here there is definite corroboration of the process of disintegration and destruction to an extent not posited for Arabia. We may cite from some writers who have studied the Sahara from personal observation. In his book *In the Desert, the Hinterland of Algiers* (1909), L. March Phillipps devotes chapter VII to a study of the desert and its effects upon the mentality of its inhabitants, and from it the following passages are cited: "The Sahara is not altogether the motionless, dead thing it looks. It is carrying on the work of destruction all the time. The means it employs are the sand itself, helped by heat and cold and wind. The variation of temperature by day and night, often 80 or a 100 degrees, causes an expansion and contraction of the rocks so sudden as often to split them asunder as if a quarryman's hammer had done the work" (p. 108). And (p. 110), "Slowly, however, the dunes are gaining ground; . . . they have invaded the old caravan routes. Year by year decomposition makes almost imperceptible progress."

Again, Angus Buchanan in his *Sahara* (1926) insists at length upon the growth of the great desert to a degree that can be measured by historical time. "It is my belief that the Sahara is increasing in size, and I think there are many conditions that go to prove it" (p. 51). "Formerly a wide pre-Saharan region of fertility once reached much farther north than at present" (p. 55). On page 57 he cites a case of a solitary well seventy feet deep, where no good grazing now exists. "The Sahara is not yet devoid of vegetation, but its poverty is advancing. . . . To-day we find the old caravan roads across Africa unfrequented. . . . These roads are still to be seen. . . . To-day they are unused, and the commerce of the Sahara is dead" (p. 66).

The same conditions must be ascribed to the Arabian deserts, which have thus been growing in historical times, and it is this physical phase that has proportionately increased the superficial aridity of the land. The rainfall may not have perceptibly changed but the area and the depth of the sandy deposits have increased, filling up springs and natural water courses, hiding the naturally fertile surface under an ever-accumulating mass of shifting sand, and so diminishing the local moisture in the air.[45]

To a certain degree, then, those historians are justified who find in Arabia a change within the historical periods from far more favorable conditions than its present dreary aspect. This is not necessarily due to a change of climate, except so far as increasing desiccation must affect the water fall and tend continuously to sand up the underground springs and reservoirs. To what degree the change has come about can be measured only by historical proof, and the earlier conditions of two or four millennia ago may not be appraised by offhand climatological theory. Thus when we make comparison with the traditions or actual archæological remains of now ruined or buried cities like Ad and Thamud, Petra and Palmyra, or the glory of the civilization of the Yemen, we may not postulate

45. Cf. Glaser's observations, *Reise*, pp. 142 f., on the overwhelming movement of the sands into what was once the garden spot of Arabia.

a continuous physical degradation since that time. There have been recurrent conditions of prosperity since those early ages, as in the vast economic improvement of the Hijáz under the Omayyads noticed above, in the establishment of the notable states of Wahhábi origin in Nejd in the eighteenth century. There was the collapse of the Wahhábi state of Daraiya in the beginning of the nineteenth century (1818) when Ibrahim Pasha destroyed its civilization and laid waste its far-flung settlements even into the Wady Dawásir, now a ruined country. And a process of restoration is now going on before the world's eyes in the renewed Wahhábi state, whose ruler, Ibn Saúd, is planting his colonies of Puritans over his territories, wherever there is water and possibility of vegetation, with the intention of making the desert blossom like the rose.[46]

Thus history shows recurrent phases of prosperity, not only progressive degradation in Arabia. And this observation leads on to the consideration of an element to be reckoned with other than physical processes, namely the effect man has had upon the desert, and vice versa its malignant recrudescence when human art grows lax. To this Lammens adds (p. 178): "We have equally affirmed our confidence in the role reserved to human activity for transforming the deserts: . . . The desert is the creation of excessive salinity. We have above enumerated the forces acting in the opposite way and succeeding with diverse alternatives to reëstablish the vital equilibrium. The climatological history of the Peninsula is summed up in

46. See Philby, *Heart of Arabia*, vol. II, 299 ff. Twenty such settlements had been established upon his visit in 1918. In his more recent *Arabia*, p. 227, he cites Rihani's report of seventy-three such colonies. Ibn Saúd is now planting colonies in his new possession of the Hijáz; see the British journal, *The Near East*, for July 1929.

the struggle of these opposed elements. It is the part of man to promote the action of the conservative forces."[47]

I may cite in conclusion a statement by Walther, who speaks as a physicist with no historical presuppositions.[48] "What fertility the well cultivated and drained desert soil may produce is shown for early ages by the inhabitants of Iran and Mesopotamia, the Egyptians and Romans in North Africa, and by the Mormons at the Great Salt Lake. With the magic word *irrigation* North America is opening up enormous water operations. It has been believed that the higher fertility of the old lands of civilization was to be referred to a change of climate in the past thousands of years. But this assumption is correct only within limits." The present writer remembers maps of

47. A study of the waterworks of present and ancient Arabia would be profitable. The depth of wells often driven through hard rock for many yards is remarkable; see Philby, *passim*. The waterworks at al-Kharj and the Aflaj region in the Wady Dawásir described by Philby, vol. II, 28 ff., 104 ff., consist of underground channels miles long, tapping water holes, constructed for irrigation; these probably belong to the period of Persian domination. Glaser, *Reise*, p. 16, notes a well at Marib 47 metres deep; and Euting, *Tagbuch*, p. 93, one 68–70 metres in depth, sunk through the rock, at Kaf. Moritz, *Arabien*, p. 24, lists several deep wells in Arabia; one in the Nafúd 60–70 metres deep, sunk through sandstone and granite. Doughty frequently refers to the great well at Teima, 15 metres deep, 20 metres wide, which partly collapsed during his visit, the natives doing nothing for its repair, until finally the Emir of Háil appropriated money and engineers for the work. Note that these ancient wells in Arabia and the Sahara prove that the water conditions were much the same in antiquity as now, but the people have degraded, as Doughty's anecdote illustrates.—I add some supplementary evidence as to these desert wells and waterways. Philby, in his last book, *The Desert Quarter*, p. 136, records a well on the border of that arid region 126 feet deep, and in the same locality the presence of other wells. A subterranean canal "three hours long" is recorded by Mordtmann and Mittwoch in their *Sabäische Inschriften* (1931). Bible students are acquainted with the remarkable waterworks in Palestine, as the Siloam tunnel and the primitive enormous shaft at Gezer. Baron von Oppenheim reports for the region of his North-Syrian expeditions wells 90 metres deep (*Der Tell Halaf*, 1931, p. 29). And Professor Speiser reminds me of the well of 22 fathoms depth at Tepe Gawra in northern Iraq.

48. *Wüstenbildung*, pp. 90 f.

his boyhood days docketing a considerable area of the West of the Union, 'The Great American Desert,' to recall which sounds as mythical as the story of the Garden of Eden.[49]

The Social Degeneration of Arabia

The social and economic breakdown of Arabia as compared with its ancient history may be attributed to two main causes. In the first place, it has lost its position as the center of the world's commerce, a desert in large part always, it is true, but navigable by caravans, which are at home in it as ships on the sea. In antiquity the Peninsula and its northern extension of the Syrian Desert were crisscrossed by great avenues of commerce, extending northwards from the Yemen to the head of the Red Sea on the one hand and to Mesopotamia on the other; and by great routes traversing the desert east and west, connecting the ancient civilizations of Egypt and the Mediterranean with those of Mesopotamia and the Persian Gulf, which latter was the open door to India and the Far East. Its extended sea-front made it central to all the civilizations facing the Indian Ocean and, by portage or canal, to the Nile

49. It is the problem of water supply and the overcoming of it that produced the great civilizations of the Orient, Arabian lands, as well as of Egypt, Babylonia, and Persia, and we may add, of China. Desiccation, if it existed in historic times, has been a blessing to human genius. And this not only in material benefits, but, as Chapter VI will illustrate, in developing the communal forces of society.

Since the development of the above argument the writer has read the notable discussion by Musil on the 'Alleged Desiccation of Arabia and the Islamic Movement,' pp. 304–319 of vol. V of his *Topographical Itineraries*. In this argument he traverses the position taken by Caetani in his *Annals* and also in subsequent publications not accessible to me, taking up point after point made by the Italian scholar and denying them. The reader is referred to this authoritative argument by the distinguished scholar, one of the few Arabists who know Arabia by intimate personal exploration.

valley and the Mediterranean lands. This feature of economic
conditions brought and kept Arabia in cosmopolitan touch
with the ancient civilizations, and while in many respects the
life of the Arabs of the desert was socially much as it is today,
they enjoyed, as producers of some of the most desiderated
products of human need and as purveyors of intercontinental
trade, means of wealth and of higher civilization, which are
almost totally lacking today. The change in these earlier conditions came with the Græco-Roman development and control of the Red Sea route to the frankincense lands of South
Arabia and to "the wealth of Ormuz and of Ind." It is in the
first two or three centuries of our era that we can mark the
degeneration and dissolution of the remarkable civilization of
South Arabia, of the Sabæan states and the intermediate communities which purveyed across the Peninsula. And to this
factor is to be added the chasm made by the hostility of the
Roman-Byzantine and the Persian-Sassanian empires whose
line of demarcation ran theoretically north and south through
Arabia, producing 'spheres of control,' so that the Peninsula
became a battleground of the two states, only with loss to its
social constitution and economic prosperity. Also the strife of
religions became involved in this political rivalry. Christianity
and Judaism entered the field to combat the ancient Paganism,
the former supported by the Christian powers of Byzantium
and Abyssinia, the latter favored by Persia; for once in its history Arabia became a pivotal field of empires and religions.
In these conditions, when wealth and social stability had been
attained at least in certain fertile lands and favored oases cultivated by human art, the land and its people began to sink
back into worse than original barbarism.

The other cause of Arabia's degradation is political and

moral, and is due to Islam. This is a statement of historical fact, not dictated by religious prejudice. The moral declension of the Peninsula has come about indirectly and yet by the inner logic of the religion. There can be no denial of the religious and ethical uplift which Mohammad gave to the Pagans of Arabia. He unified the land, in large part by force, to be sure, and eliminated theoretically the wars and *razzias* of which the Arab's life largely consisted. He did away with many a barbarous and savage custom, as that of infanticide; he advanced and regulated the condition of woman. He established a basis of common law which meant a larger equity and more certain security, all conducive to a better ethic. How far this new religious constitution compared with the elder political establishment in the Yemen we do not know; there had developed in that land an economic civilization and a constitutional law which Islam never produced in Arabia. Yet that southern civilization had long since begun to deteriorate, and there was no hope from it for the future; Mohammad stepped in to arrest a process of political disintegration and moral retrogression, and, it must be said, succeeded in his program.

But there was a double-headed result in the actual development of Islam: becoming imperial and cosmopolitan, Arabia was washed aside into the backwaters of civilization; and this condition was accentuated and legalized by the creation of Arabia as a Holy Land, at least as an Arabia for the Arabs alone, even as Mohammad visualized his religion as primarily the Arabian religion. Mecca and Medina, ancient marts, the latter largely a Jewish city, were constituted sacred cities whose territories no unbeliever might tread. The Jews and Christians were exterminated or expelled from the flourishing neighboring oases of Khaibar and Nejran, which relapsed into barbarism. And the spirit that radiated from these closed and provincial areas spread over the whole of the Peninsula, adding a savage touch of fanaticism to the natural individualism and the closed mind towards the foreigner which have always animated the Arab.

The center of the Islamic empire passed to the north, to Damascus, then to Baghdad. When imperial unity disappeared, there arose the great Islamic states and civilizations of Egypt, North Africa, Spain, of India, and then of Stamboul. But the brilliant civilizations that centered in the cities of the Omayyads and the Abbasids, at Cairo, Kerouwan, and Cordova, at Samarkand, Bokhara, and Delhi, had little effect upon secluded Arabia. That external civilization was fertilized by the inheritance from Persia and Greece and Rome, by contact with and absorption of fresh elements drawn from Christianity and Judaism, Zoroastrianism and Classical Paganism, while those first two religions were allowed to keep their autonomy and so serve as a provocative and stimulus to the dominant religion. But the contacts with the outside world, with neighboring Byzantium and Persia, not to speak of Abyssinia and India, which had contributed their fertilizing currents to the culture of Arabia, were now cut off; none might pass to the Holy Cities, and even if entrée into the land were easy, there was nothing to see or do, except for the religious and the students of the Tradition.

Even the acclaimed unity of the Peninsula of the Arabs proved a fiasco. Local separation displayed itself again. The One Religion broke into many sects, which in true Semitic fashion created their own civic polities, and these were and are as rife in Arabia as elsewhere in the variegated world of Islam. Two great sectarian movements have played their part in

Arabia, that of the rabid, iconoclastic Karmatians in the ninth and tenth centuries, and that of the Wahhábis since the middle of the eighteenth century, both aimed at the destruction of the idolatrous privileges of Mecca and Medina. And in our own day up to the Great War the map showed the following separatist divisions: the Sherifate of the Holy Cities, the land of the Hijáz; the kingdom of the Yemen, possessed by a peculiar Zeidite sect; an old-established caliphate in Oman, which contains a large Ibadhite population; the state of Asír, west of Yemen, in possession of a dynasty growing out of one of the African fraternities; a Sheikhate of Kuweit on the Persian Gulf; and two rival Wahhábi dynasties and states disputing the possession of the Nejd highlands. And along with these indistinctly marked states there were the free-moving Arab tribes paying little reck to master or social organization. The map has been somewhat simplified since the War; one of the Wahhábi states has swallowed up its rival and seized the Hijáz and its sacred cities; but the other independent groups remain, with large extents of no-man's land, as in the once fertile and lucrative region of the Hadhramot, while the *pax britannica* polices all the shores on the Indian Ocean and the Persian Gulf and holds their sheikhs and sultans as political vassals. The Arab has not known how to preserve unity of religion or nation.

The effects of this social and moral degradation are evident in the lapsing of the civilization which prevailed in Arabia under the early Caliphate. For instance, only traces are left of the great road across the desert from Iraq to the Holy Cities, with its provision of wells, khans, and beacon lights, which was the object of the particular philanthropy of Harun ar-Rashid's queen Zubeida.[50] Islam never created much in its homeland; there was at first in the world's discovery of a new spiritual center an outburst of the inner spirit of the land met by the enthusiastic and benevolent interest of converted countries. But after this first spurt, artificial in its character, Arabia fell back; it would have nothing to do with the world. Only in one region does there appear any hope from within for Arabia, rather we should spell it, in one man, namely Ibn Saúd, "King of the Hijáz and Nejd and its Dependencies." By the force of his personality and wise direction of the religious ardor of his fanatic sect, he is setting his people to make the desert blossom as the rose, or in prosaic language to clean out old wells and dig new ones, to plant crops in the oases they create, to live a sturdy, moral life. And where his writ runs there is peace and security for all alike. The success of this new state is an omen of good for the future of Arabia, and for the historian an indication of what once existed in favored parts of the land, where water is to be had for digging and dyking and where there is security for the trade routes.

The point of so long a discussion is this: that we may not judge Arabia and the Arabs from their present status and appearance. Relatively speaking, that land is more barbarous and savage today than it was in ancient history. Essentially perhaps the Arab has not changed, but he has suffered psychically from the long relapse in which the land has lain for over 1000 years, in large part for 2000 years. Once he was part of the world's complex, the purveyor of some of its most treasured necessities, the transporter of its goods between oceans and continents. He carried on his raids and looted exposed cities, but then such internecine wars were the rule in much of

50. See Musil, *Topographical Itineraries*, V, 205–236; Moritz, *Arabien*, p. 30.

what we call Ancient Oriental Civilization. He was not so far behind civilization but that he kept in touch with it and was accordingly humanized; while certain stalwart virtues of the Arab made him a worthy and striking member of the international complex.

All this must be borne in mind when we think of that ancient desert, so called, which lies at the back of Palestine, Syria, Mesopotamia, and which stretches out into a great peninsula between the seas. We find its peoples spilling over into the lands of civilization, Amorites, Suti, Aramæans, Hebrews, Midianites, Nabatæans. The Bible always remembers its parentage from that stock, always insists that its religion was born in that desert, and always its puritanic character is that of the simplicity of the desert, which has born such men as Moses, Elijah, Amos, Mohammad, and which gave its discipline to Jesus Christ and the Apostle Paul. Not a land of savagery and un-civilization as we find it today—I discount its imported rifles and motor cars and brummagem goods— but a land which could hold its own in manliness and proper spiritual goods. Abraham the sheikh and gentleman, and Moses the lawgiver, and even his tempestuous tribes, could contribute something to the world that then was, as Arabs of our day can hardly be expected to do. And yet great men and great movements out of Arabia have more than once since then lightened up the world, like Mohammad and the remarkable coterie of men he gathered about him, and the modern Ibn Saúd, who is reclaiming Arabia for the Arabs.

I pass on now to a picture of one remarkable civilization which flourished as far back as the beginning of the first millennium B.C., and which is an index of the possibilities of old Arabian history, if only we might read ourselves into it. The next chapter will sketch the history of ancient South Arabia, which had its relations with Palestine with mutual reactions between both, and so is worthy of the attention of the student of the Bible.

VI

ARABY THE BLEST

FAR in the Hinterland of Arabia and a thousand miles away from Palestine by latitude, lies a land which, blessed by nature to a unique extent, was at one time the home of a wealthy and luxuriant civilization. Its Arabic name is the Yemen.[1] A remote portion of the Islamic world, it was not incorporated in the Turkish empire until the time of Suleiman the Great in the beginning of the sixteenth century, but the land always resisted the conqueror and often rose in successful rebellion,

1. I.e., the 'right hand,' that is South, even as Syria and its metropolis Damascus are indifferently called Esh-Sham, the 'left hand,' i.e., North. Dougherty, *Sealand of Ancient Arabia*, pp. 115 f., finds the land Yemen referred to by name in an inscription of Nebuchadnezzar's; and he would identify the Javan (rightly Yawan) of Eze. 27:19 with Yemen, while the same word in v. 13 would mean Ionia. The Greeks translated the word in its other *nuance* of *eudaimon*, Latin *felix* (hence Milton's 'Araby the Blest'), but applied the name to the whole actual peninsula, distinguishing the northern territories as Arabia Petræa, the land of Edom and the Nabatæans, with the capital Petra, and as Arabia Deserta, the Syrian Desert to the east of Syria. See Sprenger, *Die alte Geographie Arabiens*, pp. 8 ff.; Hogarth, *Penetration of Arabia*, p. 41, note 1.

For the history of exploration of the land see Hommel's chapter in Hilprecht's *Excavations in Bible Lands* (1903), bringing down the story into the decade when scientific exploration practically ceased; also his *Ethnologie und Geschichte des alten Orients*, pp. 120–122, and his chapter on History in Nielsen's *Handbuch* (1927); Hogarth, *Penetration of Arabia*, and most recently, Tkatsch in art. 'Saba' in *Enc. of Islam*. A useful chronological survey is given by W. Schmidt, *Das südwestliche Arabien*, pp. 117–119. Among the Dictionary articles should be named that on the Yemen by the distinguished South-Arabist D. H. Müller in the *Enc. Brit.*, ed. 9. A. Rihani gives a vivid picture of the land and its people in his *Arabian Peak and Desert* (1930).

The bibliography for South Arabia down to 1892 is presented by Hommel in his *Südarabische Chrestomathie*, continued by O. Weber in *Mitth. der Vorderasiat. Gesellschaft*, 1907, part 2; also an excellent survey arranged in sections is given by Schmidt, pp. 109–115.

For the Arabic traditions of the earlier history see Caussin de Perceval, *Histoire des Arabes*, vol. I, and the summary view in Nicholson, *Literary History of the Arabs*, chap. I.

such uprisings having been periodic since the '70s of the last century, continuing into the second decade of this century.[2]

On the Red Sea lies its ancient port of Mocha, famous for its coffee trade, on the Indian Ocean the great harbor of Aden,[3] which since its capture by the British in 1839 has become the Gibraltar of their empire on the Indian Ocean. Otherwise the land is known only to hardy travelers who have ventured its exploration, all with risk, most with hardship, several with death. Their repeated stories remain perennially interesting as news of a land which has not yet entered into the world's imagination. Inhabited by a fanatical and surly people, ruled over today by an able but jealous Imam of a long-established foreign and sectarian dynasty who regards his British and Arab neighbors with hostile suspicion, the land has evinced none of the political and economic progress which has stirred most of the Arabic-speaking countries since the Great War. It is not much better known at large nor appears to be more of a political and economic factor than it was a hundred years and more ago. Yet its soil is rich, its climate favorable, producing commodities the whole world has desiderated. Its most recent contribution to civilization is the coffee berry.[4] To the east of the Yemen lies a land, which once belonged to its economic sphere, Hadhramot, the land of the genuine frankincense, the demand for which valuable commodity bled the resources of great empires.[5] The export of

---

2. See Harris, *A Journey through the Yemen* (1893), chaps. III, IV.

3. Erroneously identified by some enthusiasts with the Eden of Eze. 27:23.

4. 'Coffee,' 'café,' = Arabic *kahweh*, 'drink'; first known in the West in the sixteenth century (first European record in 1592, according to Hogarth, p. 43, and known to the Arabs since the middle of the fifteenth century, Schmidt, p. 79). Schmidt, p. 44, notes that the mother-stock of the common fig, *ficus palmata*, is indigenous to Yemen.

5. Known to the Table of Nations, Gen. 10, along with Sheba, which is identical with Yemen. T. J. Bent, *Southern Arabia* (1900), gives a fascinating account of that

this product along with myrrh and other gums, was handled for the Western world by the Sabæans or Yemenites, until the Greeks opened the sea routes. These are the biblical spices of Sheba.

The Yemen of history includes three great physical divisions. (1) The low-lying coastlands on the Red Sea and the Indian Ocean, the former stretch being the continuation of the Tiháma of the Hijáz.[6] (2) Back of this low seacoast rise, east of the Red Sea and north of the Ocean, precipitous mountain bluffs, which are the scarp of a truly Alpine sierra, with an average altitude of 9,000 feet, and peaks of over 10,000 feet, one of them, 10,400, being the highest point in Arabia.[7] This mountainous land is one of deep valleys and precipitous slopes, of whose picturesque and amazing character the descriptions of travelers and the few pictures we possess give but a faint idea.[8] The western ridge, or Serat, is the home of the coffee culture, for which the precipitous slopes are terraced for thousands of feet. (3) The third division lies to the north and east of these mountainous escarpments and is a lofty plateau of between 7,600 feet (at Sanaá) and 9,000 feet, bordered on the east by the trackless Desert Quarter.

We are so accustomed to envisage Arabia as one great desert

fairly unknown country. For the ancient history of frankincense see Schoff, *Periplus*, *passim*. Zwemer, *Arabia*, pp. 74, 86, observes that incense is still raised in the Mahra country along the coast, but has disappeared from Hadhramot, where myrrh still survives.

6. Aden and the Aden Protectorate (a political hinterland under the suzerainty of Great Britain) cut off the modern state of Yemen from the ocean; and on the Red Sea Yemen has fared ill for a port; only in the recent events of Arabian history has it been able to recover the port of Hodeidah from the Idrísi Imam of Asír, the state that borders it to the west.

7. *Handbook of Arabia*, pp. 145 f.; Schmidt, pp. 5 ff.

8. See, for example, the pictures in Harris, *A Journey through Yemen*. The earliest pictures presented to the public are the plates of Niebuhr's *Voyage en Arabie*, publishing his exploration made in 1763.

broken only by occasional oases, that it will be instructive to learn of one quarter of the Peninsula that seems to belong to another kind of world. To this end I cite from recent travelers, and first from Harris's *Journey through Yemen*. "The track was leading us [across the Serat] along the summit of a mountain top, which to the north looked straight down into a great valley thousands of feet below. What a wonderful valley it was, full of coffee-groves, and luxuriating in all the glories of gorgeous vegetation, amongst which banana-leaves could be plainly distinguished, waving their great green heads. Amongst all this verdure, clinging as it seemed to the mountain-sides, were villages each crowned by its *burj* or fort. . . . What a land it is, the Yemen! What a world of romance and history lies hid in those great mountain valleys" (pp. 326 f.). Again, on the same route (p. 338): "Away below us, tier above tier, were the terraced coffee and banana groves; while the rocky precipices, here bare and frowning, were in other parts hung with creepers. . . . Away down the valley a silvery thread of light told the presence of a river, fed by a hundred little streams, which, issuing from the rocky slopes, leaped and danced to join the larger stream below. . . . Wild-flowers and ferns, especially maidenhair, grew in abundance round our little nook in the rocks. . . . The whole scene was so framed by shrubs and creepers and flowers, a mass of blossom and green, that one lost the effect of distance." Further along on his journey, west of Menakha, Harris records (p. 342): "The path by which we were descending zigzags down until one arrives in a sort of amphitheatre, of which the village forms an apex. The ground here is richly cultivated with coffee-trees and bananas, growing upon terraces. In one place the jungle seems to have gained possession of what was originally cultivated land, and appears in a mass of euphorbiae and other strange trees and plants. Here, too, jasmine grows in wonderful abundance, the whole air being filled with its sweet fragrance." Our traveler speaks in still more idyllic terms of another experience (pp. 237 f.): "Below me lay the great valley up the straight course of which we had been traveling for the last two nights. Over its green fields floated a transparent hazy mist, through which I would watch the river sparkling and flashing like a silver serpent, as it passed on its way to the desert and the sea. Along its banks the dark-foliaged trees stood out clear and defined. On either side of this silver streak lay terraced fields, rising step by step from the water's edge to where the mountain-slopes became too steep for cultivation. Here they were covered with thick jungle undergrowth, while above rose precipice upon precipice, crowned, thousands of feet in the fine morning sky, by broken crags and pinnacles of rock, touched with snow. At my feet, for I was on the house-top, the villagers, rejoicing in the glorious mountains, were passing out to their labours, and the flocks and the herds bleated as they sought their pasturage. Women carrying beakers wended their way to the spring; while the men, spears in hand, their long locks tumbling in unrestrained glory over the shoulders, added a fierce element to a scene of the most perfect peace and beauty. . . . This was Arabia Felix!"

Dr. S. M. Zwemer, Christian missionary and Islamic scholar, one of the few Americans who know Arabia, the only one who has lived in the Yemenite land and recorded his travels there, presents similar impressions in his *Arabia, The Cradle of Islam* (1900), from which I cull the following passages. "A country where the orange, lemon, quince, grape, mango, plum, apricot, peach, apple, pomegranate, fig, date, plaintains and mulberry, each yield their fruit in season; where wheat, barley, maize, millet and coffee are staple products and where there is a glorious profusion of wild flowers. . . . A land whose mountains lift up their heads over 9,000 feet, terraced from chilly top to warm valley with agricultural amphitheatres, irrigated by a thousand rills and rivulets, some of them perennial, flowing along artificial channels or leaping down the rocks in miniature falls" (p. 57). "The road from Ibb to Yerim has perhaps the finest scenery of any part of Yemen; never have I seen more picturesque mountains and valleys, green with verdure and bright with blossoms" (p. 65). "I took an early morning walk to Roda, a village about eight miles north of Sana, and in the midst of beautiful gardens. From Roda the direct caravan route leads to Nejran, and from the outskirts of the village, looking north, an inviting picture meets the eye. A fertile plateau stretched out to the horizon. . . . The plateau . . . is a pasture country. The Bedouins live in the stone-built villages and herd their immense flocks on the plain; camels, cows and sheep were grazing by the hundreds and thousands. . . . Fertile, cultivated mountain slopes were on every side, reminding one of the valleys of Switzerland. In one district . . . the whole mountain-side for a height of 6,000 feet was terraced from top to bottom. . . . The terraced walls are usually from five to eight feet in height, but toward the top of the mountain they are sometimes as much as fifteen or eighteen feet." "There is generally an abundance of water in the numerous reservoirs stored for irrigation" (p. 68).

The descriptions cited appear almost too idyllic, as though the contrast with the flat, hot Tihámа and the desert expanses of the rest of Arabia had startled the observation of travelers into a natural reaction of exaggeration. But I am fully willing to accept their records. Such pictures are necessary to understand and visualize the basis of the remarkable civilization which once prevailed in the Yemen, whose natural fertility and eligibility for intense cultivation still persist despite the political and economical degradation of its people.[9]

But the productiveness of the Yemen in modern days is attended by another factor than the natural fertility of the soil, namely, the intelligence and handicraft of man. The husbanding of the water supply is still the *sine qua non* of Yemenite agriculture, and even the modern primitive hydraulic engineering helps us to understand what made the wealth of the land in its ancient glory. The rainfall in the highlands is most favorable. There are two rainy seasons, the more extensive period in the summer, lasting from the middle of June to the end of September, the other occurring in April, or according to Glaser's observations, with moderate rains from March to May. The summer rains appear to come in heavy storms.[10] In the mountain lands these torrential waters are collected in cisterns on the slopes, and thence fed by irrigation channels to the terraces which have been reared with incredible labor on

9. The chief staple today, grown in the Serat, is the coffee berry. Other products, several of which produce two or three crops a year, are wheat, several species of millet, sesame, lucerne (cut every fortnight), indigo, cotton, various vegetables, melon varieties, banana. See *Handbook*, p. 156; Mansur Abdullah (G. W. Bury), *Land of Uz* (1911), chap. 11; Schmidt, *op. cit.*, pp. 47 f.; Grohmann, *Südarabien als Wirthschaftsgebiet*, pp. 203–372. As a specimen of the climate, may be instanced that of the capital Sanaá, in the plateau, 7750 feet high, upon which the *Handbook* remarks (p. 167) that "the heat is never excessive even in summer, and in winter the temperature is most agreeable," with temperatures ranging in November between 52° and 70° Fahr., in January 40° and 62°, in March 52° and 73°. For an extensive collection of data on the climate from Niebuhr down, see Grohmann's section, pp. 27–38.

10. Grohmann, *op. cit.*, pp. 27 ff.

those slopes, often for thousands of feet. All travelers since Niebuhr's day have given descriptions of their remarkable constructions. I may quote from the summary account in the *Handbook of Arabia*, p. 115: "The plantations are laid out in terraces up the hill-sides and following their curves; these are faced with stones, sometimes enclosing a strip only a few feet wide and sometimes an acre or so; the soil is often only a foot or two deep. Great care has to be taken to prevent the destruction of the terraces by accidental water-courses caused by thunderstorms. Every accessible and suitable place on the mountain-side is utilized. Many terraces were constructed centuries ago, and they give a peculiar and characteristic aspect to the Yemen landscape. The watering is done from cisterns of cemented masonry, built in every cleft or ravine where surface waters can be intercepted." And to quote again from Harris (pp. 230 f.), describing a scene near Yerím: "The land, carefully terraced to allow of more cultivation, presented from a distance an appearance of a great flight of steps, so evenly was this great work carried out. Although at this spot the terracing was comparatively simple compared with many other places, owing to the slope being gentler, it showed signs of an enormously laborious task. But compared to places that we afterward saw in the Yemen it was *nil*. At one spot I counted one hundred and thirty-seven of these terraces on the side of a mountain, one above another, and each and every one, as far as one could judge, higher than it was wide; that is to say, the stone wall supporting the small strips of cultivated land was perhaps nine feet in height, while the supported strip was only six [in width]. It struck one as showing not only a propensity for hard work not usually found amongst Arab peoples, but also no little amount of skill and engineering"—which we may opine are the hereditary survivals of the great civilizations of the past. And the caravan routes are also provided with water cisterns for use of man and beast, these evidently of ancient origin, as an account given by Harris shows (pp. 283 f.): "Several times along the road [to Sanaá, on the eastern slope of the Serat] we passed the deep rock-cut tanks that even to-day form the water-supply of the passing caravans. One that we stopped to drink at as evening was approaching bore rough designs on horseback, and inscriptions in the Himyaric language cut in the plaster that lined the rock walls. Like so many of these tanks, a flight of steps led to the water's edges, at the summit of which was a smaller pool, to be filled by hand for the beasts of burden to drink from, and, like the main reservoir, circular in form."[11]

Also in plateaus and especially the depressions in these highlands, called in Arabic *jauf,* perennial waters are tapped by wells. Harris describes such wells in the neighborhood of Sanaá (pp. 281, 300), speaking of them as always of great depth. This condition involves vast difficulty in raising the water, which is in part overcome by placing the mouth of the well on an artificially constructed mound, so that the drawer of water can descend its slope and balance his gravity against that of the load of water. The water so drawn is also used for irrigating the crops, being poured from the well's mouth immediately into sluices descending to the lower-lying fields. These deep wells, sunk through solid rock, as Harris notes, are doubtless of great antiquity, like those we noticed above in Chapter V, Note 47. Halévy also observed the occurrence of perennial springs in the Minæan Jauf, the waters of which

11. For such artificial terracing see the interesting article by O. F. Cook, 'Staircase Farms of the Ancients,' *Nat. Geog. Magazine,* May 1916, pp. 474 ff.

Araby the Blest

are caught in great basins, in which the people bathe, wash their clothes, and catch small fish.[12] Doubtless this presence of abundant water on or near the surface of this Hollow-land created the old Arabian centers of civilization.

The remains of really stupendous waterworks of antiquity still survive to apprise us of the reason for ancient glories. One of these is within reach of the globe-trotter, if he can make a stop-off at Aden. It is a series of some fifty tanks, partly hewn in the rock, and constructed with dam-breasts in hollows or in angles of the steep slopes, in one of the deep ravines descending to the lowland back of Aden; they are capable of holding upwards of thirty million gallons of water. Despite local tradition of their high antiquity they are supposed to have been begun at the time of the second Persian invasion of Yemen, about A.D. 600. As late as 1538 Aden was entirely dependent upon these waterworks. They fell into neglect, and the British commenced their restoration in 1856, and thirteen of the great cisterns are now capable of holding some eight million gallons of water.[13]

12. Schmidt, op. cit., p. 39. For description of the country about Sabæan Marib see Glaser, Reise, p. 18. Rathjens and v. Wissmann, in vol. 2 of their Südarabienreise (1932). pp. 144–158, give a full and well illustrated description of the finely made cisterns which they saw.

13. See Harris, pp. 145 ff., Handbook, pp. 202 f. A description with plate is given in the Deutsche Aksum Expedition, II, p. 99, plate 24. I do not know on what historical grounds the construction is referred to the late Persian occupation. Quite a different view as to the present usefulness of these waterworks is given by Major General P. J. Maitland, one-time Political Resident at Aden, in his Preface to Bury's Land of Uz, pp. xii seq. He states (of date 1911): "At the present day the tanks are absolutely dry for four years out of five, and the heaviest rainfalls since they were discovered and cleared out have not filled them to an eighth part of their capacity." He proceeds to argue that it "seems in a high degree probable that, at the period when the tanks were constructed, the rainfall at Aden was much greater than it is in our times, and if greater on the coast it would presumably be greater also in the interior." This statement appears as the strongest bit of evidence we possess for a change in Arabian climate. Over against

Arabia and the Bible

But of assured antiquity and of far greater fame is the great Dam of Marib, the Mariaba of the Greeks, capital of the ancient kingdom of Sheba, or the Sabæans. The place lies 55 miles east-northeast of Sanaá, the modern capital of the Yemen, on the border of the Desert Quarter, and was a center of ancient fertility and enterprise,[14] but it has only seldom been visited.[15]

Two lengthy inscriptions of the dam, the one of 100 lines, the other of 136, in the South-Arabic or Himyaritic script and language, were copied by Glaser in his journey of 1888 and interpreted and published by him; these are of vast interest for the history of the dam and of events which Arabic tradition has celebrated.[16] They can be chronologically placed

it is to be weighed the fact that the construction may have been made to impound the rain waters over a series of years to counteract the dry seasons, whereas now the waters are used as they come to hand for a considerable and wasteful European colony.

14. The neighboring region of Khaulan is described by Halévy as "one of the best cultivated tracts of Arabia, having numerous villages at short intervals, abundant cereals and fruits, but inhabited by a savagely fanatical people" (cited in *Handbook*, p. 176).

15. 'Discovered' by Louis Arnaud, and his reports published by F. Fresnel, in *Journal Asiatique*, series iv, vol. 6, part 2 (1845); his account of the great dam edited by J. Mohl. with plans, *ibid.*, series vii, vol. 2 (1874), pp. 1 ff., repeated in full in *Corpus inscriptionum semiticarum*, part iv. vol. 2, 40 ff., and by D. H. Müller in his *Bürgen u. Schlösser Südarabiens*, along with description of the dam given by Hamdáni, the Arab geographer. There followed Halévy, whose 'rapport' is given in *Journ. As.*, series vi, vol. 19 (1872), pp. 52 ff.; then Glaser, the full report of whose *Reise nach Marib* appeared posthumously, Vienna, 1913 (his expedition in 1888). For these hardy explorers see Hogarth's *Penetration of Arabia*. The width of the valley dammed is some 600 paces, and there are the remains of massive sluices for dealing out the water. The Arabic for this dam, *arim*, is of the same root as the verb translated in Ex. 15:8, "the waters *were heaped up*."

16. For the first edition see Glaser, *Zwei Inschriften über den Dammbruch von Marib* (1897), and again published with full commentary in *Corpus Inscriptionum Semiticarum*, Part IV, nos. 540, 541; the full text of the second is given by Rossini in his *Chrestomathia Arabica Meridionalis* (1931), no. 64. It is difficult to obtain a clear idea of the size and configuration of the dam, with its accompanying sluices, from the descriptions and plans so far published.

as they are dated from a local era which can be equated, through Byzantine and Abyssinian records, with the Christian era. The older dam, of date 450 or 447 A.D.,[17] erected by a Sabæan king, tells of his reconstruction of the dam after it had broken down. The other, of date 542, or 539, commemorates the repetition of the same kind of enterprise, after a similar destruction of the dam, by the famous Abraha, viceroy of the Christian king of the Abyssinians, whose name is immortalized through his bootless attack upon Mecca in the year Mohammad was born, 562.[18] He, like his predecessor, details the great cost and labor to which he was put for this enterprise, and records the exact figures of the reconstruction: a dam-breast of 45 cubits (at 18 inches) in length, 35 in height, and 14 in thickness. This labor represented the repairing of a great breach only, not the construction of the whole dam, the figures for which, as we have seen, must have been far larger. The account gives a picture of the panic caused by the breaking of the dam, which pacified Abraha's subjects who were engaged in serious rebellion and the repair of which doubtless made him a father of his country.[19]

The above contemporaneous inscriptions record repairs to this mighty dam-breast in the fifth and sixth centuries. But the most serious collapse of the structure occurred some centuries earlier, 150 A.D., according to Caussin de Perceval (I, 84 ff.), or in the third century (Glaser, pp. 29 ff.). According to Ara-

17. The Sabæan era in question is generally assigned to 115 B.C.; in an Appendix to his monograph, pp. 123 ff., Winckler argues for moving back the era three years, to 118 B.C.

18. See the Koranic Surah of the Elephant, no. 105, and the traditions connected with it. The inscription is dedicated in the name of the Trinity.

19. For an account of other ancient dams in the Yemen drawn from the Arabic encyclopædia, the *Iklil*, see Sprenger, *Alte Geographie Arabiens*, p. 249.

bic tradition this disaster was epochal in destroying the country and forcing forth its inhabitants to northern territories, thus contributing to those parts the Yemenite element, which has played so large a part in later Islamic history. These continued shocks to the prosperity of the Yemen vastly affected the population of the other parts of Arabia, and hence large groups like Ghassan in the east, on the Byzantine border, the Tay and Shammar of the Syrian Desert, and in general the Yemenites of the north who carried on a bitter factional fight with the Northerners down into the centuries of the Caliphate, boast of their origin from South Arabia. Philby records an Arab proverb that "the Yemen is womb of the Arabs," and notes (*The Heart of Arabia*, II, 97), "the impulse which from ancient times has driven the surplus population of south-western Arabia in a steady stream north-eastward across the desert-peninsula," finding an example in the ruling class of el-Aflaj in Wady Dawásir, which came from the Yemen twelve generations ago. Doubtless the Arab *Völkerkammer* of the German South-Arabists is to be found in this section rather than in the deserts.[20]

Thus the civilization of the Yemen was reared upon the enterprise and ingenuity of its people in developing and controlling its water supply. The problem was the same for the

20. For these movements of the Arab tribes, generally northwards, see Caussin de Perceval and Sprenger. F. Wüstenfeld has devoted a monograph to the subject, *Die Wohnsitze und Wanderungen der arabischen Stämme* (1868). Also see De Goeje, section on Ethnology in art. 'Arabia,' in *Enc. of Islam*.

In the widening of our horizon for the archæology of Near Asia, which is now including the Punjab, the pivotal position of Arabia in the primitive period is now coming to be recognized. See the observations by V. G. Child, *The Most Ancient East* (1929), pp. 214 ff., on Arabia as a 'fourth party' in conjunction with Egypt, Mesopotamia, and India. He rightly notes the part that seafaring Arabs must have played in the distribution of civilization over the lands of the Indian Ocean.

South-Arabians, although of different mechanical solution, as for the civilizations of the Nile and the Euphrates. The wealth of Egypt, dependent upon irrigation from the Nile, far run-down through centuries of misrule and civic degradation, is being restored in part by the barrages which Great Britain's engineers have constructed in the great river so that the years of famine reported by native and biblical tradition may never recur.[21] The land of Babylonia is chemically as fertile as it was when Herodotus visited and waxed enthusiastic over the rich-ness of its soil: "Of all countries that we know there is none so fruitful in grain . . . in which it is so fruitful as to yield two hundredfold . . . even three hundredfold. The fruitfulness of the land must seem incredible to those who have not visited the country." And so with varying figures but equal admira-tion Theophrastus the botanist and Strabo and Pliny.[22] Of course the problem in Iraq is one of distribution of the water. It will be at one season a desert, where, as one prophetic oracle announces (Is. 13:20 ff.), "the Arab shall not pitch his tent nor the shepherds make their fold," and where wildcats and ostriches and satyrs and jackals and wild-dogs shall howl and dance; while another oracle (14:23) thinks of the flood sea-son when, according to the word of the Lord, "I will make it a possession for the bittern and pools of water." Such is Baby-lonia in its natural state, a desert in the dry season, a swamp when the rivers are in flood, as those who know modern Iraq describe it. These descriptions agree well with the thesis main-

21. There is a scheme on foot to flood again from the Nile the hollow of the Fayum, once a great inland lake, and one of the most fertile territories of the Ptolemaic em-pire. For the development of this great lake by Ptolemy II, see Mahaffy, *Empire of the Ptolemies*, pp. 156 ff.

22. See Rogers, *History of Babylonia and Assyria*, ed. 2, pp. 279 ff., for these and other citations.

tained in Chapter V that not change of climate but deterioration of human civilization has affected Arabian lands that were once prosperous oases or extensive districts of fertility.[23]

In the Yemen, the opposing conditions of wet and dry are somewhat the same, but the engineering problems are different, as we have seen. Here there was imposed upon man the necessity to impound the waters of the torrents, if he would occupy his heritage, to prevent their destructive ravages and to distribute them at will in beneficent streams to the thirsty lands. And it has been shown how even in the miserable conditions of this land cisterns and deep-sunk wells remain as the source of water supply, still distinguishing the country as peculiarly Araby the Blest.

These ancient waterworks and their modern successors expose the secret of the ancient wealth of the Yemen. The results of that civilization so created are visibly manifest in the broad fields of ruins, which such travelers as Arnaud, Halévy, Glaser, have reported to us, the remains of massive architectural constructions, temples and the like, and the broken works of art smashed by Muslim fanaticism. There is, for example, the great temple of the Sabæan deity Aum near Marib, an elliptical construction of 86 × 76 metres, with a wall of 3.3 metres thick, 9.5 high. It is called by the natives Haram Bilkís after the traditional name of Solomon's Queen of Sheba.[24]

23. Even in Arabia Deserta the torrential floods as we saw in the earlier chapter have been destroyers of civilization; human impounding of the waters is the only counter-agent.

24. See Halévy. 'Mission archéologique,' *Journal Asiatique*, series VI, vol. 19, 67 ff.; *Corpus Inscr. Sem.*, part IV, vol. 2, 20, and Glaser, *Reise*, p. 144, with more exact measurements. On the art and architecture of South Arabia see Grohmann in Nielsen's *Handbuch der altarab. Altertumskunde*, vol. 1 (1927), chap. 4, and his *Göttersymbole und Symboltiere auf südarab. Denkmälern* (1914). And now a Sabæan temple, at Hugga,

Araby the Blest

But we must pass on to more definite and articulate remains. These are the hosts of inscriptions in a peculiar alphabet which, as deciphered by scholars, has revealed a language closely related to Classical Arabic; it is called South-Arabic, the Himyaritic of elder scholarship, following Greek usage. It may be diagnosed into various dialects, Minæan, Sabæan, Katabanian, Hadhramotic. The inscriptions known to scholarship number nigh two thousand, of which only a part have been published or adequately interpreted. They reveal a remarkable civilization extending over some 1200 years at least, with an exceedingly elaborate and complicated civic organization, and contain the nomenclature of a highly developed polytheistic and ritualistic religion.[25]

has been excavated and carefully plotted out for its original form by the engineers Rathjens and v. Wissmann; see vol. II of their *Südarabienreise*.

25. These texts have been appearing in fascicles of the Himyaritic Part, Pars IV, of the *Corpus Inscriptionum Semiticarum*, 1881–1930 (up to vol. III, fasc. 1). Glaser's extensive material has appeared in various publications, often only in fragmentary shape. Nielsen, Hommel, and Rhodokanakis (the last of whom has established himself as the leading authority in the field) are editing the *Handbuch der altarabischen Altertumskunde*, of which vol. I has appeared (1927); it will include much of the new material along with fresh interpretations of the old. Lidzbarski's *Ephemeris für semitische Epigraphik*, 1902–15, has presented most of the new material as it has appeared, along with glossaries, as also now the *Recueil d'épigraphie sémitique*, which is especially devoting itself to this field.

For the grammar there are the early essay of Halévy in *Journal Asiatique*, Series VII, vol. I (1873), 434 ff., and the *Sketch of Sabaean Grammar* by W. F. Prideaux in *Trans. of Soc. of Biblical Archaeology*, vol. VII (1877), and the notable work of Hommel's, *Süd-arabische Chrestomathie* (1893), containing an extensive grammatical discussion— now out of print. Guidi has recently published a most useful 'Summarium grammaticae arabicae meridionalis' in *Muséon*, vol. 39 (1926), 1–32. There should be noticed here also the ample discussions by Rhodokanakis in his series 'Studien zur Lexicographie und Grammatik des altsüdarabischen' in the *Sitzungsberichte* of the Vienna Academy, Phil.-Hist. Class, vols. of 1915, 1917, 1931. For chrestomathies, Hommel's volume contains 37 inscriptions, almost all of them Minæan, with glossary; and now Count C. Rossini has published *Chrestomathia arabica meridionalis epigraphica* (Rome, 1931), containing 102 texts from all the dialects and an extensive glossary, a most useful as well as learned

Arabia and the Bible

The contents of these inscriptions are of various orders. Almost all of them possess some religious significance as even business documents were posted in the temples to give their contracts the sanction of the gods. The largest section of the inscriptions in the *Corpus* contains dedications, of various gifts, like images of bulls presented as thank-offerings, of lands, and of persons and whole families. The reason for the latter species of devotion is not evident; were the persons debtors who fell into the power of the temple estates, or did they obtain relief from secular impositions by entering the sphere of ecclesiastical mortmain? The very large number of building inscriptions, often concerning repairs and additions to palaces and temples and castles, and so honorific to the builders, are difficult of interpretation from the abundance of technical terms. There are also epitaphs and inscriptions concerning the right of sepulchre. The inscriptions celebrating the construction of waterworks and specifying the rights thereto are numerous, and are valuable for the insight they give into the technical and legal conditions of society; to their interpretation Rhodokanakis is making the greatest contribution. Many of the votive texts give incidental reference to historical events, caravan expeditions, wars, international relations.

volume. No lexicon of the language has as yet been published. 'An Index of the South Arabian Proper Names contained in the *Corpus I.S.*' has been published by W. T. Pilter in *Proc. of the Soc. of Bibl. Arch.*, 1917, pp. 99 ff., 115 ff. The Belgian scholar Ryckmans announces a forthcoming full lexicon of all proper names.

But few of the texts have been removed to Western museums; we are dependent for most of them on copies, often by necessity hastily made, e.g., by Halévy, or on squeezes, which art Glaser instituted scientifically, training the natives to procure such copies for him. A number of inscriptions in bronze are in existence, e.g., nos. 523, 525, 526, 527, 529, 532, 533, 567, 568 of the *Corpus*. This bronze casting of inscriptions is almost unique in the ancient Orient. I know only of the bronze gates of Shalmaneser's palace at Balawat and a small bronze text found at Nuzi near Kirkuk; see *Bulletin* of the American Schools of Oriental Research, April 1930.

Araby the Blest

There are some extensive constitutional texts, as they may be called, laying down fundamental law for the estates of the people. At the other end of the scale are texts with personal profession of faith and adoration for the gods and even confession of specific sins. Long historical inscriptions like those of Assyria do not occur; our knowledge of the history must be worked up from current references to reigning princes and dynasties. A dating system by eponyms was employed. Some of these inscriptions will be referred to in Chapter VII.

Until the discovery of the South-Arabian inscriptions our only sources for the history of the land were biblical references, like the genealogy of the Semites in Gen. 10 or the vague references to Sheba-Seba and its rare products; the notices of the Hellenistic and Roman geographers and historians, as observed in Chapter IV; and then the vague traditions of Arabian legend, seen through the spectacles of Islam. The accession of the South-Arabian monuments to our knowledge began in the first third of the nineteenth century, and they became the object of slow decipherment on the part of a few scholars. The greatest impetus to their study came from the hazardous explorations of the land by Arnaud, Halévy, Glaser. Since the heroic feats of the last-named scholar—his fourth and last expedition was made in 1892–94—comparatively little has been added to the stock of raw material, the Yemen having lain in a condition of continued insurrection against the Ottoman empire, while since the Great War it is only gradually opening up to the foreigner. Also many of the most important sites lie in desert country, possessed by fanatical tribes. During this long and slow period of exploration and decipherment, other new sources have been added: from the Assyro-Babylonian quarter where we have gained a few sure data bearing definitely upon South Arabia (see Chapter IV); and from Abyssinia, where inscribed monuments of the fourth and subsequent Christian centuries have been found, in early Ethiopic script and language akin to the South-Arabic, throwing light upon the close relations of Abyssinia with what was, so far as its Semitic stock is concerned, its mother-country.[26]

The greater part of the chronologically datable history of South Arabia belongs to the post-Old-Testament history. Some monuments dated according to a local era (115 or 118 B.C.), checked by some international synchronisms, enable us to obtain a general sketch of the later history of the country. The older Sabæan kingdom had established itself by conquest of earlier rivals, and by assimilation and federation of neighboring states. But whereas hitherto it had possessed the monopoly not only of the frankincense trade of the Hadhramot and of the overseas commerce with the Indies, now it met the sharp maritime competition of the Græco-Roman world which rendered the Arabian land-routes unnecessary for the world's commerce; and as its political life depended upon its economics, its stability was sorely threatened. In the fourth century it was invaded by an Abyssinian king who could call himself ruler of the Yemen. It became then a shuttlecock in the disastrous wars between Byzantium and the Persian empire and also a battlefield of religions, of Paganism, Judaism, Christianity. One of its kings, Dhu-Nuwás, became a Jew and bitterly persecuted the Christians; through Byzantium's stimulus Christian Abyssinia now invaded the land and im-

26. Recent publications on ancient Abyssinia are: Kammerer, *Essai sur l'histoire antique de l'Abyssinie*, etc. (1926); Rossini, *Storia d'Etiopia*, pt. 1 (1928); Budge, *A History of Ethiopia, Nubia and Abyssinia* (1928).

posed a Christian rule which as bitterly illtreated the Jews. It was the practically autonomous Abyssinian viceroy Abraha who made in 562 the attempt to destroy Mecca and its idolatrous religion—whose blasphemous undertaking was, according to Muslim tradition, rudely stopped by a wonderful miracle from Heaven. In the same year Mohammad was born in Mecca, and the end of autonomous Arabian states was in sight. For a couple of generations Persia intervened and held the land as against Byzantium and Christianity. Then with the rise of Islam the Yemen fell without much ado into the lap of the new religion. For the economic condition of the land in the Christian era we have noticed above the persistent Arab tradition of the bursting of the dam at Marib which ruined the land and drove the Yemenites to seek their fortunes in the far north. This legend of the Marib dam is expressive of the collapse of Sabæan culture.

But for the pre-Hellenistic period we are involved in great historical perplexities and in a sharp dispute between a higher and a lower chronology, such as have raged in other historical fields, but in this case with disproportionate variation. The dispute lies over the relations of two peoples which were the center of the South-Arabian history, the Minæans and the Sabæans, the latter located in their later history at Marib, the former at Maín (hence 'Minæans'), Karnáwu and other points, both states lying not far apart from each other to the northeast of Sanaá. The difference between the two nations is further marked by a dialectic variation, of interest to the Semitic philologist. The Minæan state was subsequently conquered by that of Saba, and appears, although this is doubted by some scholars, to have been the predecessor of the latter. The advocates of the higher chronology would hold that the

Minæan and Sabæan periods are mutually exclusive of each other, and that the chronologies of the two must be put one after the other. Then on the basis of 'blind' reckonings—for, while many Minæan kings are known, their dynastic relations are not established—the Minæan period is pushed back as far, at least, as 1300 B.C.; so now Hommel, who has previously argued for a still earlier date.[27] Back again of this would lie an indefinite, unknown period in which the Minæan civilization and its arts developed.

This 'higher chronology' however has been accepted only by a small school of scholars, almost entirely South-Arabists, who may naturally have exaggerated the importance of their subject. We may name as its leaders Hommel, Winckler, Glaser, O. Weber. Its only adherent in the English-speaking world is Professor Margoliouth of Oxford, who appears to have accepted it in his recent Schweich Lectures.[28] On the other hand, contributors to South-Arabian lore like the French Derenbourgs and the German Hartmann have steadily opposed these extreme views, while such historians of antiquity as Eduard Meyer will have nothing to do with them.

Indeed, serious objections present themselves to the extreme chronology. In the first place, the epigraphy of the texts hardly allows us such an early dating as the middle of the second millennium B.C. The type of script is the same for the earlier Minæan as well as the Sabæan, and yet the script is evidently of a secondary 'Gothic' character, and must have had a long preceding history. In order to relate it with the

27. Nielsen's *Handbuch*, p. 67.

28. *Relations between Arabs and Israelites* (1921), p. 24, etc. For Hommel see the bibliography in Note 1. He takes like position in his article 'Arabia' in the *Enc. of Islam*, while in the same *Encyclopaedia* Tkatsch under 'Saba' argues stoutly for the lower chronology.

Phœnician alphabet, there enters the problem how to articulate it in the history of that alphabet. Time must be allowed for the development from simpler forms, pictorial or lineal, as we have in the proto-Sinaitic alphabet or in the earliest known forms of the Phœnician. On the other hand, some scholars suggest that the South-Arabic script precedes the Phœnician as we know it.

Moreover, historians in general deny that the Minæans and Sabæans must be arranged one after the other, even as the Normans succeeded the Anglo-Saxons. One of the few Minæan texts which appear to give any international data is a subject of dispute; it is generally placed at the time of the Persian conquest, referring, as can most reasonably be interpreted, to the Mdy, i.e., the Medians, and to the late Babylonian province of Across-the-River, i.e., Syria to the west of the Euphrates (e.g., Ezra 4:10, 11, 17), to be dated about 525 B.C., in view of its reference to the Medes.[29] The second millennium date (its proponents have been constantly reducing it) offered by the rival school has little to say for itself except on a bundle of theories. Sabæan inscriptions do refer to contemporary Maín, and Strabo knows of its people. Late Minæan inscriptions have been found at Memphis and at Delos,[30] and inscriptions in the same dialect occur at el-Ula in

29. Halévy, no. 535, text given in Hommels *Chrestomathy*, p. 103 and in Rossini, no. 71; see E. Meyer, *Die Israeliten u. ihre Nachbarstämme*, p. 321; Hartmann, *Die arabische Frage*, pp. 130 ff.; Tkatsch, as cited in Note 28.

30. The Memphis text was published by Rhodokanakis in *Zeitschr. f. Semitistik*, II (1924), 113 ff., that at Delos by Clermont-Ganneau in *Comptes Rendus* of the French Academy of Inscriptions, 1908, pp. 546 ff.; the two are given respectively by Rossini in his numbers 82, 66. The Memphis text is dated in the reign of "Ptolemy son of Ptolemy"; the Delos text is assigned by Clermont-Ganneau on epigraphic grounds to the second century B.C.

the land of Midian, and these probably link up with the neighboring Nabatæan inscriptions. If the Meúnim of Chronicles are the Minæans (see Chapter VIII), their occurrence in the Bible is late, while the Sabæans appear in both older and younger (post-Exilic) biblical notices. Further, an invaluable but complicating datum is the Assyrian evidence for the existence of a Sabæan kingdom in the beginning of the seventh century. This was discussed in Chapter IV, where we observed the problem whether those Sabæans were still in northwest Arabia or had already established themselves in the south. In the latter case a southern Sabæan kingdom must have early existed alongside of the Minæan.

It remains then at present simplest to postulate the synchronism of the Minæan and Sabæan states for a long period, with the final absorption of the former by the latter. We have to realize that while the Yemen means to us a political entity, it was in antiquity divided into a number of independent communities, which managed to live alongside of each other in somewhat the same way as did the great commercial cities of northern Italy, or earlier of Syria. The later unity of the Sabæan land was attained only after a long political and social process, and even then no stability was obtained. We notice a succession of dynastic groups, of tribal hegemonies, with constant indications of the rise of fresh ethnical elements.

As for the chronology of South Arabia, there have been already noticed the Minæan inscription, which can best be assigned to the age of Cambyses, and the Assyrian references, *circa* 700 B.C., to named kings of the Sabæans. For a later ethnic element, which came to dominate South Arabia, we possess in the inscriptions a definite era, placed at 115 B.C. Before this period Sheba was ruled over first by *Mukarribs*,[31] or priest-kings, and then by kings. The new era, which introduces us to a dynasty calling themselves 'kings of Saba and Du-Raidan,' appears to be coeval with the rise of a fresh element which we may call Himyaritic, the Homeroi of the contemporaneous Greek geographers, by which name the South-Arabians are collectively known to them.

Before characterizing the extraordinary civilization which existed in South Arabia for at least the greater part of the first millennium B.C., and therefore coeval with the Hebrew monarchy and the subsequent Jewish theocratic state, we should recall the relations of that far-off land with the Mediterranean territories and the Bible lands. The distance for over a thousand miles, in large part through desert regions beset by the lurking Arabs, was covered by a finely developed system of commercial routes and transportation which defied the distance, in the same way as Babylonia was brought near to Syria-Palestine by caravans plying the desert. These routes ran north from the highlands of Yemen by stages which the later geographers Strabo and Ptolemy name and with definite distances, until they reached the land of Midian. Here at ancient el-Hijr, the Classical Egra of the Nabatæans, now represented by the ruinous settlements of Madáin-Salih, on the line of the Damascus-Medina railway, the convoys of the rare products of the south met a nucleus of routes: one went off east by way of Teima to Babylon; the main line went on to Petra where it forked again, the western branch going to Gaza and to Egypt, while the northerly route pressed on through

---

31. The consonants *mkrb* alone are given, the vowels are uncertain. The sacerdotal notion of the word is suggested by Ethiopic *mekrab*, 'temple.'

Trans-Jordan to Damascus, the distributing point for Syria and Asia Minor.

This settlement appears to have been the southernmost trading post of the Nabatæans and to have faced, and subsequently displaced, the most northerly Minæan colony at a site to the south, now called el-Ula, in the once fertile wady of el-Kura. Here a large number of inscriptions in the Minæan dialect have been discovered, which reveal that the settlement was a colony of the South-Arabian Minæan state, subject to its kings, some of whom are named and can be identified in the inscriptions of the South. It is to be identified with the Maín-Musran named in a South-Arabic inscription, that is, Maín of Egypt, i.e., towards the Egyptian territories.[32] Its name is now proved, from the local inscriptions, to have been the Dedan of the Old Testament, whose people are frequently cited as traffickers of the desert. We thus discover in the northwest of Arabia an ancient emporium of the South-Arabian trade. It is possible that the Meúnim, or Meínim, appearing in Chronicles, represent this northern post of the Yemen, which thus came into trade-conflict with the Palestinians. This Minæan Dedan was but one of the many entrepôts in the Peninsula by which trade was furthered and controlled by the states of South Arabia.[33]

32. Inscription cited, Note 29.

33. For descriptions of Madáin-Salih and el-Ula see Doughty, vol. I, chaps. 4, 5, 6, 13. The Minæan inscriptions at the latter place were copied by Euting in his expedition along with Huber in 1883–84 (see his *Tagbuch einer Reise in Inner-Arabien*, vol. I [1896], vol. II, edited posthumously by Littmann [1914]); they were published by D. H. Müller, *Epigraphische Denkmäler aus Arabien* (1889), and by Mordtmann, *Beiträge zur minäischen Epigraphik* (1897). These inscriptions have been recopied and added to (altogether over 200 numbers) by Jaussen and Savignac, who have published them in their *Mission archéologique en Arabie*, vol. II (1914). These explorers present as booty of their expedition in 1907 and following years a rich harvest of Thamudene,

Araby the Blest

Thus to the rear of the land of the Bible, to the far south but as integral part of the Semitic world, looms up a notable civilization, the tentacles of whose influence reached to the Mediterranean and to the lands of the Persian Gulf (where South-Arabic texts also have been found[34]) as well as penetrating throughout the hinterland of the unknown interior of the Peninsula. Like the Phœnician cities, the states of the Yemen were founded on commerce and correspondingly possessed a potent sway that far exceeded the possible limits of mere political power. As the Phœnicians threw their navies and planted their colonies along the Mediterranean and into the lands beyond the Strait of Hercules, so the merchant states of South Arabia handled a commerce even more far-reaching in its scope and immensely more valuable. They possessed, until the advent of the Hellenistic empire, the trade routes through Arabia reaching to the Mediterranean, and in the other direction they had the monopoly of the commerce to the far-off Indies. Thus in a primitive but actual fashion they anticipated that idea of an empire which should sit across the continents between the waters of the Atlantic and the Indian Ocean, that dream of empire which has been dreamed and ever and anon effected by Persia, Greece, Rome, Byzantium, the Islamic State, the Ottoman Empire, Great Britain, France, Germany. And the actual heir today of that old South-Arabian

Nabatæan, and Lihyanian inscriptions from those two localities, along with a sumptuous album of photographs illustrating the remarkable scenery and the notable remains, especially in tomb architecture, which help us to visualize the place these sites once held in the ancient life of the Peninsula. The Nabatæan inscriptions are found mostly at Madáin-Salih, the Minæan only in the el-Ula oasis. For the identification of Dedan see vol. II, 75 f. For the history of al-Hijr, Madáin-Salih, see Musil, *Topographical Itineraries*, vol. I, 299 ff.

34. See Chapter VIII, Note 9.

empire is Great Britain with its control of all the Arabian littoral from the Suez Canal to the head of the Persian Gulf.[35]

The political life of the ancient Yemen-land has its peculiar features, presenting a unique development of Semitic politics. The inscriptions we possess, some two thousand in number, although in considerable part still defying accurate interpretation, reveal, directly and indirectly, a remarkably complicated form of civic and political society. The petty states with which that civilization began, and also the later imperialistic organization of the Sabæan and then the Himyarite kingdom, were founded on a delicately poised balance. Socially there existed two factors—that perennial pair of elements which we find struggling all through Arabian history down into our own day; these were the colonists who had settled down in the lands potential of fertility through soil and water supply, and the Arabs, the Bedawin, who housed around in the desert. The inscriptions several times speak of the Arabs (*a'ráb*) as part of the composition of the body politic;[36] they appear to be feudal and subsidized contingents of the state, quite similar, we may suppose, to the loose social development of the Arabic tribes settled on the frontiers of later Byzantium and Persia, forming the Ghassanid and Lahmid kingdoms. These Arabs and their favor were essential to the safe-conduct of the great caravans which constituted the transportation system of the Sabæan commerce. From them were doubtless drafted fresh

35. Cf. Sprenger's dictum on ancient Arabia's economic position, *Die alte Geographie Arabiens*, p. 279 (an opinion now being corroborated by prehistoric research): "The frankincense region was the heart of the world-commerce of antiquity, and it began to pulsate in prehistoric times. There follows the conclusion: The Arabs, more exactly the people of the frankincense region, were the founders of international commerce as it existed in antiquity."

36. See Chapter II, Note 2.

supplies of settled laborers and citizens. The line of cleavage between the two elements was fluid, and the settled colonists easily drifted back into the nomadic life when the land was no longer able to support them. With the decay of the Yemenite civilization and polity in the early centuries, typified by the repeated bursting of the dam of Marib, the Yemenites poured forth in hordes towards the north, seeking in other lands of the desert the livelihood which was now denied them in their old home. The later northern tribes boasting of Yemenite origin were doubtless descended, as we have noticed above, from peoples that had once enjoyed a high civilization in the land of their origin. Further, the movement to and fro on the margin of the lands of the Sown on the part of the neighboring nomads must have caused a continual flux and consequent difficult balance of ethnic and social conditions.

The character of the settled population again produced a unique social order because of the highly artificial character of the bases of that civilization. The fertility of the land depended upon works of irrigation, deep wells, cunningly arranged cisterns, enormous dams, sluices and conduits for the fields. Such works could be produced and maintained only by an intense communal order, to which all the social elements had to contribute, and from which they all derived proportionally their means of subsistence. Along with this went the necessity of control of the trade-routes. The business of shipment across the dangerous deserts could not be left to individual enterprise; the necessity of safeguarding that business and providing it with armed escort and the assistance of the indispensable Arabs created the necessity of common and directed action. The state itself became a business organization, thus anticipating the modern development of economic and industrial communism which is the characteristic of our modern civilization. The state appears to have had its monopolies.[37] We know little or nothing of the inner history of the great Hadhramot valley to the east, the land of frankincense, which was the chief staple of Sheba's commerce. The production of that invaluable commodity was kept under careful restrictions, and according to the reports of the Greeks was protected by religious taboos which confined its cultivation to favored lands and cultivators—the private flower garden of the busy bees that were the merchants of Saba.[38] Rivals by land and sea had to be met and frustrated, and this required trained and mobile troops, and several inscriptions detail these dangers to caravan commerce.

The result of these conditions of the life of the Yemen was not a highly organized empire with a despot at the head as in Egypt, or as in more limited form in Mesopotamia; but a complicated system that we may call feudal, with a delicately strung balance of the different social factors. The basis of the social structure was the old Arabic idea of the tribe or family. These clans had settled themselves in the fertile lands, built their castles, settled their retainers about them—each a little principality in itself, as the condition still remains to this day in the Yemen. Larger combinations of these units were formed, doubtless on the basis of actual or artificial relations of kinship. A powerful combination, built up by a masterful aristocracy with some dominant hereditary dynasty, would obtain wider control and produce a state or 'people' (sha'b), as the inscriptions term the larger political unit. The develop-

37. We may compare Solomon's horse monopoly, and his enterprise of state for opening up the Red Sea; 1 Ki. cc. 9, 10.
38. See Schoff, *Periplus*, pp. 33, 120-126.

ment of kingship was secondary, as was the rule in the Semitic world. While the Minæans appear to have had kings from early times, the first period of the Sabæans, until their triumph over the Minæans, was under the sway of the *mukarribs*, whom we have noticed above. With the establishment of the Sabæan monarchy we find not a despotism, but rather almost a constitutional monarchy, in which the power of the king, while formally the respected head of the state, was carefully circumscribed by the great clans and castes of the state. The decrees of state, indeed, as certain most interesting inscriptions show, were enacted by representative parliaments in which those various elements were duly represented and consulted. The constitutional idea of the state appears in the recurring formula, 'God, King, and People.'

In these feudal groups there was the double duty imposed upon the mass of the tribe or clan, namely of military and agrarian service. There were also elements which, in view of the constant mention of them in the inscriptions, although in terms which defy accurate interpretation, appear as privileged castes and guilds; these may have included the civil element of artisans, merchants, etc., assembled in the towns, which form of life tended to break down the tribal distinctions, although these elements were probably integrated in some way into the feudal system. At the lowest point of the scale were the villains of the soil, who were practically unprivileged serfs, and also probably, as to this day in the Yemen, a pariah class.

Along with these secular elements existed the temple organizations, the members of which constituted a special caste. Doubtless in the Yemen, as elsewhere in the ancient world, the city-state was primarily a theocracy centering in the temple of the city's god or pantheon. Such communities, culminating in the local deity, were the original centers of social life and the creators of agrarian and economical development. The temples and their religious *clientèles* possessed their lands and privileges, and from the inscriptions we find them entering into all kinds of business. Possessed of immemorial privileges and enjoying the reverence of an intensely religious community, the political and economic power of these religious corporations must have been very large. With the 'dead hand,' which is the perquisite of ecclesiastical holdings, their power tended to increase, and was with difficulty diminished. Some scholars would hold that the rise to power of the later Sabæan kingdom (that of Saba and du-Rhaidan) was accompanied with restriction of the privileges of the religious corporations.

We accordingly obtain a picture of a highly organized and complicated social system, the like of which is not to be found elsewhere in the ancient Semitic world. Certain unique possibilities of the nature of the land and of its trade, requiring human endeavor and control, reacted in producing a remarkably well articulated, even if delicately balanced, social order, in which the state was the organizer and purveyor of all business. Something similar appears in the Phœnician states and again in the social life of medieval Europe; perhaps the likest phenomenon is that of the great trading cities of northern Italy, although South Arabia developed a much more closely knit complex covering an immense geographical area and coördinating most diverse elements.[39]

39. For the 'constitutional' or 'parliamentary' texts noted above see Rhodokanakis, 'Der Grundsatz der Öffentlichkeit in den südarabischen Urkunden,' in *Sitzungsberichte* of the Vienna Academy, Phil.-Hist. Class, 1915, pp. 25 ff., 33 ff. The second text has been summarized and considered by the present writer in a paper entitled 'An Enact-

Araby the Blest

In the next chapter I will discuss the South-Arabian religion and its affinities to that of the Hebrews.

ment of Fundamental Constitutional Law in Old South Arabia,' in *Proceedings American Philosophical Society*, 1928, pp. 207–213. A full discussion of the social and civic constitution of the South-Arabian state is given by Rhodokanakis in Nielsen's *Handbuch*, pp. 117–142. Similar social conditions prevail in the Yemen to this day; see Grohmann, *Südarabien als Wirthschaftsgebiet*, pp. 62 ff.; and W. Schmidt, *Das südwestliche Arabien*, pp. 60 ff.; observe the latter's remark, p. 61: "A long historical tradition developed within each tribe a well formed caste system," with citation of a monograph by Glaser, *Die Kastengliederung in Yemen*. The lowest stratum is a pariah class. For a lively picture of the organization of tribal groups in modern Yemen, see Bury, *Land of Uz*, chap. 10.

VII

SOUTH ARABIA AND THE BIBLE

WE have constantly observed contacts between the lands of the Bible, as we call them, and South Arabia. We will now pursue some inquiries into the more intimate relations between these distant regions.

The first line of investigation concerns possible race-relationship between the Hebrews and the South-Arabians. As observed in Chapter II, the Hebrews of the Bible claimed descent from a patronymic ancestor Eber (Heber) through his son Peleg, while the younger brother Joktan was the progenitor of Arabian peoples, some of them without doubt South-Arabian, e.g., Sheba, Hadhramot, Ophir (Gen. 10). What historical basis is there to this tradition of race which makes the peoples of the far South only some degrees more remote in relationship to the other Hebrews than are the North-Arabian stocks which, according to the same tradition, are descended from Abraham through his concubines?

Now one of the essential clues, often the only one we possess, for tracing the affinities of the ancient Semitic peoples, lies in the personal nomenclature of the races in question.[1] These clues are based on two elements in name-formation. One of these elements is the form of the name. On the one hand the name may be merely a descriptive noun or adjective, the simplest and probably earliest form like Caleb 'dog,' Jemimah 'dove,' or a compound noun expressing relation-

1. This interest is patent in the carefully prepared Lists of Proper Names which are attached to all publications of cuneiform texts, the digests based on these for certain periods or groups, and then the analytical studies springing from this material.

ship as Abdullah 'slave of Allah.' The epithet-names of this class appear to have been rather peculiar to central Arabia, the home of the later classical language, and such names can be observed at length in the Edomitic-Arabian genealogies in Gen. 36.[2] Or, and this is the peculiar characteristic of Semitic name-giving, the name contains a predicate statement with noun-adjective or verb as the element of assertion, like Abram, 'Father is high,' Elishama, 'God has heard.' The Akkadians went the farthest in the elaboration of this last class of names, which run out into long sentences, like Nabu-kudur-usur, 'Nebo, protect the boundary!' and their names stand in a clearly distinguished category.

This *form* of the names is especially a study, for the exact philologist. But the other element in the Semitic nomenclature, that of *content,* is more striking historically and is patent to the layman. Most of the old Semitic names—and this is particularly true of the fields we are considering—are theophorous, i.e., bear a divine name or epithet. As we know that Christopher is of Christian origin, and that Isidore traces back to the Egyptian Isis religion, and Isabella has journeyed down from Phœnician Jezebel through Spain into Christian usage, so from these contents of divine attribution we can learn much of the religion of the original bearers of those old Semitic names. Thus in the Hebrew nomenclature it is recognized that the element YEHO-, YO-, -YAHU, -YAH represents YHWH the God of Israel, and that a name of this formation came from Israel. And such an element serves for identification as between separated groups; when for instance we find

---

2. See Moritz, *Zeits. f. d. alttest. Wiss.,* 1926, pp. 81 ff. Arabic names under Islam have gone their own way.

the same element, as YAWA in Babylonian names of the fifth century, we know that their bearers were Jewish exiles.

Now it is somewhat of a commonplace that an identity of name-formation has been recognized as between the early West-Semitic groups in Palestine and Syria—for which the Old Testament is our chief source—and that ethnic group which produced the First Dynasty of Babylon *circa* 2000 B.C., whose most distinguished member was Hammurabi, largely reputed to be the Amraphel of Gen. 14. The ultimate geographic as well as ethnic relation of this First Dynasty group with the West-Semites is now generally allowed, and that group has been given various pertinent names expressive of this connection, West-Semitic, Amorite, Canaanite, even Hebrew. In general their names possess a fixed formula of composition and a few stereotyped elements. The divine element is generally the Semitic word for 'god,' *ilu*, identical with Hebrew *el*, or else an epithet of deity, like *ab* 'father'; *am* 'uncle' (i.e., nearest of kin); *ah* 'brother'; *hal* '(maternal) uncle'; to this is attached a predicate, noun, adjective, or verb. Thus of the eleven kings of the First Dynasty, seven have names of 'West-Semitic' formation. The element 'father' appears twice in Sumu-abi and Abieshu; 'uncle,' three times, in Ammiditana, Ammi-zaduga, and Hammurapi (Babylonian *h* replacing another West-Semitic guttural); while 'god' is found in Sumu-la-ilu ('the Name verily is God'), Samsu-iluna ('the Sun is our God'). Identically the same formations appear in the biblical nomenclature, e.g., Abram, Amram, Abiram, Jerob(o)am, and the large class of primitive names with *el*, e.g., Abiel, Ammiel, or construed with verbs, Nathaniel, Ishmael, Israel, while Jacob is shortened from Jacob-el, which occurs in the Babylonian and is vouched for from the Egyptian, while the root of the verb is South-Arabic, the name meaning 'God protects.'

Now the same formation appears as typical in the South-Arabic names. The divine element is most often in the older names either *il*, 'god,' or a divine epithet, but never in the earliest texts a divine personal name like Shams ('sun'), Sin ('moon'), Athtar, even as is the case with the early biblical names and largely so in those of the First Dynasty. The epithetical attribute is largely the same as in the West-Semitic, e.g., 'father,' 'uncle,' 'maternal uncle,' 'brother,' or abstract expressions like 'protection' (*zimr*, cf. Zimri, 1 Ki. 16:9), 'salvation' (*yith‘*, identical with the Hebrew basis of Jesus, Joshua, etc., and with -*eshu* in the First-Dynasty name cited above), 'righteous(ness)' (*sidk* or *saduk*, cf. Melchizedek, and Babylonian -*zaduga* above). Or the predicate is a verb, and while the verb roots are largely Arabic rather than Hebraic, as we know the lexicography of the latter, we find many etymological identities. Thus the biblical names Abiada, Abimelek, Elishama appear in the South-Arabic. That this peculiar name-formation came into South Arabia from an intruding ethnic group appears in an interesting fashion; to names of this character in the South-Arabic there came to be attached secondary names which are of genuine Arabic character in root and form, indicating the combination of two elements, the aristocracy preserving their hereditary names but adding to them as cognomens names of local characteristic.[3]

3. See Noth, *Die israelitischen Personennamen im Rahmen der gemeinsemitischen Namengabung* (1928), pp. 49 f.; this is the most recent work on biblical names. For earlier works see G. B. Gray, *Studies in Hebrew Proper Names* (1896), Nöldeke, art. 'Names' in *Enc. Bib.* For the comparison of West-Semitic, First-Dynasty and South-Arabic names see Hommel, *Ancient Hebrew Tradition*, chap. III; Ranke, *Early Babylonian Personal Names* (Philadelphia, 1905). For a list of the South-Arabian proper names in the *Corpus* see Pilter as cited in Chapter VI, end of Note 25.

Arabia and the Bible

There is one element in particular which is common to the three groups we are considering and which involves a suggestive theological affinity. The first two kings of the First Babylonian Dynasty are Sumu-abu, 'the Name is Father,' and Sumu-la-ilu, 'the Name is surely God.' Now this same element as a surrogate for deity appears in the biblical names Shemiada = 'the Name knows,' and Samuel = Shemu-el, 'the Name is God,' identical with the Babylonian name just cited. This element also appears in the Old-Babylonian West-Semitic names,[4] the Tell el-Amarna texts, the Elephantine papyri, and in Phœnician.[5] The name was already archaic when the book of Samuel was written, for the tradition attempts an impossible etymology as though from *sha'al* 'ask' (1 Sam. 1:21). Now this same element occurs in South-Arabic names, in consonantal forms as *smh*, which is generally vocalized as sumu-hu, 'his (the god's) Name'; e.g., Sumuhu-kariba (the meaning of *k.* is uncertain), Sumuhu-alay, 'his Name is lofty.' This usage common to the three ethnic groups we are considering is of theological interest as expressive of the religious *Scheu* before the use of the proper name of the deity. The same repugnance is illustrated at Lev. 24:11, where an Israelite 'blasphemed the Name'; in the Samaritan reading (*Krê*) of 'the Name' for the Tetragrammaton; and in the Jewish rule of absolute replacement of that divine name by 'the Lord.'

Thus both biblical tradition and philology assert the rela-

---

4. E.g., Ranke, *op. cit.*, p. 166, lists Sumu-atar, Sumu-hala, Sumu-hammu, Sumu-la-el, Sumu-rah. There is tradition of an Amalekite king named Samayda = Shemiada, of similar formation; see Chapter I, Note 37. The name of Moses' son Gershom is to be interpreted in the same way: 'Client of the Name.'

5. See Noth, *op. cit.*, pp. 122–126. The Phœnician god-name Eshmun is probably derived from it.

tion of the South-Arabians with the West-Semites of the north. The problem arises as to their common origin. What was the habitat of the original stock? There has been so much movement across the Peninsula in every direction that history gives no formula. Within historic times the movement has generally been northwards, and the Yemenite migrations gave birth to some of the most important tribes and states in the north. This movement, however, was due to the collapse of the South-Arabic civilization. On the other hand, we know of the Sabæan movement southwards from the Syrian Desert and there have been notable cases where northern conquering groups have entered the Yemen and established themselves as the ruling castes.[6] The evidence goes to prove that the ruling classes which made the South-Arabian civilization came from the north. There the Semitic genius produced in a land of unique natural possibilities an artificial civilization that compares with the civilization of Babylonia, only far more wholly Semitic, for in Babylonia the Semites built upon the alien Sumerian civilization. It is of rare interest to observe the relationship of these far-flung West-Semites, in Babylonia, Palestine-Syria, and South Arabia.

But our interest in the Hebrews must ever concern itself with their religious genius, and we naturally inquire into the relations between their religion and that of the South-Arabian culture.[7] The religion of that southern field is polytheistic, as

6. Bury, *Land of Uz*, p. 293, states: "The supreme head of a tribal confederation is the Sultan. He is never a tribesman himself, but comes of an alien aristocracy imported by the senior confederate chiefs, or is a scion of some ancient house whose founder emigrated with a small following." Grohmann, *Südarabien*, p. 72, notes Bury's statement, but denies it as far as the Yemen is concerned.

7. For a small selection of literature consult Hommel, *Ancient Hebrew Tradition*, pp. 224 ff., etc., and his chapter on Arabia in Hilprecht, *Explorations in Bible Lands*, p. 732; D. Nielsen, *Die altarabische Mondreligion und die mosaische Ueberlieferung*

we might expect, with a very large nomenclature of names and epithets of deities. Many of these gods, some who came to hold distinguished national position, are local *numina* or *els*, quite similar to the *baals* of Canaan.[8] However, there stands out a definite astral triad of highest deities, and in this respect the religion is in sharp contrast to the far more extensive pantheons of the northern civilizations, while it is distinguished from the eclectic Sumerian-Akkadian religion of Babylonia in remaining pure Semitic. This triad consists of Moon, Sun, and Morning (or Evening) Star, a family group of Father, Mother, and Son corresponding to the Babylonian trinity, Shamash, Sin, Ishtar. The Moon has the preëminence even as he had in the elder Babylonian religion, before settled agricultural society had shifted the center of gravity to the Sun; he is masculine, as is the Babylonian Sin, and as is the prevailing word for the moon in Hebrew. The Sun (*shams* = Heb. *shemesh*) is feminine; in Hebrew the word is both feminine and masculine, indicating the change of notion; in Babylonian Shamesh is wholly masculine. In South-Arabic she is mostly called by local or characteristic epithets, and the word appears in the plural denoting the *numina* of localities.[9] Their child (Classical Phosphorus-Lucifer) is masculine; his name is Athtar which in the form Ishtar-Ashtart[10] of the North-Semites has become feminine, the Classical Venus. The one

---

(1904), and his chap. V on the religion in his *Handbuch*. J. Hehn's *Die biblische und die babylonische Gottesidee* is a valuable work including the South-Arabian data. A useful summary is given by Tritton in art. 'Sabæans' in *Enc. of Religion and Ethics*.

8. The word *baal* is found in South-Arabic, and its presence there is proof of the ancient widespread use of the word.

9. For this degradation of a personal name to status of a common noun cf. the Babylonian *Ishtarati* 'Ishtars,' and the use of the corresponding Hebrew word for 'goddesses' alongside of 'baals,' i.e., 'gods,' e.g., Jud. 2:13.

10. The Masoretes vocalize this as Ashtoreth.

South Arabia and the Bible

biblical designation for the planet, *hêlêl*, is masculine (AV following Vulgate, 'Lucifer,' RVV 'day-star'), Is. 14:12.[11]

The Moon is designated by names found in North-Semitic,[12] but these designations occur but seldom, except that he is Sin in Hadhramot, and also never in personal names. He is known among the Minæans by the cognomen Wadd, 'love,'[13] in Kataban as Amm 'uncle,' and appears to be the national god of the Sabæans worshipped under an obscure name, generally vocalized as Il-mukah.[14] This anonymous, merely epithetical designation of the chief deity by different names is characteristic of South Arabia; it could lend itself indefinitely to syncretism and monism.

We have noted the occurrence of *il*, 'god,' in South-Arabic names. This word and its related *ilâh* also appear as individual god-names.[15] They are the same words as we find in Hebrew; the former as *el* only archaically and poetically and in name-formations. The latter appears generally in the plural *elôhîm*, which became the standing word for Deity in the Hebrew and in the monotheistic sense; the singular *elôh* = Aramaic and Arabic *ilâh*, is the standing name for God in Job and is so used in five other poetical passages. Of these *el* or *il* is the common Semitic word for 'god,' *ilâh* is

11. For opposite views for this shifting of gender see Barton, *Sketch of Semitic Origins*, and Nielsen, *Handbuch*, pp. 238 ff. The change of gender of this planet must be intrinsically related to the similar change in the case of the sun.

12. Warah, Sin, Shahar.

13. The same root is found in Elmodad (Almodad) of the Arabian genealogy, Gen. 10:26; see Chapter III. Cf. the Hebrew *dod* 'love,' i.e., 'Liebling,' used as meaning 'uncle,' 'next of kin,' e.g., Am. 6:10, and in name-formations as predicate of the deity, e.g., Dodo, Dodawahu (for Dodeyahu).

14. I.e., 'God of ward, reverence'? For the fullest discussion see Nielsen, *Der sab. Gott Il-mukah* (1910).

15. E.g., 'Il and Athtar,' Halévy, nos. 144, 150.

peculiar to the Aramæans and Arabs.[16] Hence the author of Job is true to historical color in insisting on this word. It is of interest to observe that the Hebrew word for Deity, *Elôhîm*, comes from a non-Hebraic element. The Arabs compounded *ilâh* with the article, producing *al-ilâh* which became *Allâh*, 'the God,' and Mohammad found this word ready at hand among the heathen Arabs, a pregnant term for his new religion. This formation is old, for in the Thamudene inscriptions of northwest Arabia the word appears with the dialectic article *ha* (as in Hebrew), producing *ha-ilâh*, and then *hallâh*. For an earlier period we possess Herodotus's testimony for the Arabian Alilat, 'the goddess.'[17] It may also be noticed that *Il* appears as a name of an individual deity in lists, a phenomenon occurring also in the north.[18]

The meaning of this word *il-el* has been widely discussed as to its implications; some theories have found in it primitive monotheism,[19] others a specific El-religion, others a simple *ad hoc* word for any object the religionist had in mind, e.g., the tribal god. It is certainly fallacious to read too much into the indefinite term. But it was a use of language which led to a fusing process of thought about the gods, and *il-ilâh* might in process of time come to be detached from other gods or else to subsume them and at last designate the One and Only God. We have the similar process in the Hebrew religion; 'the

16. The above statement is now to be corrected on the basis of the North-Syrian Ras Shamra texts of the fourteenth century, which offer *elohim* and its corresponding feminine *elohot*.

17. Her., iii, 3, as Alitta at i, 31; identical with Allat, one of the 'daughters of Allah,' named in the Koran in the reproach of Arab paganism.

18. E.g., in the Hadad Inscr. from Zenjirli.

19. See Hommel, *Anc. Heb. Tradition*, p. 76; Baethgen, *Beiträge*, pp. 270 ff.; Lagrange, *Études sur les religions sémitiques*, pp. 70 ff.

god,' *ha-elôhîm* (properly a plural!), comes to mean God; cf. Greek *Theos*.

At all events we have to bear in mind the potentialities of this word and recognize that there were possible 'tendencies towards monotheism,' as Zimmern has expressed it, working in the Arabian Peninsula. We cannot forget that out of that desert region proceeded the two great monotheistic religions of Moses and Mohammad, and we must be solicitous to discover and follow what clues we may in that obscure field.[20]

More tangible evidences of the South-Arabian religion are to be found in the epigraphic references to the cult and in the architectural remains that have been observed, although it is to be borne in mind that only the most fleeting observations have been made by hasty travelers watched by suspicious natives.[21]

The remains of the temples indicate massive constructions of small cellas and great walled areas, open-air mosques, or *mahram* as they are called. Remains of altars and incense altars have been found. A considerable part of the decoration must have consisted in the stone and bronze votive inscriptions, of which a great number have survived. The most notable of the sites examined is the Haram Bilkís, as the Arabs call it after the traditional names of the Queen of Sheba, in

---

20. Some texts celebrating the Merciful One, *Rahman* (*Corpus*, nos. 537–543—in one case 'the Merciful One who is in Heaven,' in another the Trinity being designated) are of interest as definitely Jewish or Christian, and yet with true Arab flavor and indicating an intermediate step towards Islam, which makes that title one of the crowning epithets of Deity; cf. Margoliouth, *Relations*, pp. 67 f. For the possible occurrence of the element Yʜwʜ in Lihyanian personal names see *ibid.*, p. 20.

21. See Nielsen's *Handbuch*, chaps. 4, 5, for the archæological remains, and for contacts between the South-Arabian and the Hebrew cult the excellent summary in Margoliouth, *op. cit.*, pp. 21 f.

the neighborhood of Marib; its dimensions were described above in Chapter VI.

It appears that the religion was aniconic as far as representation of the gods was concerned, although artistic representations of men and animals were abundant. In this respect the religion followed the primitive tradition of an imageless cult,[22] and corroborates the Hebrew tradition of its primitive religion expressed in the Second Commandment.

A number of parallels with the Hebrew cult and its terminology are found exclusively in the South-Arabian religion. The most interesting correspondence is the appearance, if we may accept the interpretation of some scholars, of Levites, male and female, in the North-Minæan texts of el-Ula, dedicated to the god Wadd.[23] If approved, this discovery throws great light on the Israelite Levites, whose name would indicate their cultic character, the word meaning according to its root 'follower,' i.e., of the god. And the female Levites may be compared to the 'ministering' or 'serving women at the door of the Tent of Meeting' provided for in the Levitical canon, Ex. 38:8, cf. 1 Sam. 2:22.

A temple apparatus, *mknt*, appears in the South-Arabic, which may be identified with the *mekônah* in Solomon's temple, translated in EVV with 'base,' a wheeled cart for handling

22. Cf. Wellhausen, *Reste arab. Heidentums,* pp. 101 ff.

23. See Chapter VI, Note 33. Cf. Hommel, *Anc. Heb. Trad.,* p. 278; the most extensive study is that by Grimme, 'Der südarabische Levitismus und sein Verhaltniss zum Levitismus in Israel,' *Muséon,* 1924, pp. 169–199. He holds that these persons were hierodules presented to the temple, persons who are otherwise vouched for in South Arabia. They would then be similar to the Nethinim of the Jewish cult, appearing in Chronicles, Ezra, Nehemiah. As such hierodules were largely alien captives, we may so account for the presence of Egyptian names among the early Levites; Moses, Phineas, possibly Aaron.

the *sacra*, 1 Ki. 7:27 ff. The place for 'boiling' the sacrifices, *mabsal*, appears in the sanctuary just as we learn of the cultic boiling in the primitive Hebrew rites, e.g., 1 Sam. 2:13 ff., Ex. 29:31. The *haj*, the word used for pilgrimage feasts in the Hebrew, e.g., Ex. 23:14–16, and especially for the greatest of them, the autumn feast, e.g., 1 Ki. 8:2, appears in the South-Arabic, even as it has survived as the technical name for the pilgrimage to Mecca. The religious tithe appears, and in the same word the Hebrew uses, *maʿser*; and this is corroborated by Pliny's statement (xii, 32) that a tithe of the incense trade was demanded by the priests of the god Sabis. The *kahal*, translated in EVV 'assembly' and generally expressing the ecclesiastical assemblage of Israel, e.g., Ex. 16:3, Ps. 22:22 (= our 'church,'), appears, as *khl* or *khlt*, in the South-Arabic as the national assembly, *Volkssammlung*; the word has undergone the same history as Greek *ekklesia*. A similar identity is that of South-Arabian *gw*, 'community,' with Hebrew *gew*, Job 30:5, enabling us to correct the 'midst' of EVV.[24] Of peculiar interest is a group of bronze inscriptions,[25] in which the donors do penance by this public profession for a *hattath* or trespass of sexual irregularities offending sacred places or seasons; the same word *hattath* is used in Hebrew for both sin, rather trespass, and the sin-offering; for the sin-offerings see the ritual in Lev. 4, and for the regulation of the sexual life Lev. 15. Also in the North Minæan inscriptions

---

24. For these two words see Rhodokanakis, *Grundsatz der Öffentlichkeit*, p. 41.

25. *Corpus*, nos. 523, 532, 533, 568; these all from Harim. Compare D. H. Müller, *Südarab. Alterthümer* (1899) pp. 20 ff., and Hartmann, *Die arabische Frage*, pp. 207 ff. Two more such bronze tablets have been recently acquired for Petrograd, and have been published by Ryckmans in *Revue Biblique*, 1932, pp. 393–397. Observe the durable material required for this intimate act of penance.

at el-Ula are found similar confessions of sin (*hattath*) and fornication.²⁶ Such confessions are otherwise unknown in the old Semitic world.

The present writer has published in the *Journal of Biblical Literature*, 1930, Part 4, a paper entitled 'The Year-Eponymate in the Hebrew Monarchy.' In this he attempts to demonstrate that upon a text-correction in 1 Ki. 4: 3, based on the Greek, the early Hebrew monarchy possessed a system of archons who were in charge of the calendar. A similar officialdom existed in Babylonia with the *limu*-officer and also in South Arabia with the *kabîr;* an identity of the Hebrew with the South-Arabian usage exists in the same term used for year, Hebrew *hóref*, Arabic *harîf*, thus evidently sharing in the Arabian vocabulary.²⁷

It is to be borne in mind that we possess only monumental inscriptions, and these of a limited and conventional character, but no documentary and literary texts such as we have in copious abundance from Egypt and Babylonia. And yet in these texts, although large parts of them are still obscure, we find extensive correspondences to the Hebrew ritual, which meas-

26. See Jaussen and Savignac, *Mission archéologique*, vol. II, nos. 28, 30, 32. This legal sensitiveness towards sexual offenses is unique.

27. Robertson Smith, Wellhausen, Nöldeke have abundantly registered the similarities between the religion of Israel and that of the North Arabs as illustrated in the Muslim traditions of the times of the Pagan Ignorance. To this literature may be added Nielsen, *Die altarabische Mondreligion* (1904), containing some rather venturesome conclusions. I may here simply call attention to the large number of correspondences in religious terminology, which also in many cases throw light upon the earlier history of the words. Thus there are the terms for 'priest' (*kohen*) Nazirite (*nazir*); for the pilgrimage feast (*haj*); the basis of the first element in the Hebrew refrain *hallelu-yah*; the roots for 'anoint' (*mashach*); 'devote,' i.e., 'taboo,' in Hebrew 'destroy' (*haram*); 'offer in sacrifice,' becoming in Hebrew 'pray' (*atar*); and for ritual cleanness and uncleanness (*tahar, tame*). Indeed for the religious vocabulary of the Hebrews we find the closest fellowship in the Arabic language.

ure up more than proportionately to the correspondences with other fields; indeed the actual philological identities already discovered are more numerous than those which relate the Babylonian religion with the Hebrew. The vista is open for still more 'light on the Bible' when Arabia comes at last to be scientifically explored and its monuments fully interpreted.

VIII

RELATIONS OF ARABIA WITH THE HISTORY AND CULTURE OF PALESTINE

In the present chapter I desire to discuss the bearing of our knowledge of Arabia upon the Bible. The discussion will be in part a summing up of what has been ascertained in the previous chapters, in part a gleaning of various items, and, finally, consideration of the chief elements of that relation, namely, in the sphere of religion.

We have learned that back of Palestine-Syria lay what appears to have been, in the large, a desert, yet a land which was throbbing with a fierce and energetic humanity. Out of it came clans, tribes, hordes, lusting to settle down in the Sown, constantly disturbing the peace of civilization and yet coming in not as blood-strangers but as kin. The Bible history presents the different peoples coming out of the desert, under different names, Amorites, Hebrews, Aramæans, Ishmaelites, Midianites, and innumerable smaller groups, all of whom contributed to the population of the Promised Land, refreshing its blood with more virile strains, as that civilization degenerated through luxury and inbreeding. But we have to be on our guard against thinking of that continuous invasion as one of rude barbarians, something like the incursions of the Huns and Goths into the Roman Empire or of Mongols and Turks with their catastrophic destructions of the Medieval Orient. Through those deserts ran great avenues of commerce connecting with oases and settled communities scattered over the Peninsula. The trade routes followed the lines of these oases, even as ancient shipping made its way from coast to coast, from island to island. The oasis with its water and palms and food supplies rendered such transit possible, while on the other hand the caravans kept those islet ports in touch with the larger world. They were like the junctions in our great transcontinental rail systems, growing from the status of nuclei of trade into important cities, becoming important in and for themselves. We have had occasion often to note these trade routes which crisscrossed the Peninsula, and which were better known to antiquity than they are in our own day. In all this lively business there was, as in our own world of shipping and railroading, the ugly practices of shippers in their efforts to hold their own and destroy their rivals' trade. The Arabs who manned and escorted the caravans were rough and hardy men, like the Buccaneers of the Spanish Main, when the lines were not drawn between piracy, privateering, and 'legitimate business.' But withal they were agents of civilization and themselves were affected by the culture they bore and by the larger human contacts they made. And their chiefs then as now were probably quite as much gentlemen as those they met in so-called civilization.

Nor was this civilization merely ephemeral and borrowed. At least in one quarter of the Peninsula, in the Yemen, there early developed a most remarkable culture with its arts and writing, with its peculiar theology and religiousness, and with a unique political constitution. Where the elements of this civilization came from we know not. The close association of the South-Arabians with the Hebrews and the 'Amorites' of the First Dynasty of Babylon, as their name-formation proves, would deduce them from the northwest of the Peninsula, having moved southwards, even as we learn of the Sabæan migration from the same quarter. But as we find that civilization it has become thoroughly native with its individual character, while it has gained the position of purveyor of culture throughout the Peninsula. We have then to regard South Arabia, along with Babylonia and Egypt, as a third center of civilization in the Old Semitic world. We will now examine some of those points of contact between the land of the Bible and what must be definitely admitted as Arabian civilization.

Early Arabian Letters

No truer index of the culture of a people is found than in its possession of a script in which to express its spirit; and also no vehicle is better fitted to enlarge the area of a culture, bringing outside lands under its spell. In the modern world the language-*motif* has been a subtle but powerful political element; we may think of the cosmopolitan bearing of Spanish and French and English, as at once representatives and propagandists of their respective cultures. Even the script plays its part as a sacramental sign of the spoken language; witness the Westernization of the script of Turkish in the new Ottoman State, the essays in this direction in the conservative empires of China and Japan. In the ancient Orient there was the spread of the cuneiform script far beyond the realms of Babylonia, with its adoption by all kinds of alien peoples, to the east in Elam, to the north among the Cappadocians, the Haldians, and the Hittites.[1] The invention of the so-called

1. There has been noticed above (Chapter IV, Note 43) the discovery of texts in a Hebraic dialect at Ras Shamra on the coast of North Syria near Latakia. The interest of the third text for the Arabian question is indicated in that Note. For the literature

History and Culture of Palestine

Phœnician alphabet was a powerful agent of culture with its cosmopolitan effect in suppressing the clumsy cuneiform script even in its own home and in giving writing to the peoples of Asia, of the Mediterranean, the Greeks and the Romans, and ultimately to the whole world. This alphabet was early adopted by the Aramæans and doubtless was an agent in making Aramaic the *lingua franca* of the whole northern Semitic world, reducing the ancient Babylonian language and its script to the archaic level of an esoteric holy language.

These observations lead us to weigh the significance of the early possession of the alphabet by the South-Arabians. How far back its history goes we cannot tell; the inscriptions go back into the first half of the first millennium and vouch for a culture which had arisen far earlier. Even in the oldest South-Arabic inscriptions we find a well-fixed script of unique form, of what we might style, after printer's language, Gothic characteristic.[2] Centuries must be postulated for the development of this peculiar form of alphabet. What its relations with the more primitive form of the so-called Phœnician alphabet are is still a moot question with epigraphists. There are those, e.g., Dussaud, who believe that it is to be derived rather from Greek forms of the alphabet than from the Semitic script. Some scholars, e.g., Hommel, would argue for the priority of the South-Arabian script over the Phœnician,

bearing on the two earlier texts I refer to an article of mine in the *Journal of the Oriental Society*, 1933, with a note on the bibliography, p. 97. A popular account of the excavations at Ras Shamra is presented by the excavator M. Schaeffer in the *Nat. Geog. Mag.*, Oct. 1930, and in a series of articles in the *Illustrated London News*, November 2, 1929, November 29, 1930, November 21, 1931, March 12, 1932, February 11, 1933. J. Friedrich has recently published an admirable brief survey in *Der Alte Orient*, vol. 33, parts 1–2 (end of 1933).

2. The inscriptions also refer to legal 'books' or 'documents'; see the writer's note, *Journ. Am. Or. Soc.*, 1917, p. 164.

which position would logically lead us to seek the origin of the alphabet in far South Arabia.[3] But avoiding the problems of the genealogy of the forms of the alphabet, we have to mark this significant fact that its belt was spread along the whole western littoral of Syria and Arabia as far as the Yemen, a thousand or more years before Christ. Further, in later ages we find the South-Arabic alphabet pressing north and adopted by peoples of western Arabia and the eastern confines of Palestine-Syria, coming there into competition with the Aramaic form of the alphabet until it was finally suppressed by what we call the Arabic script, itself a product of the Aramaic alphabet. This story is expressive of the far-reaching effect of the culture of South Arabia. We have, therefore, to correct our natural idea of the barbarous desert-land of Arabia and visualize centers and avenues of higher culture which surrounded and closely touched the Bible lands.

In regard to the alphabet, recent discoveries have vastly enlarged our perspective of its history. First came the discovery of the Phœnician inscription of king Ahiram of Byblos, dated by most scholars as of the thirteenth century B.C., carrying the history of the Phœnician alphabet back for two or three centuries behind the earliest known inscriptions in that script.[4] More sensational in its prospect is the discovery of a written alphabetic script in the desert of Sinai, which the Egyptian archæologists, in view of the attendant Egyptian remains, carry back to the age of the great Sesostris, about

3. For the descent of the Southern alphabet from the Phœnician see Lidzbarski's argument, *Ephemeris*, vol. I, 109 ff.

4. Discovered by Montet at Gebal-Byblos (whence the Gebalites of 1 Ki. 5:18) on the Syrian coast. It was published by Dussaud in *Syria*, 1924, pp. 135 ff.; see also Torrey for text and fresh interpretations in *Journ. Am. Or. Soc.*, 1925, pp. 269 ff. Three other texts of the same age and quarter have been since published.

2000 B.C. It must be confessed that few of the words have been interpreted with certainty, but there can be little doubt that we possess here a primitive stage of the alphabet when it was emerging from suggestions obtained from the Egyptian hieroglyphic script, while the language is Semitic.[5]

Now there is one capital bearing of this discovery upon the Bible history. We find an apparently rude people in the Sinai desert making use of an alphabet before the age of Moses, indeed for centuries, according to Egyptologists. While this invention of the Semitic alphabet need not at all be ascribed to the Sinai district, although many distinguished scholars so infer,[6] nevertheless it is of high interest that the first references to writing in the Bible appears in the story of the Exodus. After the defeat of Amalek, Ex. 17:8 ff., in a Yahwistic (J) section, we read that Moses was bidden to "write this for a memorial in a book."[7] In the subsequent narratives of the Pentateuch there are the traditions of the writing of the laws given by Moses. The elder natural skepticism, once shared in

5. For these 'Serabit Inscriptions' see the articles by Butin and Lake in the *Harvard Theol. Review*, January 1928, April 1932. For the most recent discussion of the bearings of this alphabet see Sprengling, *The Alphabet*, etc., an Oriental Institute Communication, Chicago, 1931. A fragment of similar script has been recently discovered in Palestine, and published by W. R. Taylor in the *Journ. Palestine Or. Soc.*, 1930, pp. 17 ff., 79 ff.

6. So Gardiner, *Pal. Expl. Fund Quarterly Statement*, 1929, p. 55: to south and east of Palestine, perhaps in Midian.

7. 'A book' with Greek, AV, RVV, not 'the book' with JV; the articulated noun is used generically, cf. Num. 5:23, 1 Sam. 10:21. In Dan. 1:4 it means 'literature,' not 'learning' with EVV. However in the ancient North-Hebrew inscription of Kalammu (tenth century) *sefer* means 'inscription,' and the word is so used in the Safaitic inscriptions of North Arabia (see Grimme, *Texte und Untersuchungen zur safatenisch-arab. Religion*, Glossary, p. 185); and such may well be the meaning of the word here. Evidently in Job 19:23, "Oh that my words were inscribed in a *sefer*, that with iron pen and lead they were graven in the rock forever," *sefer* must mean inscription, not book. May the ancient tradition in our passage refer to an inscription cut by Moses?

by the writer, regarding the existence of the Semitic alphabet in the second millennium, which led conservative scholars like Naville to postulate cuneiform autographs of the Mosaic laws, is now dispatched for good; the alphabet existed by the middle of the second millennium and an archaic form of it is now found in Sinai, in the very region where the Hebrew tradition makes Moses write inscriptions and laws, and antedating his age. Indeed these discoveries, pushing back the age of the Semitic or Hebrew alphabet by centuries, force upon us a very different aspect for the culture of the West-Semitic lands. The story how "a young man of (Trans-Jordanic) Succoth wrote down for Gideon the princes of Succoth and its elders, seventy-seven men," Jud. 8:14, is corroborated by this new light as to the early spread of literary culture. And the implications of the ostraka inscriptions of the Harvard excavations at Samaria reveal the widespread and ready use of the alphabet for ordinary, commonplace purposes as far back as the ninth century.[8]

We are now in a position to trace the propagation of the South-Arabic script with its language and religion northwards. We have already observed (Chapter VI) the existence of a northern Minæan colony in the northwest of Arabia with its Minæan inscriptions. And the far-flung extent of the South-Arabians appears in the discovery of their inscriptions in southern Babylonia and northeastern Arabia.[9] With the

8. See Reisner, Fisher, and Lyon, *Harvard Excavations at Samaria* (1924); J. W. Jack, *Samaria in Ahab's Time* (1929); A. W. Bertholet, *History of Hebrew Civilization*, pp. 95 ff. I understand 'the pledge' to be taken from his brothers by David in I Sam. 17:18, to have been a written receipt.

9. An epitaph found at Warka by Loftus in 1857, given by Hommel, *Chrestomathie*, p. 113 (the father of the deceased bears the biblical name Esau); two inscriptions found at Taj in Kuweit by Captain Shakespear, *Geog. Journal*, 1922, p. 59, plate opposite

Minæan group another is to be associated geographically, that of the Lihyanian inscriptions; then there is the so-called Thamudene group of graffiti scattered through northwest Arabia, the age of which is much disputed; and in the volcanic region of es-Safa, east of the Druse Mountain, the northeastern scarp of Trans-Jordan towards the desert, there exists another script, the so-called Safaitic, belonging to the early Christian era. All these three scripts are offspring of the South-Arabic alphabet. They followed the northward movement of the trade from the South and present an astounding witness to the elements of civilization in the desert borders of Syria-Palestine.[10]

This fact of early indigenous Arabic scripts involving varieties of spelling throws light upon two etymological puzzles in the Patriarchal story. According to Gen. 17:5 the Lord announced to Abram that "thy name shall no more be called Abram, but they name shall be Abraham; for the father of a multitude of nations do I make thee." Now Abram is a good ancient West-Semitic name, appearing in the Akkadian, and also elsewhere in the Old Testament as Abi-ram, Num. 16:1; it means 'the (divine) Father is high.' The expanded form Abraham is interpreted in the Genesis text as 'Father of a multitude (*hamon*) of nations,' i.e., as though *Ab-hamon*, an impossible etymology. Various attempts have been made to explain 'Abraham' from the Akkadian, but without success. But the South-Arabic shows the way out. There the letter *h*

p. 325; two texts from Ur published by E. Burrows, 'A New Kind of Old Arabic Writing from Ur,' *Journ. Roy. As. Soc.*, 1927, pp. 795 ff.

10. For presentation of this epigraphic material reference may be made, *inter al.*, to Dussaud, *Les Arabes en Syrie avant l'Islam*; Nielsen in his *Handbuch*, pp. 37–49; H. Jensen, *Geschichte der Schrift*, pp. 134 ff.; the section on Script in art. 'Arabia' in *Enc. of Islam*.

is often used apparently as designation of presence of a vowel, the exact rules for which use have not been agreed upon by scholars.[11] Now this use appears to have been followed in our name: along with the unvocalized 'BRM the Arabian spelling 'BRHM was also possible. Then finally in the course of time the *h* was understood as a consonant, the word was pronounced Abraham, consequently an explanation had to be given of the relation of the two forms, and hence the midrashic tradition that is given in the story. And interestingly enough the spelling of the name of Abraham's wife in the same story offers a similar play, v. 15: "As for Sarah thy wife, thou shalt not call her name Sarai, but Sarah shall her name be." Now the element -*ai* is the ancient Arabic feminine ending equivalent to -*a*(*h*), the equivalent Hebrew form for the feminine. That is, the two terminations mean the same thing, and as -*ai* came in Arabic to be pronounced -*a*, 'Sarai' and 'Sarah' were only different spellings for one and the same pronunciation.[12]

Another Patriarchal name, Jacob, Ya'kob, interpreted as the 'heel-man,' Gen. 25:26, can best be explained from the meaning of the root in the South-Arabian dialect of the Ethiopic; there it means 'to guard,' and 'God-guards,' Ya'kob-el (as the name actually occurs in Egyptian texts), gives an excellent name-formation.[13] Again it is of interest to note that

11. For the latest discussion, on phonetic grounds, see Rhodokanakis in *Studien zur Lexicographie u. Grammatik des Altsüdarabischen*, Heft 1, 1915, pp. 12–56 (in *Sitzungsberichte* of the Vienna Academy). Similarly the Moabite place-name Medeba is spelled in the Bible Meydeba, but in the Moabite Stone Mehdeba.

12. Similarly *meni* at Is. 65:11 translated 'Destiny' in RVV was originally vocalized *manai*, as feminine, corresponding to the name of the Arabian goddess in the Koran, Manát.

13. The root '*kb* in Hebrew otherwise means 'to supplant,' Gen. 27:36, and thence 'to deceive,' as at Jer. 9:4, and with probable paranomasia at Hos. 12:3. We have noted the occurrence of Esau in the South-Arabic; and Israel is etymologized by some scholars from the Arabic.

the word translated 'pottage' in Gen. 25:30 (not in v. 29), *adom*, on which a play is made with Esau's cognomen, Edom, is to be explained from the Arabic.[14]

More important still is the root of the Divine Name YHWH (our Jehovah). This name is interpreted in Ex. 3:14 from the corresponding form of the first person 'I am,' or 'I am that I am,' for which the Hebrew is 'Ehyeh' (see notes in RVV). That is, two roots are paired, *hwh* and *hyh*. Now the former is the actual Arabic equivalent of the latter, which is Hebrew, and while this may be only a case where we have a dialectic difference, *hawah* being older than *hayah*, it is of interest that we must go to Arabia to see the force of the Bible interpretation.[15]

The Wisdom of Arabia

This presence of a culture flung far and wide over the stretches of Arabia by an intensive and lucrative commerce and settled in oases which by man's handiwork could become themselves centers of civilization, throws light upon some obscure phrases and references of the Bible. One of these is the allusion to the 'Wise men of the East,' with whom Solomon might well vie, and who could be classed along with the sages of Egypt, e.g., 1 Ki. 4:29 ff.; indeed three such men are

14. See Skinner's *Commentary, ad. loc.* 'Edom' itself may be explained from both Hebrew and South-Arabic as the 'Man Clan.'

15. Some modern etymologies of the name, e.g., 'to cause to fall,' i.e., 'to rain,' or 'to love,' are wholly Arabian. The root *hawah* does appear in Hebrew in the sense of 'to mischance,' e.g., Job. 6:2, 'misfortune'; i.e., the original meaning of *hawah*, 'to fall, befall, become, be,' has been differentiated in the Hebrew, so that *hawah* = 'to mischance.' Cf. Arabic *haway*, 'hell.'

named, and two of these, Ethan[16] the Ezrahite, and Heman
are canonized in the tradition of the Psalter with their names
attached to certain Psalms in the rubrics. The Prophets make
similar allusions; Jer. 49:7: "Is wisdom no more in Teman?";
Obad. 8: "Shall I not in that day, saith the Lord, destroy the
wise men out of Edom and understanding out of the Mount
of Esau?"; and the Apocryphal Baruch, 3:22 ff., makes a
similar reference to the Hagarenes and the merchants of Mer-
ran (?) and Teman, who seek out wisdom and are 'mytholo-
gers.' The wise augur Balaam whom Balak king of Moab
fetched to curse Israel (Num. 22–24) appears—despite 22:5,
which localizes him at Pethor "by the River," i.e., Euphrates[17]—to have belonged to a region accessible to Moab, for in
his own words, 23:7, "Balak hath brought me from Aram
. . . from the Mountains of the East." The latter locality
must be the Mount of the East, Gen. 10:30 (see Chapter
III), and Aram must be the Aramæans of the Syrian Desert,
or better still 'Aram' should be changed to 'Edom.'[18] Also for
evidences of the extent of civilization in the Arabian land
there is the remarkable compilation of documents in Gen. 36
bearing on Edomite history, including a list of the Edomite
kings who ruled "before there reigned any king over Israel,"

16. An Arabic name doubtless, being the form *aytan*, 'steady'; the same word for
'perennial (stream)' in Amos 5:24, etc., against 'mighty' of EVV.

17. Cf. the obscure Aram-naharaim (EVV properly 'Mesopotamia') of Jud. 3:8, 10;
yet the district of Cushan-rishathaim must certainly be placed to the south of Judah.
There is no river '*nahar*,' there; a wady, *nahal*, such as the Wady ('brook') of Egypt
(e.g., Num. 34:5) could not be so designated. Original Edom may have been read,
with change of one consonant, as Aram (see next note), and this then expanded to
A.-naharaim.

18. So following a suggestion of Hommel's; see Meyer, *Die Israeliten*, pp. 376 ff.
The confusion of these two words is common in the Hebrew. Further, if we may read
Bal'am for Bela' in Gen. 36:32, Balaam was the first king of Edom.

vv. 31 ff. Again, Job's eldest counsellor Eliphaz the Temanite came also from Edom, being listed, apparently, as eldest son of Esau and father of Teman in Gen. 36:10, 11, and he speaks of traditions received "from wise men and their fathers," Job 15:18. If Edom is especially singled out as a home of wisdom, we have to remember that it lay across the great trade-routes of northwest Arabia and so could have enjoyed a privilege in culture such as that possessed by Edom's successor, the Nabatæan folk, and its ancient neighbor, the North-Minæan colony in Midian.[19]

In addition to these allusions to the Wise Men of the East there are two biblical passages which one tradition of interpretation assigns to an Arabian home, namely, Prov. 30, and 31:1–9. By a different construction the title of the latter can be made to read, more sensibly than by the Masoretic construction,[20] "the words of Lemuel the king of Massa," i.e., the latter word as the name of the Arabian tribe to the east of Palestine, instead of its significance as 'oracle' or 'burden' in EVV. In any case there is no Hebrew king Lemuel,[21] and the following passage may, as far as its contents go, be a piece of foreign origin. As for the title in chap. 30, the proper names Agur and Yakeh are not Hebraic; the former may be

---

19. See the very suggestive article by R. H. Pfeiffer, 'Edomite Wisdom,' in *Zeitschrift f. d. alttest. Wissenschaft*, 1926, pp. 13–26. Pfeiffer recalls the Arabic identification of Balaam with Lokman, the Arabian proverbialist, the counterpart of the Hebrew Solomon. The same scholar has since contributed to the same journal, 1930, pp. 66–73, an article on similar lines, 'A Non-Israelitic [i.e., Edomite] Source of the Book of Genesis,' a study of Gen. 36.

20. With the impossible 'Lemuel, a king.'

21. Lemu'el, or Lemo'el (v. 4), is a primitive name-formation, i.e., 'to God,' 'God's own'; cf. the equivalent Lael, Num. 3:24; Palmyrene Le-shamsh, 'the Sun's'; the Phœnician-Greek Leastartos, 'Astarte's (Josephus, *C. Ap.*, i, 18). Similar West-Semitic names are found in Akkadian texts: Zu-ilah, Sha-ili, Sha-Martu; see Ranke, *Early Bab. Personal Names*, pp. 26, 141 f., etc. So Methushael, 'man of God.'

found in South-Arabic, the latter can best be connected with
an Arabic and South-Arabic root.[22] The opening words of the
utterance translated by the EVV, "The man saith unto Ithiel,
unto Ithiel and Ucal," are quite obscure. The initial passage,
vv. 1–4, is of skeptical character, like the meditations of the
Arabian patriarch Job. The balance of the chapter, with exception of the use of YHWH in v. 9, belongs to cosmopolitan
wisdom.[23]

But the book above all of characteristic Arab flavor is that
of Job. A long line of distinguished scholars have claimed for
it an Arabic original. So first Ibn Ezra, the great Jewish com-
mentator of the twelfth century in his comment at Job 2:11.
The theory was taken up with massive philological argument
by the distinguished Arabist Schultens in his *Liber Jobi*, 1737,
and has never lost its supporters, among whom at present can
be named the eminent English Arabist Margoliouth and the
American scholars Pfeiffer and Foster. But it is to be observed
that the commentators find little room for this idea, confining
themselves to cases of etymology where Arabic appears to be
concerned.[24] This theory has its seductions for the present

22. It appears, e.g., in the South-Arabic name Wk'atht, and in the Sabæan god's
name Il-mukah (pronunciation uncertain).

23. For at least in one word in c. 30 there is considerable support for regarding it
as pure Arabic. This is the word *alkum*, v. 31, translated in EVV with "[a king against
whom] there is no rising up." This rendering is impossible in the Hebrew. But as
Arabic *al-kaum* it means 'the army' or tribal levy, and with the article *al* of classical
Arabic, unknown to other dialects. This interpretation is presented in SV margin: "when
his army is with him," similarly Moffatt, but more loosely. Arabists from Pococke to
Margoliouth (*Relations*, 30) accept this interpretation.

24. See Pfeiffer, *Edomite Wisdom*, noticed in Note 18, and F. H. Foster, 'Is the
Book of Job a Translation from an Arabic Original?' *Am. Journ. Sem. Languages*,
October 1932, pp. 21 ff. The book of Job appears verily to have cosmopolitan connections. There is the 'Babylonian Job,' translation in Barton, *Archaeology and the Bible*,
pp. 490 ff. G. A. F. Knight, *Nile and Jordan* (1921), presses its affiliations with Egyp-

writer, but he confesses to finding it not only unproved but also unnecessary. The author of the book is a man of culture, who on the one hand preserves the color of the *mis-en-scène*, but on the other draws from stores of encyclopedic knowledge. While the scenery is in general that of the desert steppes, the poet does not hesitate to go outside of his bounds and, for instance in his pictures of social conditions, to present features of the society of 'civilization.' His brilliant picture of mining operations in c. 28 suggests to us Arabia, the land of precious metals and stones, but no such extensive mining works as he describes are to be found there; he may have drawn his picture from travelers' tales of distant mines like those of Tarshish. He makes reference, if one favored interpretation be correct, to the pyramids of Egypt,[25] and so is not confined to local scenery.

But the book as a whole is primarily of value for our present study as presenting the intimate relation of the land of the Sown with the Desert. The land of Uz, whether to be placed in Edom with Musil, or with Wetzstein in the neighborhood of Jebel Hauran (Jebel ed-Drus), or by local tradition in Trans-Jordan, was familiar to the Palestinian as a well-known borderland by report or by personal traveled experience. The basic fold-story of Job may have arisen anywhere in the environs of Palestine; this settled its classical color and atmosphere for all time. The simple but grand portrait of the patriarchal sheikh Job admirably suited the author's purpose, while such a picture of primitive, non-Hebraic life allowed

tian literature. And C. J. Ball, *Book of Job* (1922), interprets it largely from Sumerian and even Chinese.

25. The word 'waste' or 'desolate places,' in 3:14. For 'pyramids' decide modern commentators, as Marti, Budde, and Moffatt so translates in his Bible.

the presentation of a great religious drama without conflict with Israel's particular dogmas.

In the introduction, taken from the folk-story, we have a definite allusion to the Sabæans and Kasdæans ('Chaldæans'), who once haunted the Syrian Desert to the east of Palestine.[26] But the references to desert life in the book are not such as to have lain beyond the ken of the cultured Hebrew. The classical allusion, by way of parable, to "the caravans of Tema and the companies of Sheba" losing their way in search of deceptive waters, 6:18 ff., does not require an Arabian home for the writer. Such was not a strange figure for the Israelite readers of the poem, any more than stories of ships and sailors are foreign to the knowledge of men of Anglo-Saxon blood.

The theology of the great poem is suggestive in one respect, in its claim of a monotheistic religion for the *dramatis personae*. With true instinct the name YHWH is generally avoided in the poem and in its place appear the old common Semitic word for 'god,' El; its Aramaic and Arabic equivalent Eló(a)h, originally Iláh; and Shaddai, an archaism taken from the Pentateuch, a name of God in the pre-Mosaic religion, in the combination El-Shaddai, translated in the English Bible by 'God Almighty' (Gen. 17:1, Ex. 6:3).[27] Now, as we saw in Chapter VII, *el* and *iláh* were known through the Arabian world, as inscriptions from South Arabia to the land of Midian show. In *iláh* we have the word that gave Mohammad his Allah, and there is reason to think that the notion of 'the God,' or 'God' as highest deity, or as an expression for the sum (*Inbegriff*) of Deity is of native Arabian development. At all events in putting a high theology into

26. See Chapter IV.
27. See Pfeiffer, *op. cit.*, p. 19, for statistics on the divine names.

the mouths of his actors the poet was not deserting the color
of his stage, and the work may be early evidence for considerable theological advance among the ancient Arabs.

Israelite Trade with Arabia

I leave the field of letters for that of politics. There is one
period in which Arabia played an important part in Israel's
history; and we can follow this drama of politics from Solomon's reign down to that of Azariah-Uzziah of Judah, who
died 740 B.C., that is for over 200 years. This close connection was due to the attempt of the united Hebrew monarchy
and then of the Judan state to control the Arabian trade that
had its outlet in northwest Arabia. The circumstances of the
Hebrew kingdoms have hardly been sufficiently realized. As
Semitic they were naturally commercial states, and yet they
were cut off by the Phœnician and Philistine control of the
seaports from trade expansion to the west. But the lucrative
routes of commerce running out of Arabia traversed the territories of Israel, whether to Gaza or to Damascus. It was for
the control of the Trans-Jordanic routes that Aram of Damascus and Israel fought their bitter feud for those centuries,
down to the Assyrian repression of Damascus about 800 B.C.
The actual control of the Arabian routes on the other hand lay
with the native peoples and traders of the Peninsula. What
we may call the land of Edom, the later center of the great
Nabatæan state, held the key to this nucleus of the avenues
of trade, and Edom was always Arabian in race and sympathy;
indeed the Arabs pushed forward their lines as far to the north
as possible and doubtless possessed for most of the time fairly
uninterrupted communication with Gaza. With Damascus in

possession of Trans-Jordan there was little left for the Israelite states, hardly the plums of trade tolls.

Now brief notices in 1 Ki. cc. 9, 10 report a remarkable
expansion of Israel's economics under King Solomon. He took
steps to establish his state as the principal middleman for the
overland trade between Farther Asia and Egypt, as is exhib-
ited in the trade in horses and chariots which he instituted, 10:
28 f. This commercial supremacy, short-lived indeed, was
possible because of the contemporary decadence of Assyria
and Egypt and the collapse of the Hittite empire, while the
rise of the powerful Aramæan states, notably Damascus, had
not yet taken effect. But more ambitious and inventive was
Solomon's policy of securing the Arabian trade from its
sources by developing a maritime route on the Red Sea. The
old vigor of Egypt as displayed by Queen Hatshepsut in her
navigation of those waters had long since disappeared.[28]
Meanwhile in the far South the Minæan state in South Arabia
was developing, it is a conservative estimate to say from 1000
B.C. Indeed we may suppose that Solomon's venture on the
sea was a direct challenge to this South-Arabian expansion,
which arrogated to itself the control of the whole length of
the routes of the Peninsula and probably with claims upon the
outlets of Gaza and Damascus and towards Egypt. And so
Solomon proceeded, with the technical help of Hiram and his
Phœnician shippers to "build a navy at Esyon-geber, which is
beside Eloth on the shore of the Red Sea in the land of

---

28. Trade on the Red Sea goes back to the Old Kingdom; a Sixth Dynasty text
states, "I have gone with my masters . . . eleven times to Byblos and Punt" (Somali
Land), and the Egyptian skippers on both the Mediterranean and the Red Sea appear
to have been Gebalites, sailors of Byblos, who were thus the predecessors of Hiram's
sailors by 2000 years. See Montet, *Byblos et l'Égypte* (1930), p. 8.

Edom," 9:26.[29] These ships were manned by 'Hiram's serv-
ants' (v. 27), for Israel had no sailors. The next verse tells
how "they came to Ophir and fetched thence gold, 420 talents, and brought it to king Solomon." With this there is a
parallel account from a distinct source (separated from its
place by the intrusion of the story of the Queen of Sheba and
the luxuriousness of the reign) in 10:22: "For the king had
at sea a Tarshish-navy[30] along with the navy of Hiram;[31] once
every three years came the Tarshish-navy bringing gold and
silver, ivory and apes and peacocks." Of this list the gold was
from Arabian Ophir. There is little definite information on
the presence of silver in Arabia in the *Periplus of the Erythræan Sea*. Silver always appears to have been imported into
Arabia; it may then have been obtained by Solomon ultimately from India.[32] The baboon is still found in the heights
of the Yemen and Hadhramot, but the Hebrew word for
monkey, *kop*, is Indian.[33] Peacocks, after the traditional trans-

29. Moritz, *Arabien*, p. 116, finds the older port Esyon-geber at present a watering
place with a name bearing the Arabic equivalents of the first element in the name, i.e.,
Ghadyan, by a salt marsh 50 km. north of Akaba, the former then in antiquity lying at
the ancient head of the Gulf. This identification was first proposed by Robinson, *Researches*, vol. I, 250 f. For the locality see Musil, *Arabia Petraea*, vol. II, part 1, 254 ff.,
with photographs. The name Elath, or Eloth, still survives in the spring Ayla at Akaba.

30. 'Ship of Tarshish' is technical for a large sea-going vessel. Cf. the term 'Hittite,'
i.e., Syrian, which Sennacherib uses of the ships he had built for him by Phœnician
craftsmen in Mesopotamian waterways for use in the Persian Gulf; see Luckenbill,
Ancient Records, vol. II, pp. 145, 148, 154.

31. This note distinguishes two national, but coöperative, enterprises.

32. See Index in Schoff's edition. For references to silver in South Arabia see
Grohmann, *Südarabien*, pp. 169 ff., who notes that the first report on silver mines is
found in Hamdani of the ninth century. Some silver is found in the Yemen and in Oman.

33. See Bury, *Arabia Infelix*, pp. 27 f.; *Handbook of Arabia*, p. 227; for Arabic
references, Grohmann, *Südarabien als Wirtschaftsgebiet*, p. 46. Hatshepsut's expedition
brought back monkeys from Punt; Breasted, *History of Egypt*, p. 276. But earlier than
this enterprise in the Story of the Shipwrecked Sailor, preserved in a Middle Kingdom
papyrus, the hero tells how he brought back from Punt, on the Red Sea, incense, ivory,

lation of the last term in the list could have come only from India. Another Indian product would be the 'sandalwood' with which the king inlaid his buildings and musical instruments, 10:12 f.[34] This commodity was brought from Ophir along with gold and precious stones, and the latter item appears in the Arabian trade of Eze. 27.[35] We have not to think that the Israelite-Phœnician navy sailed as far as India to get Indian products; they made their purchases and exchanges at Arabian ports whither the Indian merchants had brought their wares. As remarked in Chapter IV, the knowledge of the monsoons of the Arabian Sea must have been common in very early times to the sailors of those shores, although first made known to the Western world and so 'discovered' by the Greek Hippalus.[36]

This profitable commercial enterprise could not have outlasted Solomon's reign. There came the division of the king-

greyhounds, monkeys, apes, etc.; see Erman, *Literature of the Ancient Egyptians* (1927), pp. 29 ff. Monkeys and birds were brought from the far Orient in Roman days; see Warmington, *Commerce between the Roman Empire and India*, pp. 147, 152.

34. *Almug* in Ki., *algum* in Ch. The word is derived by philologists from Sanskrit-Tamil *valgu*; see Schoff, *op. cit.*, pp. 36, 152, 175. Another Indian wood may be the ebony of the Arabian trade in Eze. 27:15, but it may also be African in origin; see Schoff, pp. 36, 153.

35. V. 22. For the semi-precious stones, onyx, etc., of the Yemen, see Grohmann, *op. cit.*, pp. 175–181.

36. A Phœnician dedicatory inscription engraved on ivory has been found by Woolley at Ur and is studied by E. Burrows in *Journ. Royal Asiatic Soc.*, 1927, pp. 791 ff. (cf. Savignac, *Revue biblique*, 1928, pp. 257 ff.; Dussaud, *Syria*, 1928, pp. 267 ff.). It is to be placed between the eighth and ninth centuries. It may be a bit of booty from Phœnicia, or possibly represents a Phœnician trading colony, come from overseas. For early Phœnician advance towards Indonesia see the suggestive paper by the Dutch scholar E. Schröder, 'A Phoenician Alphabet,' *Jour. Am. Or. Soc.*, 1927, pp. 25 ff., i.e., Phœnician in contrast with the Aramaic origin of the Indic alphabets in general.

We may simply note the problem of the relation of the Judgment of Solomon, 1 Ki. 3, with the similar story in the Mahoshadha Jataka, Cambridge ed. of the Jatakas, vol. VI, 163; see Rawlinson, *Intercourse between India and the Western World*, p. 11.

dom, the hegemony of the Damascene state in Syria, which for the most part held Trans-Jordan, and the Edomite movements for freedom from Judah, e.g., the revolt of the Edomite prince narrated as for Solomon's reign in 1 Ki. 11:14–22, 25.[37] When at last Judah and Israel came together in peace and marriage-alliance between Jehoshaphat and the dynasty of Omri (c. 860 B.C.), and a better front could be made by the Hebrew states against their common enemy, Syria, there is recorded, 1 Ki. 22:48 f., the attempt of Jehoshaphat to build 'a ship' at Ezion-geber on the Red Sea for the resumption of the Ophir traffic. But the ship was wrecked. Then Ahaziah, son and successor of Ahab, offered to coöperate in the expensive and hazardous enterprise, but Jehoshaphat refused. So another attempt at the Arabian trade was frustrated.[38] Once again we learn of Judah establishing itself on the Red Sea. The able and successful Azariah-Uzziah (died 740 B.C.) "built Elath and restored it to Judah," this new port replacing the old Ezion-geber (probably now sanded up), 2 Ki. 14:22. 1 Ch. 26:7 tells of the same king's successful operations against the Arabs and the related Meúnim (see below). But this seaward expansion was short-lived. In the reign of his son Ahaz, Aram, the hereditary enemy of Israel, in the person of its king Resin (or Rason) "recovered Elath to Aram and drove the Jews from Elath; and the Edomites came to Elath and dwelt there, unto this day," 2 Ki. 16:6, i.e., until the composition of the book of Kings in the sixth century. But before that period Assyria entered into dominion over all those lands, succeeded by Babylonia; the

37. Read 'Edom' for 'Aram' ('Syria') in the last verse.

38. The Hebrew has plural, 'ships,' but the Greek reads singular, 'ship,' which is actually supported by the singular of the Hebrew verb.

Judæan state never again, even in its ages of restoration under the Maccabees and Herod the Great, recovered the head of the Red Sea.[39]

The Sabæans and the Minæans in the Bible

The record of Solomon's expeditions on the Red Sea is accompanied with another which is generally dismissed as a romantic tale, the story of the Queen of Sheba's visit to him, 1 Ki. 10. There was once the objection that no such cultured Sheba existed at that early date; with the discovery of its civilization it seemed to be the Minæans and not the Sabæans who had the priority; while with the abundance of royal inscriptions no queens appear in the lists. But, as observed in Chapter IV, on the basis of Assyrian inscriptions from Tiglath-Pileser to Sennacherib the Sabæans were still in northwest Arabia, in the very neighborhood where the book of Job locates them, 1:15, and they were purveyors of the South-Arabian trade, whether or not they had as yet ensconced themselves in the Yemen, even as the Queen of Sheba brought precious gifts of the South to Solomon. Moreover, the Assyrian inscriptions name 'queens of the Arabs' in conjunction with the listings of the Sabæans and other Arabian tribes in the northwest; we have noticed the names of two such ladies, Samsi and Zabibe, while a number of other queens appear in early North-Arabian history.[40] Accordingly, the biblical *mis-en-scène* is quite correct.

39. The British have imperiously drawn the lines of their Mandate in Palestine and Trans-Jordan so that both impinge on the Red Sea, thus offering possibilities of over-land transportation between the Mediterranean and the waters of the Indian Ocean through all-British territory. Ibn Saúd has refused to accept this arbitrary delimitation.

40. Besides the two queens mentioned there are named: Yati'e, Luckenbill, *Ancient*

History and Culture of Palestine

These northern Sabæans of the Syrian Desert were then those who in conjunction with the Aramæan Kasdæans ravaged the possessions of Job's family. We have no reason, as with some scholars, to change the reading 'Sabæans' or to regard them as southern Sabæans, with the result that such distant raiding expeditions would be absurd.[41] On the other hand in the post-Exilic books of the Old Testament we have references to the contacts of the Jews with the Sabæans of South Arabia. In Joel 3:4 ff. is a long condemnation of the Phœnicians and Philistines for plundering the treasures of the temple and for selling Jews into slavery to the Greeks; in retribution the oracle declares: "I will sell your sons and daughters into the land of the Sons of Judah, and they will sell them to the men of Sheba, a distant nation." This is another testimony to the great overland slave-trade which passed across Arabia, an earlier reference to which is found in Amos's denunciation of the similar trade between Gaza and

Records, vol. II, 130; Telhunu, *ibid.*, p. 158, under Sennacherib; Tabu'a, imposed as queen by Esarhaddon over the oasis Adumu, biblical Dumah, *ibid.*, p. 214 (also an unnamed queen, p. 222). A North-Minæan queen, Udbay, queen of PSMM', is recorded in Euting, no. 57, given by Hommel, *Chrestomathie*, p. 113; and a Lihyanian queen in Jaussen and Savignac, II, 391. A 'queen of the Nabatæans' appears, Schürer, *Gesch. d. jud. Volkes*, vol. I, 741; there is the famous Zenobia, queen of Palmyra, in the third century; and a Christian Ghassanid queen, Mawia, who reigned 373–78 A.D., Caussin de Perceval, *Histoire*, vol. II, 218; Kammerer, *Pétra*, p. 331. This history of queens comes down to our own day; the empress Judith of Abyssinia, alleged descendant of Solomon and the Queen of Sheba, died April 2, 1930. To be sure the biblical figure of the Queen of Sheba may be a composition of various Arabian elements. Zwemer, *Across the World of Islam* (1930), p. 94, notes the presence of women judges in ancient Arabia.

41. Dhorme, *Revue biblique*, 1911, p. 105, would locate these northern Sabæans at Dedan, i.e., el-Ula; Musil, *Topographical Itineraries*, I, 288, both here and at Maon east of Petra; Glaser, *Skizze*, pp. 387 ff., in the Jebel Shammar of Nejd and also at the Wady ash-Sheba near Medina. A village, 'Pool of the Sabæans,' is named in a Greek inscription of the Leja, Dussaud, *Les Arabes en Syrie*, p. 10. So uncertain are the identifications of ancient Arabian geography!

Edom, and, if the passage be authentic, between Tyre and Edom, Am. 1:6–10. According to the passage in Joel the Jews will become the middlemen for this trade southwards to the Yemen. This nefarious traffic between Arabia and the Mediterranean was of ancient and vast character, and Gaza was its Asiatic emporium.[42] For this trade we have interesting testimony from the Sabæan quarter, in an inscription which details the devotion to a temple of female slaves, whose names and origin are given.[43] The mutilated list shows the following identifiable localities from which dedicated slaves had been bought and forwarded: Gaza, whence three persons, Yathrib (later Medina), Dedan, and two from *Msr*, probably Misraim, Egypt. It is interesting to observe that this trade moved both ways between north and south, and as Jewish slaves were shipped to the Greek lands, so, in the pious expectation of the Jews, their neighboring adversaries were to be sold into slavery to far-off Yemen.

There is yet another people named in post-Exilic books, the Greek renderings of which have induced many scholars to find in them a South-Arabian folk. These are the Minæans, who according to the accepted view originally held the hegemony in the Yemen, until the Sabæan state dispossessed them. Their chief capital was Maín, whence the Greeks formed their word Minæan.[44] The following biblical data are cited for possible identification with these Minæans: Jud. 10:12, Maon, where

42. For Gaza as the northern end of the Arabian trade, see Schürer, *Gesch.*, vol. II, 110 ff. The center for the Greek trade in slaves was Delos (where a Southern-Arabic inscription has been found), Moritz, *op. cit.*, p. 82; cf. Dussaud, *op. cit.*, p. 79.

43. Halévy, nos. 190, 231–234, in Hommel, *Chrestomathie*, p. 117; cf. Hartmann, *Die arabische Frage*, pp. 206 ff.

44. For the Greek references see Sprenger, *Alte Geog. Arabiens*, p. 211. The name 'Maín' is etymologically identifiable with the biblical 'Maon' discussed below.

however the Greek reads 'Midian'; 1 Ch. 4:41, 2 Ch. 26:7, Meúnim, in the former case the consonants (not the Krê) spelling Meínim, and so exactly identical with the South-Arabian name; the Greek at 2 Ch. 20:1, correcting the Hebrew repetition of 'Ammonites' and reading, "the Sons of Ammon and with them some of the Minaeans;" the Greek at 26:8 replacing 'Ammonites' with 'Minaeans.' Also in Ezra 2:50 = Neh. 7:52 a family of Meúnim is mentioned among the Nethinim or temple-slaves, hierodules, at Jerusalem—possibly obtained through the South-Arabian slave traffic. In all these cases this people appears on the southern frontier of Judah and are named in conjunction with Philistines and Arabs, or at 2 Ch. 20:1 with Moab and Ammon. Now in Chapter VI we have noticed the Minæan colony at el-Ula in northwest Arabia, and also a Minæan inscription probably of the age of Darius I recording the successful resistance of a Minæan caravan against their assailants in the borderland of Egypt and Syria. Hence it is argued by some that we must postulate a potent northward extension of the Minæan empire.[45] But such a pressure as is indicated by the biblical references was hardly in the power of the distant Minæans; the caravan inscription does not imply a military expedition. Possibly the Minæan colony at el-Ula in coöperation with its neighbors, Arabs and Edomites, was able to make considerable aggression on the southern borders of Judah. Or, as the word Maon is good Hebrew, we may look elsewhere for these Meúnim, and locate them possibly, along with Musil, at Maon to the east of Petra.[46] Then a later tradition would have identified the people with the famous Minæans of the South.

45. E.g., Hommel, *Ancient Heb. Tradition,* chap. 8.
46. Musil, *Topographical Itineraries,* vol. I, 243 ff.

A similar process is seen in the Greek rendering of 'the Naa-mathite,' tribal epithet of Job's friend Zophar, by 'Minæan' (actually 'king of the Minæans' at Job 2:11 and in the Greek colophon to the book).[47]

Hebrew and Arabian Religion

There remains for the Bible student the question of most profound interest: What is the bearing of Arabia upon the Hebrew religion? At first the sources at hand for an answer appear very small. There are the testimonies handed down through Islamic tradition and Classical sources.[48] Surface explorations have been made in northwest Arabia, where the desert and human barbarians have swallowed up the records of the past. Only Petra remains there as a Pompeii of a one-time flourishing Arab civilization. In the far South the archæological discoveries that have been made reveal vastly greater possibilities, with the picture we can now sketch of a highly developed social and economic system and an elaborate religionism. We can follow the traces of this civilization extending northward by the western shores of Arabia till it is well abreast of the boundaries of Palestine and Syria. Our prospect takes in one-time flourishing oases in the heart of the Peninsula, like el-Ula in the land of Midian, or Teima the midway station to Babylonia. We fill out these scattered pieces of evidence from the reports bearing upon Arabia from the Greek, Akkadian, and Hebrew records. We observe the in-

47. The Hebrew at 1 Ch. 4:41 was then an editorial change in the same direction.

48. E.g., as given by W. Robertson Smith in his *Religion of the Semites*, Wellhausen in his *Reste arabischen Heidentums*, and Nöldeke in art. 'Arabs,' *Enc. Religion and Ethics*.

sistence which the Bible makes upon the racial, political, and economic relations with Arabia. We come to realize that Israel had its face turned towards those quarters we call the Desert, and that this was its nearest neighbor. With the Arabs they were more closely related in original and ever-replenished stock, in common religion and social formation, than with Philistia, Phœnicia or Syria, while the civilizations of Egypt and Mesopotamia were distant and alien. We may not speak of a civilization of Arabia in the same terms as for the fertile and populous lands of the Nile and Euphrates. The Arabian civilization was one of scattered market towns and caravan stations, which possessed in their peculiar way the competitions and stimuli that are the prime factors of civilization. In denying these possibilities the fault lies with us moderns; it were as fallacious to deny an Ægean or a Phœnician civilization in the Mediterranean on the ground that such was not spelled in the later terms of empire, and could not consist only of fragile ships and small trading factories. The camel and the oasis make Arabia a similar.

If we honor the scattered facts in our possession, attempt to piece them together, and withal use our imagination to get 'a vision of the whole' as Koheleth says, then we obtain the complement to what the tradition of the Bible has to say about its religion. According to its own consciousness, expressed again and again in legend and the Prophets, it was desert-born.[49] It is somewhat the fashion to scoff at the legends of the Wanderings in the Desert, but it is these items, without

---

49. A protest may be made against the exaggerated emphasis laid by Assyriologists upon Abraham's associations with Ur of the Chaldees. Moses is more historical than Abraham, and all we know of the latter's association with that city of hoary civilization is that his father early took him away from it. According to the oldest source (J) Harran was "the land of his nativity," Gen. 24:7.

discrimination as to so-called 'sources,' which are illustrated from actual Arabian life, both contemporary and of historical record. If that region is one of 'the simple life,' it was not a land of unmitigated barbarism as we innocently depict it. Out of barbarism a lofty religion could not have arisen; but on the other hand religion is not a product of high civilization. There was enough of a culture among the tribes of the desert, Amorite, Hebrew, Aramæan, Arabic, that came to constitute the complex of Israel, and a sufficient measure of civilized contact with the peoples of the desert in the later biblical history, to honor the tradition of the Hebrew religion that it came from the desert. There still remains an unsolved x in the problem of the origin of 'Yahwism,' as it is sometimes tagged; other sources have failed, Arabia supplies, secularly speaking, much of the solution.

Renan maintained the thesis that the peculiar metaphysics of Arabia is sufficient to explain the birth of the three great monotheisms which the Semites have given to the world; this position is now noticed only to be denied. But there is the unavoidable fact that out of the land of Midian and the Hijáz to the south arose Israel's religion and Islam. General problems of the history and philosophy of religion do not concern us here, while the rise of Islam lies beyond our purpose. But none can adequately study the Mosaic religion without comparing with it the growth of its later compeer. In both, although with difference in spatial quantity and moral quality, we observe a movement arising within an Arab population, under a great leader who imposes law in the name of his God upon his people and establishes a theocratic state with visions of conquest over the world, while both remain Semitic. The movement was of religious inspiration, as history proves for

Islam, and as the Hebrew poets and prophets since Deborah celebrate the fact for Israel. Mohammad had the advantage in building upon Jewish and Christian foundations; but it is being increasingly recognized[50] that the doctrine of the One Allah had its native Arabian roots, and that Mohammad appealed to an autochthonous religious consciousness. Allah did not arise out of Mohammad's original summation of all gods into one God. This was already posited in the Arab consciousness, and Mohammad's diatribes against polytheism are similar to those of the Prophets against the cult of strange gods; their polytheism, he argued, was illogical in view of their fundamental belief in One God. We may not offhand deny that similar hidden forces were operative two thousand years before Mohammad, for in certain respects Arabia is a land of static character, nor may we make objection on ground of primitive barbarism.[51] The ascent to a vital monotheism has not been made through elaborate polytheisms. In Arabia it may have come more simply and directly through charging the indefinite words *il, ilâh* with a definite and exclusive potency. The compact unity of the Arab group focuses upon its tribal god; the simplicity and austerity of life led to single-eyed purpose;[52] perhaps some credit is to be given Renan's ingenious theory and the unity and monotony of the desert led, as soon as the belief in local *els* and *jinns* was surmounted,

50. E.g., by Brockelmann, 'Allah u. die Götzen,' *Archiv. f. Religionswissenschaft,* 21 (1922), pp. 99 ff., in criticism of Wellhausen.

51. A timely caution against the current rough and ready attribution of 'primitivism' has been expressed by Söderblom in his recent book, *Das Werden des Gottesglaubens,* chap. 1, 'Die Primitiven und wir.'

52. Somewhere Lawrence speaks of the sharp contrast of light and shadow in the Arabian desert, and takes it as a symbol of the Arab mind which can think things only in the extreme.

to a notion of the Unity above. So we may attempt to argue, doubtless without boot. But the fact remains that not from the wisdom of the Egyptian, Babylonian, and Greek civilizations came our Western religions, but out of Arabia.

INDEX OF SCRIPTURE REFERENCES

OLD TESTAMENT

Arabia and the Bible

Index of Scripture References

Index of Scripture References

Arabia and the Bible

INDEX OF SUBJECT MATTER

A

Arabia and the Bible

Index of Subject Matter

Index of Subject Matter

H

Arabia and the Bible

Index of Subject Matter

Index of Subject Matter

R

S

Index of Subject Matter

Index of Subject Matter